Children, Religion and the
Ethics of Influence

Bloomsbury Philosophy of Education

Series editor: Michael Hand
Bloomsbury Philosophy of Education is an international research series
dedicated to the examination of conceptual and normative questions raised by
the practice of education.

Also available in the series

A Critique of Pure Teaching Methods and the Case of Synthetic Phonics,
Andrew Davis
Cherishing and the Good Life of Learning, Ruth Cigman
Philosophical Reflections on Neuroscience and Education, William Kitchen

Also available from Bloomsbury

Learning to Flourish, by Daniel R. DeNicola
Teaching Virtue, by Marius Felderhof and Penny Thompson

Children, Religion and the Ethics of Influence

John Tillson

BLOOMSBURY ACADEMIC
LONDON • NEW YORK • OXFORD • NEW DELHI • SYDNEY

BLOOMSBURY ACADEMIC
Bloomsbury Publishing Plc
50 Bedford Square, London, WC1B 3DP, UK
1385 Broadway, New York, NY 10018, USA

BLOOMSBURY, BLOOMSBURY ACADEMIC and the Diana logo are trademarks of
Bloomsbury Publishing Plc

First published in Great Britain 2019

A catalogue record for this book is available from the British Library.

A catalog record for this book is available from the Library of Congress.

ISBN: HB: 978-1-350-06679-3
ePDF: 978-1-350-06680-9
eBook: 978-1-350-06681-6

Series: Bloomsbury Philosophy of Education

Typeset by Deanta Global Publishing Services, Chennai, India
Printed and bound in Great Britain

To find out more about our authors and books visit www.bloomsbury.com
and sign up for our newsletters.

For Michael and Christine Tillson

Contents

Acknowledgements

My deepest debt of gratitude is to my parents, Michael and Christine Tillson, who have sometimes encouraged, sometimes tolerated, but always supported me through my spells at university and the gaps between them. My next debt (also of gratitude and fortunately not of money) is to the Irish Centre for Religious Education for the award of a doctoral scholarship which enabled me to conduct much of the research on which this book is based. I am grateful also to my PhD supervisors, Gareth Byrne and Ian Leask, who helped me develop a thesis from a shadow of an idea. Patricia Kieran and Jones Irwin are to thank for a thorough and thoroughly enjoyable viva voce.

While working on the thesis, I benefitted from discussing its ideas with Dave Aldridge, Richard Bailey, Julian Bennett, David Boylan, Kevin Currie-Knight, Scott A. Davison, Mark E. Jonas, Colm Kenny, Kevin McDonough, Andy McGrady, Bernadette Sweetman Morris, Joseph Rivera, Jonny Scaramanga, Claudia Schumann, Patricia Smith, Rebecca Taylor, Ruth Wareham and Kevin Williams. I have learnt much since defending my thesis, and my list of educators has extended further. In particular, at Warwick I learnt much from members of Warwick's Centre for Ethics Law and Public Affairs and from Matthew Clayton in particular. Since moving to Liverpool Hope I have benefitted from working with David Lundie and John Shortt as well as from being nested within the Centre for Education and Policy Analysis.

I should like to single out two people for special thanks. First, Michael Hand, who has proved a critical and encouraging mentor since supervising my MA thesis in 2009. Secondly, Reviewer 2, whose stern rejections and merciful requirements for revision have been both legion and (almost) always justified. I don't know who you are, but I think you're great. Such papers as I have produced are, without exception, much better for your discerning observations and demanding standards. Finally, I would like to thank the Philosophy of Education Society of Great Britain for the inestimable benefit of its monetary and spiritual support since I first joined its ranks in 2009. Long may it and its global cousins continue to grow and nurture the field! Without the help of these many people and institutions, this book would not have such qualities as it has. It is customary to say that its remaining faults are my own fault, and so they are.

Chapter 6 is derived in substantial part from articles published in the *Journal of Philosophy of Education* (copyright Wiley) and in *Ethics and Education* (copyright Taylor & Francis): 'Towards a Theory of Propositional Curriculum Content'. *Journal of Philosophy of Education*, 48, No. 1 (2014): 137–148, and 'Is all Formative Influence Immoral?' *Ethics and Education*, 13, No. 2. (2018): 208–220. Part of Chapter 10 is derived from my chapter, 'Rival Conceptions of Religious Education' in the *International Handbook of Philosophy of Education*, ed. Paul Smeyers (Dordrecht: Springer, 2018): 1059–1082.

John Tillson, Liverpool, 2018

Series Editor's Foreword

Bloomsbury Philosophy of Education is an international research series dedicated to the examination of conceptual and normative questions raised by the practice of education.

Philosophy of education is a branch of philosophy rooted in and attentive to the practical business of educating people. Those working in the field are often based in departments of education rather than departments of philosophy; many have experience of teaching in primary or secondary schools; and all seek to contribute in some way to the improvement of educational interactions, institutions or ideals. Like philosophers of other stripes, philosophers of education are prone to speculative flight, and the altitudes they reach are occasionally dizzying; but their inquiries begin and end on the ground of educational practice, with matters of immediate concern to teachers, parents, administrators and policy-makers.

Two kinds of question are central to the discipline. *Conceptual* questions have to do with the language we use to formulate educational aims and describe educational processes. At least some of the problems we encounter in our efforts to educate arise from conceptual confusion or corruption – from what Wittgenstein called 'the bewitchment of our intelligence by means of language'. Disciplined attention is needed to such specifically educational concepts as learning and teaching, schooling and socialising, training and indoctrinating, but also to the wider conceptual terrain in which educational discourse sits: what is it to be a person, or to have a mind, or to know or think or flourish, or to be rational, intelligent, autonomous or virtuous? *Normative* questions have to do with the justification of educational norms, aims and policies. What educators do is guided and constrained by principles, goals, imperatives and protocols that may or may not be ethically defensible or appropriate to the task in hand. Philosophers of education interrogate the normative infrastructure of educational practice, with a view to exposing its deficiencies and infirmities and drawing up blueprints for its repair or reconstruction. Frequently, of course, the two kinds of question overlap: inappropriate aims sometimes rest on conceptual muddles, and our understanding of educational concepts is liable to distortion by ill-founded pedagogical norms.

In terms of scholarly output, philosophy of education is in rude health. The field supports half a dozen major international journals, numerous learned societies and a busy annual calendar of national and international conferences. At present, however, too little of this scholarly output finds a wider audience, and too few of the important ideas introduced in journal articles are expanded into fully developed theories. The aim of this book series is to identify the best new work in the field and encourage its authors to develop, defend and work out the implications of their ideas, in a way that is accessible to a broad readership.

It is hoped that volumes in the series will be of interest not only to scholars and students of philosophy of education and neighbouring branches of philosophy, but also to the wider community of educational researchers, practitioners and policy-makers. All volumes are written for an international audience: while some authors begin with the way an educational problem has been framed in a particular national context, it is the problem itself, not the local framing of it, on which the ensuing arguments bear.

Michael Hand

1

Introduction

Introduction

The primary question of this work is this: How may we ethically influence children with respect to religions? In particular, by what means, and towards what ends (if any) may we do this? More perspicuously still, what ethical claims (if any) do children have over us when it comes to our influencing of them with respect to religion, and what ethical claims (if any) have we over them in the same regard?[1] I ask about *influence*, instead of upbringing, education or schooling, since similar considerations are relevant to deciding both what kinds of upbringing and education children are entitled to, as well as to deciding whether schooling embodies an appropriate expedient in their service. That is to say, in my view, the ethics of education and upbringing are best discussed in tandem, as parts of the ethics of influence.

Different ethical claims that children are thought to have in this domain include the following: to be initiated into their parents' cultural commitments, truth-claims and all (Giussani 1997; Vryhof 2012); to know what beliefs about religious matters are best justified (Hand 2004); to be empowered to develop an informed, autonomous judgement about whether any religious claims are true (Wright 2000); to be made aware of the variety of religious identities and affiliations as part of an education about diversity quite generally; to gain a comprehensive narrative, as a precondition of gaining evaluative knowledge (Cooling 2012); to become acquainted with the transcendent, or form a

---

[1] This 'we' and 'us' captures those who are both capable of influencing children, with respect to religions, and capable of controlling how they do so. Subsequent investigation may reveal that different people have different ethical burdens in this domain, but that is part of what is to be established. By an ethical claim that A has over B, I mean a demand that can be made on A's behalf which B is ethically obliged to satisfy.

relationship with some particular deity or deities (DfE 1994);[2] to know what it's like to be part of a religion so as to make a more autonomous choice about whether to be religious (McLaughlin 1984).[3]

Generally, we may ask whether children ought to be initiated into a religion, encouraged and prepared to evangelize, forewarned and forearmed against religion, encouraged and prepared to denounce religion, insulated from religion, not deliberately influenced with respect to religions, at all, or some more fine-grained combination of these possibilities concerning particular religions and particular aspects of religion. The maximally permissive answer to my question is that we can do no wrong when it comes to influencing children with respect to religion; that whatever we do will be alright. In this case, children would have no ethical claims over us when it comes to our influencing them with respect to religion. The maximally impermissive answer is that children have a claim to be left to develop according to their un-perverted nature, or even a duty to resist all influence in order to best realize this nature. As I shall argue in Chapter 6, neither the maximally permissive nor the maximally impermissive answer stands up to scrutiny.

I argue that religious initiation is morally wrong whether conducted by parents, teachers or others. The reason is that, very plausibly, it comes at a high opportunity cost – that of being ready to recognize and respond to the truth and to avoid error. This interest is compounded by the fact that 'religious traditions are so comprehensive and all-encompassing in their claims' (Taliaferro 2013). Further, it very plausibly comes at the further cost of collateral errant belief formation (i.e. beliefs formed on the basis of premises which don't simply disappear when one later rejects the premises). Instead, children have a powerful interest in being made aware of range of religious and non-religious answers to the question of how we have most reason to live, what we have most reason to value and how we ought to treat one another, developing the capacities to appraise these for themselves.

---

[2] In a 1994 circular, 'the UK Department for Education explained that one of the purposes of the daily act of Collective worship legally required in all state maintained schools was "to provide the opportunity for pupils to worship God"' (DfE 1994, 20).

[3] This claim would seem more plausible claim if a circumscribed anti-realism were true of religion (as opposed to global anti-realism, or realism about religion), since whether religious beliefs are true or false is not best rationally evaluated from a position in which one already believes them. On the other hand, if religions do not contain propositional content, and understanding them consists in knowing what it is like to indwell, then a 'don't knock it 'til you try it' attitude seems more appropriate.

The argumentative strategy

The argument begins by identifying seven sub-questions, answers to which will contribute to answering the primary question. These seven questions are as follows:

1. What are the sources of ethical responsibility? (Chapter 2)
2. What is the most general content of ethical responsibility? (Chapter 3)
3. In what respects are we apt to be formatively influenced? (Chapter 4)
4. What means of formative influence are available? (Chapter 5)
5. What ethical obligations and restrictions are there on the means by which and the ends towards which we formatively influence children? (Chapter 6)
6. What is a religion? (Chapter 7)
7. How rational is religious belief? (Chapter 8)

Each question will receive consideration in a chapter of its own, and in the order listed above, before, in Chapter 9, our conclusion, we come to summarize our answers to each, and explain what import, taken together, they have for answering our primary question.

A minimally comprehensive answer to our primary question must consider how we can determine the difference between what is and what is not ethical, and how one comes to have ethical responsibilities at all. It must consider what sort of thing influence is, where influences fit on the ethical/unethical distinction, and indeed, what ethical difference it makes when we are talking about influencing children, as opposed to adults. It must have a notion of what counts as a religion, and in what respects we may possibly be influenced, with respect to it. It will also need to consider what the value of religion is. Having satisfied these desiderata, we should be in a position to answer our primary question.

These desiderata require a framework for prospectively selecting and rejecting kinds of acts and for retrospectively evaluating acts and omissions.[4] Such a framework requires two parts. First, any plausible answer to our primary question must identify specific parties that have responsibilities to children, together with the content of those responsibilities. If either were lacking, it would be as though an unsigned, blank check were made out to children. For this reason, we require an account of the sources of ethical responsibilities which identifies the bearers of responsibilities (benefactors), the beneficiaries of

---

[4] On the notion of selecting *kinds of acts* rather than *particular acts*, see Dancy (2012).

responsibilities, and the things that benefactors are responsible for. Second, an account of benefits and harms (or of well-being) is required to give content to the responsibilities.

I will argue in Chapter 2, what we *can be* morally responsible for is those of our actions and omissions which bear on the well-being of intrinsically valuable objects, such as human beings. Following Peter Singer, I accept the principle that 'if it is in our power to prevent something bad from happening, without thereby sacrificing anything of comparable moral importance, we ought, morally, to do it' (Singer 1972, 231). As to who is responsible for what, I argue that the best person for the (ethical) job is responsible for making sure that it is done (an onus they cannot abdicate, but which falls simultaneously on the next best person if they drop the moral baton). While plausible, this answer does not easily accommodate the view that biological parents have a prima facie responsibility for their children's well-being. I argue that it can, in fact, accommodate, and even ground, this view. The conception of well-being that I develop (in Chapter 3) is one which holds that the nearer an act brings human beings towards becoming like God, the better it is for them; the more it keeps them from becoming like God, the worse it is for them. This view is able to account for why humans should value knowledge and rationality; it is also entirely available to non-religious people.

In Chapter 4, I argue that children and human beings in general can be formatively influenced in the following five respects:

1. The degrees and kinds of one's physical and mental powers
2. One's stock of concepts
3. Those propositions which one understands
4. One's cognitive attitudes to those propositions, such as belief and disbelief
5. One's affective attitudes to those propositions and to other objects.

In Chapter 5, I argue that, morally, influence should take a basically rational form so far as that is practicable, but that non-rational means could be used where people, such as small children, are insufficiently rational to benefit from rational influence. The import of Chapter 3 is that people are better off the more rational they are (i.e. the more competent and inclined they are to apportion belief to the evidence, and to seek evidence and suspend judgement in its absence). In particular, we should equip children to be in a position to rationally form and revise opinions about those matters which are momentous to their lives.

In Chapter 6, I argue that for each prospective formative influence, which a child could adopt, influencers have the following range of options: to ignore it, to promote it, to demote it or to draw attention to it as something worthy of consideration to adopt. The theory of ethical influence that I develop holds that for each prospective formative influence, it ought to be promoted, floated or demoted respectively, according to the following three sets of criteria, and where none of these apply, it might be fairly ignored:

1. (a) That it is momentous; (b) that it might well not be adopted without intervention; (c) that it is certain.
2. (a) That it is momentous; (b) that it might well not be understood and rationally evaluated without intervention; (c) that it is plausible.
3. (a) That it is momentous; (b) that it might well be adopted without intervention; (c) that it is false or unfounded.

In Chapter 6, we note that the influences which may be had may be more or less comprehensive depending on just how many respects it is in which we are influenced. The increased comprehensiveness of a set of influences imparted raises its moral stakes. Furthermore, while it might be alright morally, on some occasions, to favour the practical rationality of the beliefs that one imparts over their theoretical rationality, in so far as those beliefs are highly comprehensive, it becomes significantly morally costly to sacrifice theoretical rationality (e.g. to sacrifice truth in the hopes of promoting happiness), in part because the downstream effects become hostage to fortune. These same considerations will be seen to preside over both formal educators and informal educators such as caregivers. Also, in Chapter 6, we will see how this theory of ethical formative influence can be used to select curricula content where a planned programme of learning delivered by pedagogues is the sort of intervention that would be required to rationally encourage and discourage prospective influences in children, or to enable children to better judge their rationality.

Chapters 7 and 8 develop the foundations for the application of this theory of ethical influence to religion. To give content to the question of how children ought to be influenced with respect to religions, we will have to develop an account of what religions are. The answer to be developed in Chapter 7 is that a religion is a system of beliefs which is premised on the existence of at least one super-being to whom adherents should defer as having rightful dominion. Chapter 8 discusses the extent to which religious belief is rational from a practical and theoretical perspective, finding that theoretical considerations must trump practical considerations on such comprehensive matters (even from a practical point of view). It concludes that, from a theoretical point of view, while there may be scope for some people to sustain religious beliefs rationally, the problem of evil poses a credible enough defeater to religious belief systems that one cannot think it unreasonable to deny religious belief.

Chapter 9 then explores the import of these answers for answering our primary question of how children ought to be influenced with respect to religion. Religions are doctrinally speaking, highly comprehensive, that is to say that they are often close to a theory of everything. That would be fine if they were well enough justified to make denial irrational, but as I argue in Chapter 8, it seems that they are not. At the same time, it seems entirely possible that some children do already believe rationally. Where children are not irrational in their beliefs, it is not acceptable to aim to disabuse them of these.

2

The Sources of Parental and Extra-Parental Responsibility

Introduction

We want to know how (if at all) children may be ethically influenced, with respect to religions. Any plausible answer to this initial question must enable the identification of specific parties that have responsibilities to children, together with the content of their responsibilities. The alternative is to address an ethical cheque to children with either or both of the amount and the patron missing. What is needed are answers to the questions: Who (if anyone) has duties to act so as to influence children, with respect to religion, and who (if anyone) has duties of omission on influencing children, with respect to religion, and in virtue of what do they have them? In this chapter, after defending both moral objectivity and contextual sensitivity of moral principles, I discuss two foundational issues regarding ethical responsibility:

1. What sorts of things *can we properly* be morally responsible for at all? (Part of which involves establishing who or what can possibly have ethical claims over us, and part of which involves what sorts of claims can be had.)
2. In virtue of what is it that people have the specific responsibilities that they in fact do?

In answer to the first question, I argue that what we *can be* morally responsible for is our actions and omissions which bear on the well-being of intrinsically valuable objects, such as human beings. I first criticize the view that the specific moral responsibilities that people have emerge from the nature of relationships that they happen to have. Next I introduce the view that the specific moral responsibilities that people have emerge from whether or not they are best person for the (ethical) job. While plausible, this answer does not easily accommodate the view that biological parents have a prima facie responsibility for their children's well-being (for trying to avert harms to them and to ensure some benefits). I then discuss various attempts to say in virtue of what it is that biological parents ought to accept responsibility for their children's well-being. These include principles of fairness, ownership, naturalness, being best equipped, and, finally, whether responsibility for the well-being of children being occasioned by biological parentage makes for a plausible moral axiom. I conclude that the principle of being the best person for the (ethical) job can, in fact, accommodate the view that biological parents are *usually* morally responsible for their children's well-being. I argue that the principle of 'the best person for the ethical job' is able to ground both *parental* and what I shall call *extra-parental* responsibility to children. Before summarizing, I consider some problematic cases for the thesis of the primacy of biological parental responsibility for children's well-being. I shall address the content of parental and extra-parental responsibilities in the next chapter.

Moral objectivity and context sensitivity

I want to defend the claim that value judgements may be right or wrong irrespective of what anyone happens to judge valuable. We act as if things were valuable; we refrain from acting in ways that damage those things which we take to be valuable, and we act in ways which advance and preserve those things which we think are most valuable. We act as if beholden to obligations we perceive, and refrain from acting in ways that seem to us impermissible; we act in spite of what we might prefer to do, for instance. It seems, furthermore, that we cannot jettison our evaluations entirely, or take ourselves to always merely 'project' value rather than recognize it. While it might be *psychologically* hard or even impossible to switch all of our evaluations at random, I want to suggest that it is not a *logical* possibility to think that it would be *alright* to change our judgements at random (in a hypothetical, random attitudinal-amendment machine, say). To think that it would be alright would already mean that these were not *really* our judgements at all. To make sense of a sincere civil rights advocate being willing to undergo the risk of becoming a racist, say, there would need to be some other sincerely held value that would be well served by entering the machine. Similarly, to think that all of our judgements merely reflect arbitrary preferences would be to have already abandoned them. It seems that we cannot step outside of our values. In having values, we are committed to our value judgements being right irrespective of what we happen to think, otherwise we would already be judging the objects that we value to be worthless. That said we will likely find that our values can be made to form a more coherent whole than they do, by amending them in light of one another. Indeed, this process of mutual amendment (or Reflective Equilibrium) seems to be the best method for the rational vindication of one's ethical views as being what they seem, to the valuator, to be, namely, accurate appraisals of value (Tillson 2017).

While I readily acknowledge that value judgements have varied across time and place, and between cultures and individuals, I deny that whether or not these judgements were correct has been determined by any of these facts. At the same time, I also acknowledge that judgements can be properly sensitive to contextual features. In understanding how both things can be so, we will do well to contrast *primary* and *secondary moral entitlements*, with the latter emerging from the former. We may say that all morally significant beings have primary moral entitlements to life and liberty (if only defeasible ones) no matter who they are, or where or when or to whom they were born, but that there are some secondary moral entitlements that emerge from these primary moral entitlements and which vary between contexts. For instance, while nobody could plausibly have had a right to brain surgery in prehistoric times, since there was no such thing, they might more plausibly have had a claim to be looked after as well as possible (without thereby sacrificing anything equal moral importance). A secondary entitlement to brain surgery emerges from one's primary entitlements only in contexts where brain surgery is (among other things) a real option.[1] I offer these remarks only by way of showing the compatibility of moral objectivity and contextual sensitivity. Misunderstood, the contextual sensitivity of objective and universal moral principles can sometimes generate bad questions about what is appropriate to certain contexts.

It is common to ask what kind of education is appropriate in liberal democracies.[2] However, it seems bizarre to ask what kind of education is

---

[1] Some may say that there were no rights in prehistoric times, and certainly there were no legal rights, no United Nations' Universal Declaration of Human Rights or European Union Charter of Fundamental Rights. Indeed, laws are a social construct, but one may argue that there is a moral reality of rights that laws can reflect, or fail to reflect. Some argue that morality itself is a social contract (notably, Hobbes and Rousseau), but it seems that immoral contracts can be created. What I mean to contend is that in drawing up a contract which defines the good, the right and the just, some evaluative judgements have to be presupposed to justify those procedures, and indeed the fact that immoral contracts can be drawn; this shows that morality cannot just be defined into existence by contracts themselves. Indeed, a breach of contract (where one can get away with it, without damage to their reputation) cannot be written into the contract as bad thing without circularity, since it is presupposed by the very existence of contracts.

[2] See, for example, Alexander and Agbaria (2012).

appropriate in an illiberal theocracy, or in a totalitarian state. One might more reasonably ask how an ethical education might be possible in the context of such an unjust state. But one does not ask what kind of education was appropriate to children in Nazi Germany, as if the official views of the country somehow made it all right to teach children the things that it did, and in the way that it did. One might argue that a liberal democracy is the only morally acceptable form of government, and then ask what forms of education are morally demanded within it. It might be that a moral kind of education prepares children to live in and be supportive of what is the best kind of government, morally speaking. Indeed, the factual circumstances about the kind of society we do happen to live in do, to some extent, determine the sort of education that children should have; a morally acceptable education in Nazi Germany and present-day liberal democracies will both involve forcefully criticizing anti-Semitism, but it will likely only permit secrecy about this criticism in Nazi Germany.[3] The context of Nazi Germany created a moral compulsion for a secretive, politically subversive education; a context of liberal democracy might more likely create the moral compulsion for a more politically allegiant education. Deep political questions exist about how society ought, ideally, to be organized; about whether states ought to exist, for instance. While I will defend the notion of extra-parental responsibilities to children from the wider community, this need not be thought of as presupposing or requiring the existence of a state. That said, in contemporary liberal democracies, for instance, it will not be alien to regard existing state infrastructure such as taxation and government funding as the natural means to satisfy extra-parental responsibilities (i.e. those ethical entitlements that reach beyond parents' capacities to satisfy).

By whom, to whom, and in virtue of what are ethical duties owed?

Children plausibly have different ethical claims to particular acts and omissions over people corresponding to the different relationships they have to them. For instance, they seem to be owed distinct kinds of care (unique profiles of act obligations) by their parents, teachers and doctors. Indeed, we commonly think of parents as having special duties to their own children, rather than to other

---

[3]   It would be singularly inappropriate to reproach the White Rose group for the anonymity of their anti-Nazi graffiti and pamphleteering, since six were (as they could reasonably expect) beheaded for treason when they were apprehended.

people's children, for instance. While we might regard all people as having duties not to harm children (duties of omission), it seems that parents have a lion's share of duties to promote their own children's well-being (duties to act). On these views, what obligations of acts and omissions we have to children (and indeed to adults) turns on the character of our relationships to them. However, to assert that some relationships are special requires an account of how and why they are ethically special, how it is that they entail different ethical obligations (if they are not to be merely prejudicial). While we may be quite happy with the notion that one has special obligations to family and friends, this notion becomes darker when we speak about special obligations to countrymen, or to members of our sex, gender, class, race or species, simply in virtue of our belonging to the same categories. Furthermore, if demands are made of us in light of these relationships, we may reasonably ask why they are being made.

Independent of the notion of special relationships is the plausible principle articulated by Peter Singer that 'if it is in our power to prevent something bad from happening, without thereby sacrificing anything of comparable moral importance, we ought, morally, to do it' (Singer 1972, 231). Notice that this principle does not turn on the nature of relationships. Whoever we are, we ought to prevent what harm we can from coming to others, whoever they are to us (so long as it doesn't come at the cost of 'anything of comparable moral importance', that is).[4] It is to argue that we have *act obligations* to ensure basic benefits for others – friends, family, countrymen and distant strangers alike.[5] Brighouse and McAvoy suggest that while 'it is good for a child to have music lessons', this good would entail no claim right since 'providing them might take away money being spent on a parent's education towards a more fulfilling career' (Brighouse and McAvoy 2010). Here, an appeal is made to the comparable moral worth clause. But an appeal might have been made to the basic goods clause; music lessons are not a basic good, the absence of which constitutes a form of harm (something bad).[6]

---

[4] Bernard Williams (1981a) has argued powerfully that bracketing motivations caused by our special relationships can seem pathological and require 'one thought too many of us'; as when I save my wife instead of a stranger, where there is nothing else to choose between them for both reasons, when it seems that I should just save my wife because she is my wife, without thinking any further.

[5] In fact, the idea is not as circumscribed as this. To say we ought to act to prevent bad things from happening is not yet to specify what counts as a bad thing. So it might be that we have moral reason to prevent bad things from befalling non-human animals, plant life, human artefacts, and so on, not because of their import for human animals, but for their own sake. Cf. Davison (2012).

[6] Some might suggest that harm consists, to some extent, in the loss of goods, so that if one already enjoys music lessons, to lose them would constitute harm, while not being given music lessons in the first place would not count as a harm. On the other hand, this same analysis could not plausibly to starvation and nourishment.

I take it that coming to harm is a bad thing, although more substance must, and, in the next chapter, will, be given to this rather bare notion. On Singer's principle, we owe the prevention and avoidance of harm to others whoever they are, and so owe them action, rather than just omissions of action such as not harming them. But why should we accept Singer's principle?

An argument for singer's principle

When we have a principle which is conceived of as a source of explanation, it need not be amenable to explanation itself; it may be ethically basic. What can give it some credibility for the sceptical is its use in explaining other things which they are ethically committed to. What then can Singer's principle explain to lend it credibility if it is to be conceived of as ethically basic? I think that Singer's principle can explain the intuitive appeal of both the Problem of Evil and of apologists' best responses to it. The problem challenges theists by asking why it is that the terrible suffering of the innocent persists, if God is able to prevent such suffering, knows about the existence of such suffering, and is morally good. Here, the suppressed premise seems to be that knowledge of suffering (i.e. something bad), in addition to the power to end it, generates the moral responsibility to do so and that failure to act on such a responsibility undermines one's claim to being morally good. This requires no special relation of God to those who suffer. This looks like an application of Peter Singer's aforementioned principle. In challenging the suppressed premise, apologists' usual responses – that (1) suffering is an unavoidable consequence of allowing free will and that (2) suffering allows for moral growth – appeal to Singer's qualification regarding the non-sacrifice of 'anything of comparable moral importance'.[7] One might say that, being our creator, God would have a special reason to relieve our suffering, but that relationship is not mentioned as part of the traditional problem, and there is no suggestion that, were God not our creator, he would be relieved of any onus to relieve innocent suffering. We have said something about the source of responsibility, about who can be responsible and in virtue of what, but what can they be responsible for?

---

[7] These responses have been advocated by Plantinga (1989) and Irenaeus of Lyons (1885) respectively.

Objects of responsibility

What things and people are we responsible for the well-being of (in as much as our actions and omissions can ensure it)? Put differently, what things are we morally required to keep bad things from befalling? It must, I think, either be a bearer of intrinsic value[8] and have scope for harm and benefit, or it must be required to keep a bearer of intrinsic value from coming to harm. Nobody can be responsible for something that doesn't matter. Nor can anyone be morally responsible for something immutable. Since no harm or benefit can come to immutable objects, there is nothing that one can ensure and therefore nothing that one can be responsible for ensuring.

What is it to do a moral wrong?

There seem to be two different kinds of wrong for which we can be blamed, namely acts (such as harming), on the one hand, and omissions (such as allowing harms and failing to ensure basic goods), on the other.[9] While an act can *cause* harm, an omission is not a cause of anything.[10] However, omission can thereby allow some harm or constitute a failure to procure some basic benefit, without playing a causal role; for instance, failing to feed one's child allows them to starve (a clear case of coming to harm).

Things are a little more complex than this, though: intentions, risks and outcomes are also important. For the moment, I shall talk of causing harm, and leave the matter of allowing harms, and failing to procure basic goods, to one side. We can distinguish the following: someone's intending to do harm (whether or not their act makes harm likely, and whether or not it causes harm), someone's acting in such a way that doing harm is likely (whether or not they intend to

---

[8] I do not have an account of what it is that distinguishes something as being an intrinsic value bearer. I need only to be allowed that children count as bearers of intrinsic value. It seems to me that having a benefit/harm profile (or 'a good') is a necessary condition of being of moral worth, but not a sufficient condition; furthermore, something immutable might be of intrinsic value, but not of moral significance – since it cannot be harmed or benefitted.

[9] I speak of failure to ensure basic goods, rather than failure to ensure goods tout court, since ensuring some goods, such as exotic holidays are surely supererogatory. A basic good might be that of proper nourishment, the negation of which would constitute a form of harm, that of being malnourished.

[10] There is lively debate in metaphysics as to whether we bring about states of affairs through omissions. However, Helen Beebee (2004) has argued convincingly that there is 'no need to think of [for instance] Godzilla's lack of impingement [in our world] as a kind of causation'. My not feeding a plant doesn't cause it to die, even though my feeding it causes it not to die. But this in no wise means I was not morally culpable for allowing the plant to die.

do harm, or realize that harm is being risked), and someone's actually causing harm (even if they hadn't intended to, or even done something that significantly risked causing harm). It seems that too much of an emphasis on actual outcomes obliterates the importance of the nature of our actions, and their underlying intentions, since whether or not we acted well comes down to how things may (even freakishly) turn out. I want to emphasize risk and intention, rather than outcome.[11] So, more accurately, we are liable to do wrong when

1. we *intend* to frustrate basic goods or bring harm
2. we *fail to intend* to bring basic goods or to prevent harm
3. when we *risk* frustrating goods or bringing harm,
    3.1 unknowingly, but negligently
    3.2 knowingly, but regardless.

We do wrong even if (through luck) no harm comes. Stipulation 3.2 captures the following scenario: I might greedily eat all of the food that my family has, and not feed my children because I enjoy gorging myself. In doing so, I did not intend for my family to come to harm even though I knew that they would; rather, their coming to harm was a byproduct of my intended outcome. Still, my action seems no less wrong for that. Here, my action of eating all of the food was in part a knowing forbearance to feed my children, and that omission to feed my children and grant them a basic good is a wrongful aspect of both my intentions and actions. While it is what outcomes *actually obtain* for us that are good or bad for us, it is for what outcomes we intend, and for what outcomes we risk, that we are culpable for in producing those outcomes. The next stage of our enquiry is to establish in virtue of what is it that people are responsible for averting such harms and ensuring such benefits as they are.

Who is responsible for what actions pertaining to whose well-being, and in virtue of what are they so responsible?

We know what sorts of things we *could possibly be* responsible for (at least for our actions and omissions which bear on the well-being of vulnerable, intrinsic value-bearers that are not self-sufficient). But how do we know what things (if any) we *are in fact* responsible for? It is certainly an interesting question as to

---

[11] See Nagel (1979) and Williams (1981b) for a critique of this view.

how one acquires responsibility for a child's development (and for other forms of influential practices, such as providing public information and offender reform). Indeed, it is an interesting question as to how one comes to have *any* moral responsibilities at all, whether, for instance, they are always or ever a matter of choice. In the next section, I shall argue that the responsibilities arise from being the best person for the moral job. However, first, I want to argue that moral responsibilities do not arise from roles, as is often thought.

We might say that a little league coach should attend all of their team's training sessions, and that if they were unable to, then they ought not to be in that role. Indeed, we expect doctors to be good *qua* doctors and everyone else to be good in their role, but why have these roles and the duties that come with them in the first place? It seems that one takes on a responsibility distinctive of a role through a choice, and that one can opt out of that role (the first half may often be true in becoming a biological parent, though not always). Plausibly, however, the primary functions of roles address the vulnerabilities of value-bearers that create an ethical demand for those roles in the first place, vulnerabilities which place ethical demands on members of societies to fill the roles. Indeed, in the case of one's role being a bad one, we should hope that its occupier sabotages their purpose as best they can; concordantly, Oskar Schindler is (rightly) admired for being a terrible munitions manufacturer for the German army during the Second World War. Bernard Williams points out that some people's successes in their roles are precisely moral failings, even by their own lights:

> It is said of certain German Generals who during the war were appalled by Hitler's policies that they were for a long time inhibited from setting to work against him by considerations of the oath they had taken, as officers of the Wehrmacht, to obey him. Let's suppose obedience to the oath could be established as certainly part of one's duties as a German Officer; then what the Generals needed was to form the conception of things they had to do which were contrary to what they were supposed to do as German Officers; that is to say, it was no longer under the title, and in the role, of German Officer that they had to act. And this was a conception, which it seems, some of them found very difficult to form. (Williams 1993, 51–2)

Some have suggested that the relationship that teachers have to students makes certain demands of them (e.g. Cooper 2008). But I do not think that it will do to start by explaining the nature of a relationship, and then proceeding to explain what responsibilities flow from that relationship. This is because what are understood to be the responsibilities are constitutive of the relationship. For instance, it would be absurd to suppose that just because someone was in a role that they ought to satisfy it. Rather, it is because they ought to assume a role that they ought to satisfy its duties. Indeed, we can think of cases where those playing a certain role in a relationship have no responsibility to stay in it, because there was no need for the role in the first place; think of a subordinate younger sister waiting hand and foot on her lazy slob of an older brother, the fact that they have such a relationship implies no duty to sustain the role.

There are many diverse kinds of relationships: husband–wife, civil partnership, parent–children, grandparent–grandchildren, godparents–godchildren, neighbours (in the sense of people living nearby), doctors/nurses–patients and so on. Some of these relationships feature saliently in responsibilities that we expect people to fulfil, with respect to one another, other relationships do not feature so prominently ('lives two doors down from', for instance, or 'wears the same colour hat as'). Some of these roles are more obviously social constructs than others, and the question is whether the roles have any moral basis for the creation of the institutions in which they exist in the first place.[12] I want to ask about a stage, logically prior to actual existing arrangements, which has to do with what arrangements should be brought into existence, that is to say, asking about whether the ethics of influence ought to have implications for upbringing and schooling, and not vice versa. In the next section, I consider an answer, that the best person for the ethical job is responsible for making sure that it is done, a view which, I shall argue, has considerable plausibility.

The best person for the job

It seems reasonable to leave tasks to those best placed and equipped to perform them, where they need to be performed (the best person for the job, as I will call them) so that the person nearest to the elderly person that fell over ought to help them up, and where they cannot provide sufficient care to them, to call out for someone that can (again, the nearest person whose powers will suffice). This is an onus that they cannot abdicate, but which falls simultaneously on the next best person if they drop the 'moral baton', so that in not bothering to help up the elderly person, the most able person thereby puts the next most able

---

[12] It is reasonable to say that they are created because people are (a) not able to meet their own needs and responsibilities unassisted and (b) unable or unwilling to respect other people's needs unpressured, or at all.

person under an obligation to take up the slack, without excusing themselves. Here, we have two rival goods to weigh up in the service of expedience, namely, proximity and competence. We often hear of people in need of complex surgery being flown to distant hospitals which specialize in such treatment (a case from 2012 is that of Nobel Laureate, Malala Yousafzai, who, as a young girl, was shot in the head by a Taliban gunman, being flown to Birmingham, England, for specialist treatment). There is a balance of immediacy and competency to be weighed up, since someone may be nearest by but least competent, or furthest away but most competent. There will be gradations in between, and, indeed, those most competent to a task may be equipped well above the level of expertise required for a task for it to be done sufficiently well. We may distinguish between ability and opportunity (more on this distinction in Chapter 3), and we may say that modern-day doctors would be best able to look after the needs of ancient peoples in ill health, but have no opportunity to do so, being separated by ages. Needs here (and throughout) are to be understood as basic goods of vulnerable, value-bearers. The thought here is that being best able to do something together with having the opportunity to do it (through some combination of proximity, liberty, expertise, equipment and availability) is what obliges someone to meet needs.[13] We might also add another clause: that of knowing about the need to be satisfied. It seems unreasonable to blame anyone for failing to help out in a disaster that they had no way of knowing to have been occurring.

It is possible to cultivate expertise and obtain equipment (and, indeed, we can advance expertise and develop equipment). It is interesting as to whose job it should be to step up and fill the required expert roles (those roles dictated by needs). On the one hand, it is not as though it is alright for everyone to do just whatever they want (thus societies do well to reward those jobs most needed so that people are more inclined to take on those roles). On the other hand, it is not as though it is alright for society to allocate the needed places and then draft people into those roles. This undermines the plausible principle that people ought to have an open future, and ought to be free to choose what that should be. Perhaps drafting teachers and doctors should be done if their need desperately outweighed their supply, in spite of inducements. Indeed, it is

---

[13] The reference to 'availability' harks back to Singer's principle: 'If it is in our power to prevent something bad from happening, without thereby sacrificing anything of comparable moral importance, we ought, morally, to do it', since it seems that one cannot neglect to help simply because one would prefer not to; one needs to have been doing something at least as morally important which was incompatible.

often (falsely) attributed to Aristotle that one's vocation is the overlap between one's talents and society's needs (some versions have it that it is the overlap between one's talents and the world's needs). A vocation here is thought of as being how one could most valuably employ one's abilities in a career (which would hopefully be highly rewarding), whereas we want to know whether some people might have a duty to become certain types of professionals, or for certain professions to be created. This difference aside, it is a plausible enough starting point to consider that one may have an obligation to satisfy those roles at which our talents and society's need intersect. Before going on to look at parent–child relationships, I want to defend my conception of ethics against a Kantian objection.

The very idea of imperfect obligations

I have argued that any ethics of influence must identify specific parties that have responsibilities to other specific parties, together with the content of those responsibilities. I claimed that the alternative was to address an ethical cheque to children with either the amount or the patron missing. But this claim of mine is something that Kantians, such as Onora O'Neill, are concerned to deny. Following Immanuel Kant, O'Neill distinguishes between perfect and imperfect obligations, perfect obligations having set benefactors and imperfect obligations having unset benefactors. A set beneficiary is a specific person who is due a benefit from a specific benefactor. Where the beneficiary is unset, there is no specific person who is due a benefit. But 'so long as recipients of the obligation are neither all others or specified others, there are no rights holders and nobody can either claim or waive performance of any right' (O'Neill 1988, 448). However, I cannot even make sense of owing something to nobody in particular. If I ever owe anything to anybody, it must be in virtue of their qualifying for the benefit somehow. But this seems to make it a perfect obligation. I may not owe you something in all circumstances, but I may owe it you in some particular circumstances: I don't owe the time the train leaves at (if I know it) to everybody or anyone in particular, but I owe it to people who ask. If you ask, and I refuse to tell, you can object that I breached your right to know. We will now explore how these considerations might help us with deciding how (if at all) parents are responsible for their children's well-being. Having defended my conception of ethics against a Kantian objection, we can go on to look at the import of my account for parent–child relationships.

The nature of parent–child relationships

'Really', my dad said. 'I wouldn't bullshit you about this. If you were more trouble than you're worth, we'd just toss you out on the streets.'

'We're not sentimental people', Mom added, deadpan. 'We'd leave you at an orphanage with a note pinned to your pajamas'.

Green 2012, 166

These comments are made in jest and are funny. The suggestion that attachment to one's child is mere sentiment that ought to be trumped by a negative return on a cost/benefit analysis is laughably absurd.[14] Indeed, it is almost universally held that a child's biological parents should, where possible,[15] assume primary responsibility for their child's upbringing. The emotionally charged word 'abandonment' is used where parents give their children up for adoption, for instance (though it should be noted that many young mothers have been coerced into giving their children up for adoption or do so for their child to have a better life), and the word 'neglect' is used where parents fail to invest time, energy and consideration into their child's upbringing. There is a powerful scene in the film *There Will Be Blood* which illustrates this.[16] There, the protagonist, Daniel Plainview, is brought to confess in an outburst of emotion in front of a Baptist congregation that 'I've abandoned my child! I've abandoned my child! I've abandoned my boy!'

Biological parent–child relationships are not defined by proximity and expertise (although it is often thought that parent–child relationships ethically demand proximity and the cultivation of some expertise, among other things).[17]

---

[14] To laugh, it seems, is to evince one's position, without making an argument. Certainly the joke has some persuasive force, but it is not rational. It may be regarded as an intuition pump which shows up one's feelings.

[15] Few other responsibilities could trump their responsibility for bringing their child up. One recalls Sartre's example of a young man who had the choice 'of going to England to join the Free French Forces – which would mean abandoning his mother – or remaining by her side to help her go on with her [difficult] life' (1973, 35). This decision can be paralleled with that of many fathers (and fewer mothers) who have gone to war or pursued other projects which took them away from their children.

[16] *There Will Be Blood* (dir. Anderson 2007).

[17] In fact, saying 'biological parenthood' is ambiguous between two or perhaps three senses, as I shall explain now. The sense in which I meant it is: genetic parentage. There are disputes over the proper definition of motherhood, where that means who should be presumed in the first instance (sans defeaters, such as severe mental illness) to be female guardian, (or female primary carer or parent) to bring up the child. The possible definitions are genetic, contractual (or 'intent' based), and gestational. The complexity emerges where a 'traditional surrogate' agrees to be both the genetic and gestational mother to a child, but to give them up to another woman to raise the child (the contractual mother). On the contractual (or intent) definition, the surrogate cannot renege on the contract. On the gestational definition, the child would be supposed to be that of whoever carries

Indeed, there are many things which we call needs that we do not think that all parents would even be capable of meeting; medical needs being the most obvious example. We might further suggest that children can have educational needs which outstrip what most parents can provide (especially parents working in non-educational contexts), and thus have to outsource the satisfaction of some of their child's educational needs to others.

Proximity and ability would be relevant considerations for relieving parents of their parenting commitments, but it seems that parenting's own commitments come from a source other than ability and proximity.

It is interesting to reflect on those cultures which place the responsibility for upbringing on the state and took it from the parents. One reason for this might have been egalitarianism, as Rawls makes clear:

> It seems that even when fair opportunity (as it has been defined) is satisfied, the family will lead to unequal chances between individuals. ... Is the family to be abolished then? Taken by itself and given a certain primacy, the idea of equal opportunity inclines in this direction. (Rawls cited in Brighouse and Swift 2009)

But it seems bad to break up families in favour of egalitarianism: we feel that harm is done to both parents and children. Indeed, Rawls thought that 'the invocation of his other principles, which he takes to soften the conflict between the family and "justice as a whole", prevents this counterintuitive result' (Rawls cited in Brighouse and Swift 2009). And here we seem to shift the emphasis from responsibility to an entitlement. But since entitlements can be waived, it seems to be a responsibility that we are seeking.

One might hope to resist this line of reasoning by drawing on Bernard Williams' paper 'Persons, Character and Morality' in which he characterizes the person who saves the life of his wife over that of a stranger for the reason that 'it was his wife and in situations of this kind it is permissible to save one's wife', as having had 'one thought too many'. It might have been hoped 'for instance, by his wife' that he had saved her *just because* she was his wife (Williams 1981a, 18). Williams argues that most people have reasons to live in the form of projects which they aspire to undertake, and that these can be intimately related to close, preferential relationships with other people. Where we must give up on these in favour of impersonal requirements of what he

---

and births the child. On the genetic definition, the child would be supposed to be that of whoever's DNA it is that they share. It seems that where the concept of a biological mother comes apart, we should simply say that children can have two biological mothers: namely a gestational and a genetic mother. See Mulligan (2014).

calls the morality system, we thereby lose what are our interests in living and 'generally one shouldn't take advice if, were one to take it, one would have no reason to go on living' (Millgram 2008, 144). But here again we have an argument not for a responsibility, but an argument for a 'free pass' on some moral responsibilities. The worry is that this approach ultimately amounts to nihilism, with our only having those responsibilities we like, and our not *really* having those anyway.

The source of parental responsibility

In virtue of what is it that a biological parent has a specific set of act obligations to their child? There are various principles in virtue of which people potentially ought to accept responsibility for their biological children's well-being, which we shall now assess. These include principles of fairness, ownership, naturalness and being best equipped. I will ultimately defend an argument from them being best equipped to them having a specific set of act obligations. First though, perhaps responsibility for the well-being of children being occasioned by biological parentage makes for a plausible moral axiom, just as Singer's principle seems morally axiomatic.

Moral axiomaticity

A responsibility to act as guardian might be thought to arise from biological parentage axiomatically, just as being best able to satisfy some need might be taken to be an axiom of moral responsibility. If it is, then there may come times when rival parties have the same moral responsibilities, and one will need to trump the other, or else they will need to share the responsibility somehow. In the case of parenting, we want to say that the initial responsibility goes to the parent over the best equipped; indeed, if it did not, then there would hardly be room for special responsibility of biological parenthood at all. If we cannot find another principle in which it is rooted, then we may have to admit this.

It would seem wrong for anyone to take a child away from a biological parent, other things being equal. Indeed, it would often seem wrong for someone to take the child away from a biological parent, other things being unequal; wealth or social status, for instance. There is a strong presumption that the person or people that a newborn child would 'go home with', so to speak, from a maternity ward is the mother, or mother and father, in the first instance. One consideration is the well-being of the biological parent; whether or not they want to be a parent, and if they do, it would seem cruel to the parent to take them away. This suggests that parents have some rights of parenthood that can be distinguished from responsibilities of parenthood. Suppose it made no odds to the child's well-being whether they stayed with the parent or not, it would seem odd, other things being equal, to say that there was no valance in the parent's favour that their child should stay with them.

Fairness

It might be thought unfair for anyone to take on responsibility for a child that they did not create. It is least unfair that parents raise their own children. Here, then, one would expect that where a parent was keen, but moderately less able to parent their child than another person who was also keen to raise them, that they ought to leave the parenting to that person. But this consequence also seems too counterintuitive. Furthermore, it seems that this case overlooks the well-being of the child in the first instance, instead looking to keep people free of unbidden responsibilities. But it seems the nature of responsibility that it comes unbidden. This is nicely expressed by an exchange from Peter Jackson's adaptation of Tolkien's *The Fellowship of the Ring*, when Frodo confides in Gandalf, his mentor, that he wishes he had never come to have the responsibility of destroying an evil, magical ring:

> Frodo: I wish the ring had never come to me. I wish none of this had
>   happened.
> Gandalf: So do all who live to see such times. But that is not for them to
>   decide. All we have to decide is what to do with the time that is given to us.
>
>   (dir. Jackson, 2001)[18]

Ownership

The parent–child relationship has sometimes been characterized as one of ownership, where parents are entitled to sell their children, or use them as any other piece of property. It is perhaps in virtue of one's having in some sense *made* one's children that one might be thought to own them. It has been the

---

[18] The remarks look different to those in the original text: 'I wish it need not have happened in my time.' 'So do I', said Gandalf, 'and so do all who live to see such times. But that is not for them to decide. All we have to decide is what to do with the time that is given to us' (Tolkien 2012, 50).

case one cannot be held accountable for how one treats one's own property. While it might be foolish to destroy or harm one's own property, one cannot be morally blamed for it. But this result is hugely counterintuitive. Indeed, on this model parents would not be responsible for their child's welfare at all. This is to construe childhood as a form of slavery. One might urge that this is a false consequence of ownership. Modern UK and Irish law regards pet owners as being responsible for their pets' welfare, while still being their owners. So too might one urge that this is true of slavery. However, there would seem to be something terribly wrong not only with whipping, raping and murdering slaves but with owning people in the first place. One wonders why adulthood should release one from slavery, or whether one would remain the property of their parents until they both passed away, and whether they could transfer ownership before passing away. One might resist the notion of property altogether and urge along Marxist lines that all property is theft. Alternatively, we might allow for the possibility of ownership and try to draw a distinction to separate those things which may be owned from those that may not. This is not easy to do. It is very tempting to suggest that the capacity for self-determination makes one's ownership unethical, but sleeping people do not have it, nor do people in comas, nor perhaps some severely disabled people. We might say then that the capacity for self-determination is a sufficient but not a necessary condition for why one shouldn't be owned. Notice that many non-human animals ought not to come under our ownership either, under this definition, since they too are self-determining.

Naturalness

Another raison d'être for parents being responsible for their children is that it is in some sense, *natural*. The Irish constitution is written with this in mind:

> The State acknowledges that the primary and natural educator of the child is the Family and guarantees to respect the inalienable right and duty of parents to provide, according to their means, for the religious and moral, intellectual, physical and social education of their children. (Article 42, 1)

Presumably, not to allow this would be a perversion of nature, of how things would go in a state of nature or without interference. But it does happen in nature, to the extent that we can understand the expression 'in nature'. Moreover, it seems that we can distinguish between what is natural and what is morally acceptable. It seems that vindictiveness, jealousy and blood feuds are perfectly natural, but certainly not morally acceptable.

Having discussed the prospects of parental responsibility being understood as morally axiomatic, and as a consequence of more basic principles of fairness, ownership, naturalness, I will now defend an argument from them being best equipped to them having a specific set of act obligations.

Best placed

It might be urged that it really is their ability to be best able to care for their children that makes biological parents responsible for their child. Parents usually love their children and want to do what is best for them; their desires overlap with what they think is in their children's best interests (including satisfying their perceived needs and keeping them from coming to perceived harm). It may be argued that this motivational drive makes parents the best equipped to nurture their children, or at least counts in favour of their being so considered. Kleinig and Hobson both argue for this conclusion:

> There is some reason to think that the developmental needs of children are likely to be met most successfully in an environment in which primary responsibility, and the authority that is derivative of that, lies with the parents. There are grounds *for* believing that parents, more than anyone else, will have the kind of commitment to their offspring that will safeguard and promote their welfare interests. (Kleinig 1983, 145)

> Parents should be the prime agents in their children's upbringing, other things being equal, because they are the ones most likely to best promote the welfare of their children. It is the parents who have the most direct interest in their children's welfare and the parent-child bonds of affection are more likely to ensure the continuous care and attention needed, even under the most difficult of circumstances. It is generally agreed by psychologists that the developing child benefits greatly from the intimate relationship with its parents and the sense of belonging and being loved that is normally present. (Hobson 1984, 64)

It may be objected that what parents think is in their children's best interests may not be. Jehovah's Witnesses having refused to let their children to have blood transfusions in life-threatening situations arguably demonstrates this. So too does the practice of female genital mutilation. It seems that there are reasonable expectations of a good upbringing, connected with proper development that parents should be held accountable for, and not just any earnest upbringing will do. Indeed, both Kleinig and Hobson acknowledge this. It seems to be their contention then, that those who are in the best position to raise children have the responsibility to do so, and that (usually) that is their biological parents because (usually) their parents love them. If this works, then they will have placed the allocation of upbringing responsibilities within the context of the 'best person for the job' principle.

This argument really only establishes that it is biological parents who *love* their children who have a responsibility to them bring them up. This can seem strange in that a parent who chose to have a child, and then frivolously decided that they did not want to bring them up, had not broken some duty. Here, what would be wrong is the frivolity of the decision to have a child, rather than their giving up their child. Indeed, there is something worrisome about a biological parent who are parents out of a sense of responsibility alone, and not out of a sense of affection and concern. Consider an emotionally indifferent parent, or indeed a parent who did not like children, or their child in particular, one who perhaps resented being responsible for them. It is hard to imagine such a person actually raising a healthy and happy child. It might be a rare case, perhaps the case of a psychopath, since it would be hard for most people to resist forming strong bonds with anyone that we spend a large amount of time with and aim to care for. But still, it seems false to say that children who are unloved and unwanted have no ethical claims over a world that is able to care for it; it seems that their parents in the first instance and anyone else who is most able after that has the responsibility to help. But willingness is important. Willingness seems to be part of the ability profile. A begrudging carer is hardly a real carer at all. It is contingent whether affections will grow or not, and perhaps one can take steps to make them do so – by spending time together, for instance, by enjoying activities together. It would only be when a person both willing and able to facilitate their well-being cannot be found, that a begrudging carer is to be drawn on.

Some might deny the idea that primary caregiving responsibilities going first to biological parents is anything but a social construct, devoid of moral character; biological parents just happen to be expected to be a primary caregiver in our society. But this is extremely implausible: this intuition can be encouraged by asking people what they think of a case of a child being taken away from biological parents and given to some other people for no special reason. This simply looks like a case of kidnapping, with wrong done both to parent and child. There may be social arrangements in which child care is diffuse, with no clear primary carer; these might include polygamous societies in which men have multiple wives, all of whom take on responsibilities for raising one another's children. And indeed these do seem to erode the somewhat atomistic sorts of responsibility which appear to be recommended on Singer's principle.

Non-biological parents as primary carers

There are cases where we should not look to biological parents to take on the role of primary carer. By 'primary carer', I mean the parental role in the normative rather than the biological sense of the word. There are instances where, plausibly, it is not shirking of moral responsibility that they do not take up this role. Some might even be concerned that I am outlining a sort of hierarchy whereby the best sort of upbringing is that facilitated by one's two biological parents, and any other permutations of this are inferior in quality. This is not at all what I am defending. Furthermore, I am not arguing that initial responsibilities of primary caregiving always originate with parents, but only that, on Singer's principle we can understand why they often do. There are many cases where it is not at all obvious that primary caregiving responsibilities go first to biological parents. While one can imagine speculative cases, such as where a child spontaneously came into existence without biological parents, there are actual cases. Let us consider some of those cases now.

The first of these cases is a parent who feels that he or she is not capable of being a primary carer – an example of such a parent could be a rape victim who carries her child to full term pregnancy, perhaps out of a moral belief that her unborn child is entitled to live. Other cases could include mentally ill people who do not believe that they could raise their children properly. In this case, there will be some questions over whether or not they could in reality raise their children properly, and perhaps they could be persuaded that they could be good parents where that is true. But if someone does not believe they could be a good parent, that is ground to take their worry seriously, and could very possibly become a self-fulfilling prophecy due to the stress that child-raising while holding such a belief would likely cause.

There are cases where couples have more children than they were prepared for – say a poor couple who saved up to be able to afford to raise one child, but unexpectedly had octuplets. It might be that the wider community should facilitate their raising these children where they want to serve as primary caregivers – by giving resources, time and energy, for instance. But where the task outstrips their abilities, that task could not possibly fall on them as a duty.

Consider cases where the parent does not want to raise their child. One may wonder why they had the child. An explanation could be that the child had been unplanned and had in a country where abortion is illegal. Alternatively, they might have been naïve about what having children involved, have felt pressured into having a child, or have found that circumstances since trying and succeeding in conceiving had changed dramatically. One might ask: if they gave their child up for adoption, would they be doing the wrong thing? On the account that is sketched above, it not clear that they are; indeed, they would more likely be doing the wrong thing in raising a child with a sense of duty and resentment, since this is unlikely to be conducive to the child's well-being.

There are cases where biological parents enable others, such as gay or infertile couples, to become primary carers, through the donation of sperm and egg, and through 'traditional surrogacy' (as distinct from 'gestational surrogacy'). Think of a surrogate mother, who agrees to have a child that she will not mother, although she will be that child's biological mother in both a gestational and genetic sense. Suppose that the surrogate mother decides that she would rather raise the child that she has borne. It is not obvious whether she is doing the right or wrong thing; she is backing out on an agreement and she may disappoint those with whom she has made the agreement. She may be damaging her own well-being by going through with her agreement, and handing over her biological child.[19] On Singer's principle we say that we ought to stop bad things from happening; breaking a contract would seem to be a bad thing, giving up a child that one loves would be a bad thing, refusing a child to someone who dearly wants, and has prepared, to be a parent would seem to be a bad thing. Weighing up which of these is the least bad thing to do is no easy task. However, it does not seem at all obvious that there should be a presumption of primary caring responsibilities falling on the traditional surrogate – especially not when one considers the person who requested the child refusing to accept responsibility for their upbringing, perhaps because the child is disabled or other than anticipated. There is an important question unaddressed by this chapter, and indeed, book – should there be a presumption in favour of the mother when there is a dispute

---

[19] We might say: no traditional surrogate mother can sign a binding contract in which she says she will unreservedly have a child on behalf of another person. That any such contract will have no ethical commitment on her to do so, any more than signing oneself into slavery ought to.

over who the primary carer should be. Where does the moral onus for childcare fall? Some might criticize the 'naturalization' of motherhood and regard it as a form of oppression. Against this, I urge that, if in essence 'first refusal' to bring up a child goes to a mother over a father, this is a form of freedom which is clearly not extended to the father, and hardly looks like a form of oppression at all. It might only be defended by a thesis of manufactured consent on which mothers are persuaded against their interests to want to bring up children. More importantly we can imagine a case where a DNA donor and gestational surrogate agree in a contract that a third woman should be the mother, and that all three claimants disagreed as to who should raise the child at the birth. It is this case that is of interest later.

3

The Content of Parental and Extra-Parental Responsibility

Introduction

In the previous chapter, we discussed the *sources* of responsibility. In this chapter, we shall discuss the *content* of responsibility. I have agreed with Peter Singer that 'if it is in our power to prevent something bad from happening, without thereby sacrificing anything of comparable moral importance, we ought, morally, to do it' (Singer 1972, 229). I also argued that it is the person best placed to prevent something bad from happening that should morally do it. Singer's principle requires some idea of what constitutes a bad thing. In this chapter, I contend that, other things being equal, an intrinsically valuable object's coming to harm is a bad thing, while its being benefitted is a good thing. It will be argued that the nearer an act brings us towards becoming like God, the better it is for us, and the more it keeps us from becoming like God, the more it harms us. We shall also discuss the parental role, and extra-parental roles, which we can be responsible for playing in virtue of our being the best person for the ethical job. The justifications of paternalism are discussed, as is the value of autonomy, and the values of truth and truthfulness, before we summarize our findings.

The good and the bad, harms and benefits

Singer's principle requires some idea of what constitutes a bad thing (his own example is famine). It seems that coming to harm is a bad thing and being benefitted is a good thing. But what is of harm and what is of benefit to human beings (and to children in particular)? The answer that I want to elaborate and defend is that the nearer an act brings us towards becoming like God, the better it is for us, while the more it keeps us from becoming like God, the more harm it is to us. God is 'that than which a greater cannot be conceived',[1] and that which helps us towards being in the greatest conceivable state, by giving us more powers, opportunities, knowledge and goodness, for instance, is *in fact* in our interests, rather than just what we might happen to *think* is in our interests. Atheists need not think that any such being exists to understand that being in such a state is properly desirable.

Adams on God and excellence

The view advanced here is to be distinguished from that of the prominent theist R. M. Adams. For Adams, 'God is … that which best plays the role of the referent of *the Good*'. 'God is a particular, not a Platonic form or universal; but God is the Good, and so Adams suggests that the excellence of created things might consist in some kind of resemblance of God' (Davison 2012, 118). The view I defend is different from this. According to my view, God would be excellent and in the best possible state. There is a God role; that being, or those beings, which have all perfections, and anything which satisfies that role is maximally excellent. Things are more excellent by the degree to which they approximate the role. On this view, God's condition (if the God role were satisfied) is not excellent because it happens to be satisfied by that particular individual (while whatever other conditions that individual might have been in would be equally good), but because there is some standard of excellence which that individual exemplifies. Atheists may accept the standard while denying that anything satisfies it.

Omnipotence, abilities and opportunities

In order to better understand this conception of well-being, we should distinguish between powers and opportunities, understanding that God would have maximal powers and maximal opportunities to exercise them. The distinction is brought out in the following example. While I might be *able* to learn a foreign language in the sense that, were I to go to abroad and immerse

---

[1]   St Anselm, *Proslogion*, trans. Clement C. J. Webb, https://en.wikisource.org/wiki/Proslogion, Chapter IV (accessed 18 June 2015).

myself in the language, I would indeed learn that language. I still might not have the *opportunity* to go abroad, and so my ability to learn a foreign language (given the opportunity) would seem pointless. It should be admitted that some abilities and inabilities are two sides of the same coin and a choice must to be made as to which ability/inability pairing to have. For instance, one cannot be optimally good at long distance running and optimally good at sprinting (contingently, if not necessarily); indeed, God cannot logically do everything, since claims that God is omnipotent can present us with a paradox as to whether God could thereby make a stone that he could not lift. Consider an example about a trade-off in mental powers offered by Kevin Currie-Knight in a personal correspondence:

> One trait (speed of processing) may be desirable but require a trade-off with another desirable trait (faster processing often means a less nuanced or less accurate processing). Consider ADHD-like processing (that sees bigger pictures over details and oscillates focus rapidly) and non-ADHD focusing (quicker to see details and pay attention to one thing at a time, for longer). It is fantastically difficult to say which of these is better, because the answer is almost surely contextual.

We can easily reply to this valuable insight that, while there are almost certainly trade-offs to be made, one would be more nearly omnipotent, and thereby better off, in being able to process well, both quickly and slowly, as one thought appropriate. While one may have a constitutional penchant towards doing one more effectively, it is no reason not to train oneself in the other. As finite beings, it is true that we have to make choices about which of our talents to develop and must develop one or some to the exclusion of others. But that is no objection to the conception of excellence, but only to our being able to ultimately satisfy it.

Four objections to well-being construed as Godliness

There are some other difficulties with this conception of well-being that I ought to address. First, in emphasizing Godliness, we seem to be emphasizing independence, but it may be both impossible and undesirable to emphasize these over socialization and functioning well within teams (to emphasize independent labour to the division of labour into (fulfilling) specializations). Second, being human involves inhabiting a point of view on the universe, whereas being godlike may seem to involve transcending any parochial point of view and seeing the universe under the aspect of eternity.[2] But it would seem strange to recommend this as an ideal. In particular, it would seem strange to emphasize radical transformation out of human biological limitations: such as being uploaded onto computers to become maximally disembodied, for instance. Third, emphasizing truth, power and beneficence (in the sense of maximizing truth and power in others) seems a little paltry, as it lacks much of a reason to live. Fourth, the conception of well-being that I have in mind may register a note of insensitivity and political incorrectness. First, one may think of blind people having heightened senses of smell and hearing as a result of lacking sight. Furthermore, human beings with disabilities may prefer to think of themselves as simply *having* disabilities, rather than *suffering with* them, regarding their situation as an alternative way of being in the world, even regarding the word 'disability' as stigmatizing and condescending. A good example of such an attitude is demonstrated by some members of the deaf community, who take pride in their way of being in the world. Alternatively, lacking certain powers can give people a sense of purpose in overcoming their inabilities: in respect of gaining powers (the power to walk again, perhaps, or the ability to read), with the journey having been more worthwhile than the destination. Indeed, one may think of the virtues which one cultivates by way of adjusting to life as being more important than how one is in the world. There is much truth in these objections, but I still want to maintain that (other things being equal) the more abilities one has, the better off one is, and the greater one's abilities, the better off one is (and where things are not equal, it is because these *access goods* give one access to yet more goods). John Rawls expresses this point well:

> Regardless of what an individual's rational plans are in detail, it is assumed that there are various things which he would prefer more of rather than less. With more of these goods men can generally be assured of greater success in carrying out their intentions and advancing their ends, whatever these ends may be. The primary social goods, to give them in broad categories, are rights and liberties, opportunities and powers, income and wealth. (Rawls 1972, 92)

Rawls' list of 'rights and liberties, opportunities and powers' and 'income and wealth' seems to be collapsible into the categories of abilities and opportunities described above (with wealth, rights and liberties providing opportunities to exercise powers or abilities). I want to add knowledge, and understanding to

---

[2] This description is in terms taken from Williams (1985), especially Chapter 8.

this list of access goods, as well as the ability to expand one's knowledge and understanding. This is not just because opportunities to pursue projects require knowledge; indeed conceiving of projects, inventing or choosing between them requires knowledge too; but instead because knowing is partly constitutive of well-being.

Well-being and a sense of purpose

We might say that it is all well and good being better natured, more powerful and having more opportunities, but wonder what should we do with our increased power and opportunities. This is to ask the question that has been variously formulated as: What is best in life, how ought one to live, what is the meaning of life, and what is the good life? Should we simply make other people more powerful and freer to use their powers or are there some goods which powers and opportunities give us access to (they are after all *access goods*). While being given powers and opportunities is of benefit to us, and being disempowered and having opportunities restricted harms us, I have as much as acknowledged in my last paragraph that these cannot possibly be all that there is to value, even morally. Powers and opportunities are valuable because they enable us to avail of goods, to pursue worthwhile projects. I have said nothing about this so far. Further, good character is surely to be valued for itself and not for the effects it has, as the following consideration demonstrates. Imagine a moral monster plugged into a virtual reality machine living out all of their fantasies of wanton cruelty and destruction, convinced that it is real, without any possibility of actually harming anybody. Even without there being any possibility of their actually harming anybody, the content of their character and desires seems bad in itself. However, good character certainly does not promote harm or undermine benefits, and so is not a rival good.

Satisfying preferences is not the only good

So far we have given answers to the questions 'What sorts of things *can* we be morally responsible for?' and 'What counts as a harm or benefit for a human being?' In answer to the first question, I argued that what we *can be* morally responsible for is those of our actions and omissions which bear on the well-being of intrinsically valuable objects, such as human beings. My answer to the second question was that the nearer an act brings us towards becoming like God, the better it is for us, and the more it keeps us from becoming like God, the more it harms us. In contrast to the account of well-being offered here, Peter Singer has defended the goal of maximizing the attainment of people's ultimate, informed and rational preferences. The problem with this notion is that people may cut their preferences to fit what is available to them, that is, they may start to want what they get, where they do not get what they want. Indeed, one already has to admit at least one objective good on Singer's view, namely the satisfaction of rational desires. But this seems implausible, because it makes what people's preferences are completely arbitrary, with none better than any other; people don't want good things because they are good, they just have wants, and these ought to be respected (it is nihilistic about all but one value, and then that value seem dubious in its solitude). Indeed, the specification of 'rational' preferences only seems contentful if there are objective values to rationally track. That said, it does seem that a person's ability to get their own way is (other things being equal) a good, together with their having a range of ways that they might possibly get available to them, but that is so because there is a range of things which are in fact valuable or that might reasonably be thought 'valuable'.

An additional claim right

As per the arguments of the last chapter, we have rights to omissions of harms, and actions which keep us from coming to harm over each other. It may be that education and upbringing could help to cultivate characters of the sort that would respect these rights (it would be a bad thing if people didn't stop bad things from happening and if we can stop that from happening through education, then we ought to (from Peter Singer's principle)). But if that is so, then it is someone's responsibility to raise children to respect these rights. Whose responsibility would it be though? Plausibly, it is something of a collective duty to enable this (to fund it, for instance), and (again, as per the arguments of the last chapter) the duty of those best placed to execute the role to do so.

The content of parental responsibility

It is the content of the parental (or guardian) role that generates the need for it in the first place. It seems that children's welfare needs require the generation of at least one person to play what we might call the parent role. The parental role is not to provide every type of care, but to have an overview of the care which children need, and ensure that they receive it; that they see a doctor when they are ill, get to school, that they eat and drink, and rest, that they are growing in powers, knowledge and beneficence (indeed, knowledge seems to be a precondition of power, if not sufficient for it (as shown by the case of Casandra)). The idea is that it is good to have an overseer of the beneficiary's well-being. This role described thus far is administrative, but it further requires a depth and pervasiveness of concern. It seems that children need stability, and strong loving relationships, both as a good in itself, and as a model of how to develop relationships in the future, and as a basis for enabling growth of powers, knowledge and beneficence. These are the well-being needs, and scope for their best satisfaction that generate the parent role, a role which, as I argued in the previous chapter, is often (but by no means always) best satisfied by biological parents. There are also extra-parental responsibilities generated by the potential harms to which children are susceptible: responsibilities that outstrip the abilities of people who play the parent role, *qua* occupants of that role, to minister to.

The content of extra-parental responsibility

It seems that people who are not parents can either have duties to take over, or supplement parental responsibilities.

Taking over parental responsibility

While it is overwhelmingly agreed that, other things being equal, biological parents ought to raise their children (and indeed, other things being unequal, they often ought to do so, too), it is also widely held to be incumbent upon wider society to relieve parents of their charge if they are abusive or negligent, or to assume some responsibility if they are overburdened. Biological parenthood is (we argued in the previous chapter) usually the point from which responsibilities of childcare originate, and from which they transfer over to others. What counts as sufficient reason to take a child into care is a point which is contested, but one which every society has a de facto answer to evident in its policy, or lack of policy. Boris Johnson, then mayor of London, controversially argued in a London newspaper that extremist parents and guardians ought to have their children taken away on the grounds that they ought not to be able to teach children doctrines of hate and violence; 'radicalism is a form of child abuse', he argued (Johnson 2014). In his article, he focused on radical Islam and was accused of Islamophobia. His *exclusive* identification of Islam seems unfortunate given that Islam is not the only broad category within which there exist factions promoting doctrines of hate and violence, but it is surely one reasonable example among others (including the Christian group the Ku Klux Klan). Let us accept that often (usually, in fact) biological parents have a primary and original ethical responsibility to and for their own children. Original, in that the responsibility is theirs in the first instance and taken from them where they are unable or unwilling to fulfil it, and primary in that, while others may owe some kinds and degrees of responsibility, theirs exceeds the kinds and degrees of responsibilities that anyone else owes to them. Responsibility of parents can temporarily be transferred over to others who act in loco parentis, such as carers, coaches, tutors, teachers, baby sitters and so on (but it is still thought that providing for the child financially, for buying food for instance, is a responsibility that falls on the parents' shoulders, except where they are not able to or where others are happy to).

We might say that this responsibility cannot be abdicated, that it is inalienable (as the Irish constitution does).[3] But that does not mean it cannot be shared and to some extent be mitigated (as when a parent leaves their child in the care of a reliable childminder or teacher). Furthermore, it seems that, since parents can neglect their responsibilities (can be abusive and do harm beyond allowing harm to happen, and failing to bring basic benefits), a duty can fall upon others to relieve parents of their charge.

Indeed, it is not just whatever parents thinks is in their children's interests that is indeed in their interests. It may be reasonable to give parents a large margin for error in determining what is in their children's interests. This is partly because what counts as an error may not be always obvious, partly because some errors matter less than it matters that parents maintain a close relationship with their children. However, we cannot reasonably think that parents are infallible in this regard; even sincere, well-intentioned parents can be mistaken. While an important question is indeed when parents ought to be relieved of custody, it is not our question.

---

[3] '42: The State acknowledges that the primary and natural educator of the child is the Family and guarantees to respect the inalienable right and duty of parents to provide, according to their means, for the religious and moral, intellectual, physical and social education of their children.' The Irish Constitution, http://www.irishstatutebook.ie/en/constitution/ (accessed 28 June 2015).

Supplementing parental nurture

It seems that often there are many aspects of children's well-being that parents cannot adequately minister to or provide for. Health and education are obvious examples of both. Where keeping children from harm in these domains outstrips the means and abilities of parents, it seems that responsibility falls beyond parents to the wider community (where that community is able to meet those basic elements of well-being). This would be the arguable basis for free healthcare, and, more importantly in this enquiry, free education (at least for those unable to secure it for themselves). I shall argue in Chapter 6 in some detail that children have extra-parental claim rights to be educated, and in Chapter 9 will explain how this relates to religion.

Paternalism, autonomy and entitlement

I will now argue that children's having claims over their guardians to some good does not (by itself) mean that guardians have an entitlement to compel their children to avail of that good. Additional paternalistic arguments are needed to make that case. Guardians might well have such an entitlement and it may be closely connected to their responsibilities; however, the two are not identical, and must be separately justified. The thought is this: children have certain ethical claims over their parents in the first instance that they do not have over anyone else (until their parents seriously and obviously fail in satisfying these), for instance to be physically nourished. But supposing that they did not want to be nourished, it would not *follow* that children ought to be force fed by their parents. Again, it might be that children should be force fed, but not just from parents' responsibility to satisfy claims that their children have, for it seems that claims are things that their holders can waive.

More naturally, we would think of justified compulsion as requiring some good for others; we think of ourselves as having obligations to others rather than to ourselves, or at least of having the right to veto our own obligations to ourselves and others' obligations to us, but no right to veto our own obligations to others. To take an example given by Jonathon Wolff during a conference keynote address: a more compelling reason to wear seatbelts in cars than to avoid doing damage to oneself, is to avoid doing damage to someone sitting in the seat in front; this example was used in a UK public advertising campaign in which a young boy without a seatbelt crushes his mother's chest when he is flung forward into her seat during a collision, while he himself comes off comparatively unscathed. Concordantly, it raises few eyebrows when it is suggested that criminal offenders ought to be compelled to undergo a process of rehabilitation in order to reintegrate into civil society. To motivate compulsion to receive entitlements, plausibly we should begin by contrasting wards and wardens. If one ever properly has wardenship over somebody else, one's ward, rather than being entitled to have their own decisions regarding their own well-being respected completely, one has a responsibility to commit their ward to what one thinks best for them. This might well take the form of compelling one's ward to benefit from an entitlement.

To leave it to children to exercise and waive claims is to respect their autonomy, and at this point in our investigation, it is an open question as to whether, and if so, adults ought to respect children's autonomy. Arguably, while children have rights to well-being, they do not have rights to self-determination, where they are not yet competent choosers:

> Children often do not grasp the ramifications, for them or for others, of the choice they make. This is true even of very simple decisions (what to eat for lunch; how long and with whom to play after lunch; how early to go to bed), let alone decisions about whether to waive or claim their rights. (Brighouse and McAvoy 2010, 76)

> For adults, because they generally have a better sense of what will serve their well-being than any other agent does, we think that they should have a great deal of control over how and whether these interests are met. Young children are in a different condition, and do not have an interest in controlling as much of their lives as adults do. (Brighouse and McAvoy 2010, 81–2)

Still, according to Brighouse and McAvoy, children do 'have a powerful interest in the conditions and resources needed for them to develop into the kinds of beings that have agency interests' (Brighouse and McAvoy 2010, 81–2). Where they are not competent choosers, those best placed to oversee the satisfaction of children's well-being needs (to keep them from harm and ensure that they receive basic benefits) have a duty to do so.

Champions of promoting autonomy and reason sound a little unrealistic in the case of small children whom in practice they would prefer to be obedient, to follow instructions and complete set tasks. Lest anyone should think that children are naturally good, and are poisoned by a corrupt world, one is tempted to point to a brilliant website which chronicles the poor reasons for which children throw a tantrum (e.g. the reason one young boy is bawling is that 'he is not allowed to put his hand in the toilet').[4]

Indeed, young children's consent counts for less than adults' consent, since children give their consent much more readily than adults do. Adults, just by virtue of the accretion of knowledge through experience, are in a stronger position to make judgements about what will secure their own well-being (although, they may not make good decisions, and may act contrary to what they know is in their interests, perhaps through giving in to the pull of addictions, or the attraction of a nearer good at the expense of a more significant, longer term good).

Harms and benefits to children

We might say that children have rights to actions which prevent their coming to harm, but no right to self-determination, because they are not competent choosers. But since this is not true of all and only of children, the morally relevant category would seem to be 'incompetent choosers', rather than 'children'. Another point about children is that they are going through a formative phase. It's a phase in the sense that one passes through it before adulthood, and that it has an effect on one's adulthood:

> There has been a tendency among moral and political philosophers to regard children as proto-adults and to see their interests primarily in those, future oriented, terms. (Brighouse and McAvoy 2010, 81)

> Thus they consider the fundamental responsibility they bear toward their children to be the obligation to provide the kind of supportive environment those children need to develop into normal adults, where normal adults are supposed to have the biological and psychological structures in place needed to perform the functions we assume that normal, standard adults can perform. (Matthews 2014)

We can overemphasize these points, since adulthood is not a formative terminus (as Kevin Williams has emphasized).[5] Indeed, we can think of all

---

[4] 'Reasons my kid is crying', http://www.sunnyskyz.com/blog/119/36-Reasons-My-Kid-Is-Crying-Temper-Tantrums-You-Can-t-Help-But-Laugh-At (accessed 23 June 2015).
[5] 'An irony about the ascription of authority to adults is that it introduces a sharper distinction between the worlds of children and adults than can be justified. Adulthood should not be envisaged as an emotional, intellectual or career terminus' (K. Williams 2014, 133).

of life as constituting a process of growth and becoming, or as constituting a phase (before death). Furthermore, as Brighouse and McAvoy point out, even supposing that we know a child to have a terminal condition which will prevent them reaching adulthood, they will still have 'interests in the present day', 'there are goods available to her in childhood ... the value of which is not reducible to the role they play in human development' (Brighouse and McAvoy 2010, 81). Matthews argues that children are more able at some things than adults (such as learning a second language) and are not to be understood as adults minus certain abilities (Matthews 2008). But we cannot allow the pendulum to swing too far in this direction: children are vulnerable and impressionable. Childhood is a period which comes before adulthood (barring the tragedy of childhood fatality) in which people do well to develop their powers (especially those that are more easily acquired then). It is a period in which one does well to promote those learning objectives that constitute a well-formed adult for this reason. The thought is not that when people reach adulthood they no longer have something to learn, or have no obligation to learn, but simply that learning happens best in childhood, and those who do not receive such tutorage suffer for it in later life. However, children finish schooling at a certain age (which varies from country to country in which schooling is enjoyed (or endured)), not when they achieve certain required capacities. And indeed, those who have reached this age and not even been through those formal educative procedures are not thereby denied autonomy-rights, are not compelled to attend school or kept from voting or drinking. It is disingenuous for any such system to stress capacity-based autonomy-rights or to attempt to justify its practices on their basis. It is perhaps reasonable to think that it would be cruel to keep people in schools until they have attained certain standards, especially if they show no sign of likely doing so: at some point, the benefits of schooling (such as powers) do not warrant the costs of restriction (namely, opportunities). For instance, it would be absurd to compel schooling until old age if a student had failed to attain the minimal standards generally desired of students in order to graduate. Indeed, it would seem that students who had not graduated by adulthood would not have a claim right to such an education, since it would extend beyond what anybody would reasonably be expected to offer.

Young children are more impressionable than adults. They are more deeply and more comprehensively receptive to influence than adults. Early influences are thereby too easily irrational, and too hard to shake, and so more is at stake than with the formative influence of adults. Early influences enter deep, permeate subsequent learning and are harder to separate out and reject rationally. Indeed, 'Socrates was tried by the Athenian courts in 399 BC and executed, on charges, among other things, of "corrupting the youth"' (Williams 2009). The charge was corrupting *the youth*, and not corrupting people of just any age. The motivating consideration here is likely that the youth are more impressionable and need to be protected by laws whereas adults do not.

In summary, children are best able to learn while young and may reasonably have a paternalistic attitude taken to them to further their own benefit, and while adults might benefit from compelled learning, it is especially cruel to restrict opportunities into adulthood, with childhood being understood as a period of time rather than a physical or mental state. But since children are more impressionable than adults, special concern needs to be paid when exercising influence over them.

Knowledge, rationality, autonomy and well-being

What do knowledge, rationality and autonomy add to one's well-being? When exercising one's autonomy in voting for leaders, or government policies, or choosing what products to buy or which school to send our child to it is (all other things being equal) better to be informed than to be uninformed or, which is a special case of being uninformed, misinformed. There seems to be something special about informed decisions, and its specialness consists in having valuable real options, theoretical rationality (which tracks the truth), and practical rationality.

First, informed decisions rely on real alternatives in order to be meaningful. We need only mention Henry Ford's edict that his customers could have his cars in any colour they wanted, so long as they wanted his cars in black, to illustrate this idea. Second, there are general prohibitions on lying, on not checking one's sources, on not verifying results, on failing to gather information, on not telling the truth, the whole (relevant) truth and nothing but the truth. It might be thought that the premium on informed consent creates the need for truthfulness: for gaining someone's consent through misinforming them looks like a case of manipulation. But theoretical rationality is required for us to track the truth and is required for the possibility of informed consent. Third, informed choice means nothing if we do not know what to do with the information we have; for example, how to derive a good choice from the information available.

A few tempering considerations should be raised at this point. First, we can be spoiled for choice, and this can worsen our choice; we will likely choose better between three options than between three hundred. Second, all other things are not equal, when it comes to informing our decisions, informing ourselves requires time, energy and all the more so the less are our talents at doing so (by research and critical reflection). Indeed, it can be well to defer to expert opinion on the questions of what to think, and on the question of what to do. Third, there is a powerful value that can conflict with these values, namely happiness. We might say that an informed choice can still undermine our well-being, and we would have been better off having had the choice made for us. It is cited as an example in Thaler and Sunstein's book *Nudge* that parents are happier when they are not given the decision of whether or not to artificially preserve the life of their child who will never have any reasonable quality of life. Another example might be *Sophie's Choice*, from William Styron's book of that name (2010), in which a Nazi officer forces a Jewish mother to choose between saving the life of one or the other of her two children.

These important considerations notwithstanding, there still seems to be something special about informed decisions. Having the power to make a decision and the political freedom to do it is to be called autonomy of action. And it requires rationality, truth-tracking and real options. Enabling informed consent ought to be one aim of upbringing. Ensuring real options is more a matter for political and economic theory. Cultivating practical and theoretical rationality is the other matter. All of this is so because (as argued earlier) of the existence of many valuable options and the difficulty in appraising them decisively.

Why seek and share truth?

It may be that knowing the truth is often beneficial, but not always so. Is benefit what justifies truth telling, or is benefit something extraneous which perhaps sometimes trumps whatever it is which justifies truth telling? Sometimes, it seems better to believe a falsehood, which has some pragmatic approximation to the truth, when we are not able to understand the complexity of the truth. This comes out in Michael Hand's example of telling young children that 'all berries are poisonous' (Hand 2002). Here a falsehood goes proxy for the truth; it is not as useful as the truth, if that was attainable, but it will do where it is not attainable.

The value of truth was powerfully challenged by Nietzsche in *Beyond Good and Evil*, where he asked, 'granted that we [happen to] want the truth: why not rather untruth? And uncertainty? Even ignorance?' (Nietzsche 2009, §1) 'The falseness of an opinion is not for us any objection to it', he continued, more pertinent is the matter of 'how far an opinion is life-furthering, life preserving, species-preserving, [or] perhaps species rearing' (Nietzsche 2009, §4).

> We are fundamentally inclined to believe [that] the falsest of opinions … are the most indispensable to us; that without a recognition of logical fictions, without a comparison of reality with the purely imagined world of the absolute and immutable, without a constant counterfeiting of the world by means of numbers, man could not live – that the renunciation of false opinions would be a renunciation of life. (Nietzsche 2009, §4)

The most obvious response to Nietzsche is this: objecting to truth in this fashion, presupposes access to the truth. Thus, when he comments that 'we are fundamentally inclined to believe the falsest of opinions are the most indispensable to us', we are fundamentally inclined to believe this (if indeed we are) because it is true. Indeed, if Nietzsche truly recognizes 'untruth as a precondition of life', he is put in the awkward position of vouching for the untruth of certain propositions, while at the same time depending on thinking they are true in order to live at all (Nietzsche 2009, §4). This objection can be mitigated somewhat, however, in that Nietzsche might respond that he is only able to embrace the truth at a great cost, and one which is not worth the price to anyone else; and perhaps then, only briefly, before he must shun the truth. Further, one might bear the truth in order to better protect others from it. This latter option is paternalistic to be sure, but so too is education altogether.

More generally, the thought is that practical and theoretical reason can recommend contrary beliefs. Indeed, whether to employ theoretical reason appears to be a question for practical reason, as does how long to spend thinking about something is also a practical question. While theoretical reason might suggest assent, dissent or agnosticism, whether or not to believe truly appears to be a matter for practical reason. Consider the case of Pascal's wager. Pascal argues that it is less costly to believe wrongly that god does not exist than it is to believe wrongly that god does exist. I do not think that the argument works in this instance, but it could work in some other instances (Pascal 1925, Section III, §233). He concludes that where theoretical reason is indecisive, practical reason is not. Some might doubt that one can, as a matter of fact, convince oneself of a proposition which one self-consciously does not think is true. It is perhaps easier to imagine at the level of the subconscious. It is matter of some puzzlement but an empirical matter, and one we have reason to believe is both possible and not uncommon.

Sympathetic examples of paternalistic lies (and not mere over-simplifications) include the following. A soldier who is moments from dying on a battlefield may be better lied to about the severity of his condition. But here the misinformation will not likely affect the autonomy of his decisions (such as changing his will). Similarly in the film *Titanic* (dir. James Cameron, 1997), a mother in a third-class compartment puts her children to bed, reading them a story as the ship goes down, with no hope of their escaping, judging it better that they should pass away without the anxiety of knowing their fates. 'An omission', some might object. True, but a lack of truthfulness and the illusion of safety may easily require the support of lies. Somewhat differently, in *Interstellar* (dir. Chris Nolan, 2014) the protagonist decides to leave his daughter on Earth in an attempt to save all humanity without telling her that humanity is in peril, since 'when you become a parent, one thing becomes really clear, and that is you want to make sure your children feel safe'. Here he has withheld information. Were he pressed on it, he might have had to lie in order to preserve his daughter's sense of safety. Here, it is his child who he is protecting from the truth; perhaps were she an adult, he might have been less inclined to conceal the truth from her, since it would figure significantly in what decisions she would go on to make. For these examples, T. S. Eliot's words come to mind:

> Go, go, go, said the bird: human kind
> Cannot bear very much reality. (Eliot 2000)

Indeed, Timothy D. Wilson (whose work on narrative we shall consider in a Chapter 4) emphasizes happiness over truth; after an initial emotional upheaval when a lover leaves us 'we can take a step back and put as good a spin as we can on what happened', he says (Wilson 2011, 13). 'Our wellbeing is intimately tied up with the way in which we think about ourselves and our place in the world' (Wilson 2011, 40). 'What kinds of perspectives [narratives] make us happy? Research reveals three key ingredients – 'meaning, hope and purpose':

> First, it helps to have answers to the most basic questions about human existence and our place in the world ... to make sense of why bad thing sometimes occur.

> Second, it helps to be optimistic … because optimistic people cope better with adversity. Third, it helps to view ourselves as strong protagonists who set our own goals and make progress towards them' (Wilson 2011, 51).

Perhaps what matters is that people are happy, not that they are informed. Some information will disrupt people's lives and make them unhappy. It might be the case that, in practice, nobody ever knows well enough what will happen when people are informed and so one can't use the balance of probable happiness to dictate whether or not to inform. It is sometimes said that what one does not know, cannot hurt them. This is clearly false in the case of smoking: not knowing that smoking causes cancer does not mitigate the effects of smoking.[6] In many cases, it may be that the information would help them make decisions which will more likely benefit them (as with the smoking example). On the other hand, if one's wife had cheated on one but feels ashamed and would never do so again, being told of the infidelity might only ruin the relationship that it is in one's interest to preserve. Indeed, it may be in the interest of one's wife to delete her memory of having done so, should that be possible. Some are wont to respond that the relationship was already ruined, and that this would merely make it apparent. But this is not from either one of their points of view, but only from some third-personal perspective which may remain un-manifest for the duration of the relationship. The point is put (rather gratuitously for this context) by John Stuart Mill's remark that 'it is better to be a human being dissatisfied than a pig satisfied; better to be Socrates dissatisfied than a fool satisfied' (Mill 1906, 260). If one really pushes the disruption line of thought by suggesting that one's suicide was an inevitable result of one's being informed, Mill's 'better to be Socrates satisfied' line might begin to look a little pale, but this is rarely the case. There would seem to be a duty to inform, paired with informing sensitively.

So how can one respond to Nietzsche? One approach is that which R. S. Peters took, with his transcendental arguments. These were designed to show that truth is hiding in the background of everything we value, that an interest in truth is presupposed in valuing anything at all. Another is offered by Robert Nozick who asks whether we should rather live our lives in an experience machine,

---

[6] On the other hand, it is clear that sometimes beliefs are self-fulfilling, and would not have been true, had they not been believed: a soldier's conviction that he would make it out of the war alive, for instance increases their likelihood of survival.

than encounter reality. We will look at each of these in turn after starting with a consideration due to E. Jonathan Lowe.

Truth is unitary

If truth is, as E. Jonathan Lowe argues convincingly, unitary, then it is no good hiving off one area of inquiry to be insulated from requirements of truth, or systematically attempting to so insulate it, since all facts must be consistent with all other facts. 'Truth is single and indivisible or, to put it another way, the world or reality as a whole is unitary and necessarily self-consistent' (Lowe 2002). Indeed, lies multiply to maintain the illusion, the more so, the more our world view is compromised with untruths.

Transcendental arguments

R. S. Peters' Transcendental Arguments attempted 'to establish the worthwhileness of theoretical activities by demonstrating the value of truth' by arguing that 'the person who seriously asks "Why do this rather than that?" must, in order to answer her question', (a) 'find out what this and that involve' and (b) 'have made some preliminary assessment of her situation, distinguished this and that as options for herself, and judged the choice between them to warrant careful consideration' (Hand 2009, 113–14).

However, Hand holds that the justificatory problem is merely deferred: 'The problem, then, is that having shown commitment to truth to be presupposed by serious engagement in practical discourse, Peters now needs to justify serious engagement in practical discourse' (Hand 2009, 115). But denying that we should be committed to tracking the truth seems unstable: it seems to require a justification of the sort that it says is not required and won't allow that such justifications are required unless one is provided. If it could, that might give us pause for thought, but otherwise it seems merely prejudicial. While Peters attempts to say that serious engagement in practical discourse is unavoidable, because in failing to engage with it seriously, one would find themselves living by 'procedures which are inappropriate to demands that are admitted, and must be admitted by anyone who takes part in human life' (Peters 1973, 253). Hand speculates that such demands might possibly be ignored; however, anyone who did this would be a nihilist, which is surely a rare, if not altogether inconceivable, case (Hand 2009, 115).

The experience machine

If truth is only instrumentally worthwhile, one ought to plump for a life of good that the truth is ultimately instrumental to (perhaps pleasure). Consider the following thought experiment presented by Robert Nozick:

> Suppose there was an experience machine that would give you any experience you desired. Super-duper neuropsychologists could stimulate your brain so that you would think and feel you were writing a great novel, or making a friend, or reading an interesting book. All the time you would be floating in a tank, with electrodes attached to your brain. Should you plug into this machine for life, preprogramming your life experiences? … Of course, while in the tank you won't know that you're there; you'll think that it's all actually happening. … Would you plug in? (Nozick 1971, 44–5)

Intuitively, the answer should be 'no'. In seeking reasons to value truth, one is necessarily subordinating truth to some other value. The question is: as a matter of fact, do we appreciate the truth as good in itself? Answering Nozick's thought experiment as we do, it seems that we do appreciate truth as a good in itself, as an anchor which we may or may not be inclined to stray from. Where we respect others equally, we will endow them with that truth. In fact, given my procedure of reflective equilibrium, what is important are my own intuitions. In the absence of an error theory explaining why my intuition is misleading, and in the absence of any more fundamental value with which it conflicts, I must accept its dictates as being rationally compelling.

Duties of truthfulness

Rational beings, as rational beings, have a duty, it seems, to believe the truth, and to disbelieve falsehoods or, more accurately, to believe and disbelieve only on rationally adequate grounds.[7] They have a duty to pursue the truth, and correct their false beliefs. They have a practical reason to tell others the truth and to correct their false beliefs, namely the mutual epistemic benefit gained from this activity. Since pursuit of the truth requires sensitivity to the

---

[7] This claim is denied by David Papineau (2013), who argues that there are no doxastic norms, but he allows that we still have moral reasons not to misinform others which seems to create a drip-down moral obligation to avoid believing falsely so as to avoid misinforming unknowingly.

sorts of considerations which render a proposition more likely true or more likely false, the further duties to sensitize ourselves to such considerations is entailed by the duty to pursue the truth, and a practical reason to sensitize others to such considerations. Call these the duties of truthfulness. Children come to recognize and observe these duties chiefly through the guidance of their parents or carers and those who act in loco parentis. Adults have a duty to promote the duties of truthfulness in the children for whose development they are responsible.

It seems that the duties of truthfulness have the following implications for determining and teaching propositional content: in the absence of defeating conditions, teachers ought to attempt to *impart* a given belief to children where it is known to be true, and ought to *make it known* to them as *possibly* true, where it is thought to be a reasonable possibility. On the question of when beliefs should be taught to be false or unfounded, it seems that the educator is only *entitled* to do this where they know the belief to be false or unfounded, but should only *bother* to do it when it is something that they know the child believes.[8] Thus, on the assumption that Young Earth Creationism (which takes the book of Genesis to be literally true) has been decisively falsified, it may still have a place in the science classroom just insofar as its inclusion enables any student adherents to come closer to a more scientific understanding, and to leave behind their false beliefs. The question ought to be raised as to whether it is particular people's beliefs sets, or something more impersonal and encyclopaedic that we ought to have in mind when we speak of imparting beliefs which are known to be true. The question is crucial since it will have implications as to the universality or teacher-relativity of the content of education. If it is personal belief sets that we have in mind, then one might wonder whose estimation of the truth is to be drawn on, and, very arguably, it is the educator who has the responsibility of making the judgement call as to what is known. For an educator to teach anybody else's estimation of the truth would seem to be a dereliction of the duties of truthfulness and inauthentic. Of course, this encumbers them with a weightier onus to adopt and revise their beliefs rationally. On the other hand, that onus may be too weighty, and expertise as pedagogue in no way guarantees that subject matter expertise is sufficient to make robust judgements oneself. Indeed, experts will have to be identified by non-experts, and there is no shortage of claimants.

---

[8] See Tillson (2011a).

Underlying the above account of the duties of truthfulness, there is one obvious and important question for the curriculum which we should address, namely, whether we should seek and promote the truth about everything. What is worth correcting people on, informing other people about and testing our own beliefs about? Some things are true but are trivial and not worth knowing. Indeed, there may be some mistakes which are not worth correcting. Whether or not I have seventy-three hairs on my left eyebrow should be the least of anybody's concerns. Thus, we need a criterion of importance. In Chapter 9, I will develop and defend the following criterion: In order to decide *how important* it is that a particular belief appears on curricula, educators ought to ask how much of a practical difference would it make to the student's life if they were *not correctly informed* about that belief's truth (if they were wrong, or had no opinion, for instance). Supposing that Christianity were true, it would obviously make a practical, if eschatological, difference to their lives if children are not *correctly informed* about whether Christianity is true, just as much as it makes a practical difference if children are not right about how to ensure their physical health. The more 'foundational' a piece of information is, the more of a practical difference it is likely to make in the following ways: to undermine or recast much of what is already believed, or to provide a platform for the future assimilation and interpretation of further information. In the sciences, for instance, evolutionary theory is foundational in just this sense for much of biology, zoology and anthropology.

4

Those Respects in Which People Can Be Formatively Influenced

Introduction

My question is how (if at all) we may ethically influence children, with respect to religions. More particularly, we have in mind the ethics of deliberate, formative influence. Although not mutually exclusive, formative influences are to be distinguished from behavioural influences. Whereas behavioural influences make a difference to what people do, formative influences make a difference to those of their mental characteristics in virtue of which they are what they are: their beliefs and desires for instance or, more generally, their dispositions. Others may like to say that these dispositions constitute our character, our identity, or *who* we are.

One may think of the threats of fines and prison (and of hell) as being deterrents and of the promise of financial rewards (and of heaven) as being inducements which might affect our decisions, but not our decision making apparatus. To put it another way, these things will affect our decisions, but not us. One might think that creating deterrents involves creating a belief, but it doesn't, even though informing people about a deterrent is wise since otherwise the deterrent cannot deter. Instead, the relevant thing to the ethics of influence *qua* mental characteristics that determine action is not the creation of a deterrent but informing people about the deterrent. It should be said however, that sustained conditioning through incentives and disincentives may affect a formative influence; if we take away the incentives and disincentives after a while, like scaffolding from a building, they may have helped to form habits and attitudes which make their continued presence unnecessary.

We should be clear that the sense of 'identity' that is of interest here is not that which has to do with people's persistence conditions. We may assume that individuals have synchronic and diachronic identities which distinguish them from other individuals at any given time, and in virtue of which they are identical with some spatiotemporally distinct individual from an earlier time (e.g. those conditions in virtue of which Eminem is numerically identical with Slim Shady, but distinct from Dr Dre, and again why a contemporary Eminem is numerically identical with a young Marshall Mathers). When we speak of identity such as that which is cultivated by formative influence, we do not have this in mind at all. Indeed, the same individual might undergo a deep and comprehensive transformation, while retaining their diachronic and synchronic identity. That is why it is possible to say of an individual, without paradox, that he is a changed man or a different person. Furthermore, an individual could have exact clones made who would share all of their attitudes and beliefs and so on, but who are yet numerically distinct individuals who must therefore have distinct persistence conditions.

It is obvious that there are limits to what influence we can have over one another. For instance, some attempts to influence people to be a certain way are superfluous, as people would be thus and so *anyway* (e.g. encouraging people *not* to grow wings), other attempts are idle because no influence *could* make them thus and so (e.g. encouraging people *to* grow wings). There may then be some *rigid* internal conditions in virtue of which people do what they do, and in virtue of which they cannot be brought to do other things. Our interest will be in the *malleable* internal conditions in virtue of which people do what they do, as these are respects in which people *can* be formatively influenced by one another. The point about *internal conditions* is to distinguish them from *external conditions* in virtue of which people do what they do: say, being asked, ordered or coerced into acting, all of which constitute behavioural influences.

The *malleable* internal conditions in virtue of which people do what they do may come with default settings which can be altered (e.g. we may naturally feel disgust at some things, but then later no longer feel disgusted by them), or they may come with no default settings, but empty value fields, which may be given some input (e.g. we may have no beliefs about whether God exists, and yet come to hold some). Malleability may vary by degree in different people, and one may think of one's plasticity as registering on some kind of scale with an inability to change at one end, and an inability to avoid change at the other (between maximal and minimal impressionability). However, before one thinks of an inability to resist the force of an influence as always being a sign of weakness, gullibility or undiscernment, one ought to reflect that a rationally decisive argument will compel an agent to accept its conclusion insofar as that agent is rational. Any ability to resist such compulsion appears obtuse.

While our particular volitions to act may be affected by what I have termed 'behavioural influences', more intimately with our personhood (and hence 'formatively'), those of our dispositions which incline us towards actions and volitions may also be influenced; dispositions being 'those properties picked out by predicates like "is fragile" or "is soluble", or perhaps more accurately by sentences of the form "*x* is disposed to break when struck" or "*x* is disposed to dissolve when placed in water"' (Maier 2011). Ultimately, we are interested in the ethics of influencing those of our malleable yet stable internal conditions which incline us towards our actual volitions and actions. What are those conditions (i.e. in which respects can we be formatively influenced)?

Learning versus formative influence

The question 'In what respects can we be formatively influenced?' is distinct from the question, 'What can be learnt?'. It seems that the latter is a subset of the former, for, in principle, there could be forms of formative influence in which nothing is learnt. Perhaps knowledge could imaginably be uploaded or implanted, for instance.[1] Short of such speculative possibilities, learning and being formatively influenced might seem to be coextensive. However, we should reflect that people have often been formatively influenced in ways that can't naturally be classed as teaching or learning. Michael Hand has suggested the examples of foot binding and female genital mutilation to me in a private correspondence, remarking that 'they are certainly things that are done to children that change them, or affect their development, in significant ways'. A more positive example might be confidence-building exercises.

Focusing on just the case of what can be learnt, Hand has convincingly argued that it is broader than 'skills and factual knowledge' (contra D. W. Hamlyn), since we can learn falsehoods, and truths, but without *knowing* them to be true. It is also broader than propositions (be they true or false, justified or unjustified), skills and 'control by paying relevant attention' (contra John Wilson), since 'learning to be compassionate or just does not seem to be a case of coming to

---

[1]   For a defence of this claim, see Tillson (forthcoming).

know something, nor does it appear to be a matter of acquiring self-control'
(Hand 2010, 51). Ultimately, Hand judges that he knows of no satisfactory
answer to the question of what can be learnt and recommends the question for
further attention. This question is part of our concern insofar as we want to
identify those things that can be learnt, and in virtue of which people do what
they do. We want to know how we can best characterize and classify the different
kinds of malleable internal conditions in virtue of which we do what we do.
We are attempting to identify discrete *respects* in which we may be formatively
influenced. These seem to be somewhat wider than those things which we can
'learn', and which can be 'taught', but they are susceptible to influence.

In this chapter, we shall critically survey and attempt to synthesize the best
parts of some notable answers to our question. We will consider potential answers
from the work of Timothy D. Wilson, E. J. Thiessen, Daniel C. Dennett, Benjamin
Bloom (et al.), E. Jonathan Lowe and Herbert Kelman. I will defend a critical
synthesis of these proposals. Before we begin by discussing the work of Dennett,
by way of a brief, advance summary, I argue that we should regard the following
as constituting those respects in which we can be formatively influenced:

1. The degrees and kinds of one's physical and mental abilities
2. One's stock of concepts
3. Those propositions which one understands
4. One's cognitive, propositional attitudes, such as belief and disbelief
5. One's affective attitudes to propositions and objects

Memes

In his 1995 book, *Darwin's Dangerous Idea*, Daniel C. Dennett defends the idea
that human beings are (in Suzanne Blackmore's memorable phrase) 'meme
machines' (Blackmore 1999). Although definitions vary, a meme is, roughly,
'an idea, behaviour, style, or usage that spreads from person to person within
a culture' (*Merriam Webster*).[2] The term was coined by Richard Dawkins in his
book, *The Selfish Gene*:

> We need a name for the new replicator, a noun that conveys the idea of a unit
> of cultural transmission, or a unit of *imitation*. 'Mimeme' comes from a suitable

---

[2] http://www.merriam-webster.com/dictionary/meme (accessed 23 June 2015).

Greek root, but I want a monosyllable that sounds a bit like 'gene'. I hope my classicist friends will forgive me if I abbreviate mimeme to *meme*. If it is any consolation, it could alternatively be thought of as being related to 'memory', or to the French word *même*. (Dawkins 1989, 192)

One way to think of this is to conceive of the brain as a piece of biological hardware, capable of supporting software, that might be called ideas, beliefs and so on (although the extension of the phrase 'so on' is precisely the issue at stake), but that may be captured under the general heading, 'memes'. Memes go beyond this, expanding to any respects in which humans are imitable by one another (or indeed any respects in which one entity is imitable by another entity). Question: What can go on the curriculum? Answer: Memes! Dennett gives a fascinating example of this way of thinking during a talk entitled 'How Did the Humanities Evolve?'[3] 'Whenever you hear a philosopher use the word "surely" a little bell should ring "ding", because you've probably just located the most weak point in the person's argument … he doesn't want to argue for it, he's trying to nudge you along with a "surely".' Dennett then announces 'I have just downloaded an app on to your neck top'. Dennett's 'application' is a habit, one that is apt to pass through cultural transmission such as conversation.

Dennett observes that 'our normal view of ideas is a normative view. … In brief, we ought to accept the true and [admire] the beautiful.' And, says Dennett, it is because a claim is thought to be true, and a painting beautiful that they are believed and admired respectively. In contrast, for Dennett, the proper explanation of why a claim is believed, or why an artwork is approved of, recasts claims and artworks as memes, and says that 'meme X spread among the people because X is a good replicator' (Dennett 1995, 363–4). However, we may worry that this claim is either rationally self-defeating (if it is thought to explain everything) or true but trivial. Memetics (the study of memes) seems to claim the following:

1. That the entirety of the intellectual economy is formed of replicable units
2. That the entirety of human behaviour is made up of replicable aspects
3. That the entirety of the explanation as to why they are replicated has to do with whether they are suited for replication, and is no different in character to the explanation of why some genes are successful in particular environments

---

[3] Daniel C. Dennett, 'How Did the Humanities Evolve?' https://www.youtube.com/watch?v=A2er4N5hzKA, @ 44:56 (accessed 23 June 2015).

The question arises as to how anything like rational thought enters into evaluating these three claims. If it doesn't, then it seems that this whole way of talking is itself a meme which has no rational foundation and it would be a staggering coincidence if it turned out that the flow of memes produced a correct explanation of itself. Indeed, it may seem that the very notion of truth drops out of the picture as memes, like genes, become mere coping mechanisms to navigate the environment, rather than representations of a mind-independent world. But the question arises as to whether that picture is true, and if it is, then it cannot be true after all (its truth is not even possible). As Anthony O'Hear explains: 'As with every other belief or theory we should be minded to accept it only if we have genuine reasons to think it true – which is just what the meme analysis leaves no room for. So we should reject it' (O'Hear 1997, 157–8).

If a weaker hypothesis is suggested, that while some ideas are rationally spread, others are spread in a more gene-like fashion, we could be more sympathetic. These evolutionary stories could be mobilized to explain non-rational trends in a rational fashion. But that much seems trivially true. While some philosophers of education, such as Smeyers, Smith and Standish might be expected to scorn the very notion of memes, declaring 'the reconstruction of the pupil or student as a collection of programmable skills' to be part of the lamentable condition in which education finds itself in valuing 'performativity', an argument is required to say how it is wrong (Smeyers et al. 2007, 4). It might well be suited to the performativity agenda, but that does not show it to be wrong; indeed, it need not be adopted for the performativity agenda. For our purposes however, we may say that it leaves the most interesting question open, namely: 'What kinds of memes are there?' Thus, for us, Memetics has little to offer for the moment (indeed, we might even hope that we have something to offer it). One other limitation is that memes are not coextensive with those respects in which we can be formatively influenced since while we might become more or less confident, these are not acquired through imitation or transmission but through such practices as encouragement, praise and deference.

Wilson and narratives

Timothy D. Wilson argues that 'in order to understand why people do what they do, we have to view the world through their eyes and understand how they make sense of things' (Wilson 2011). Wilson cashes out the ideas of how people 'view the world' and 'make sense of things' with the concept of a 'narrative'.[4] For instance, Wilson contends that 'people have core narratives about relationships that are rooted in their early interactions with their primary care givers', furthermore, 'our interpretations are rooted in the narratives we construct' (Wilson 2011, 9). In sum, our interpretations of events are rooted in narratives that are constructed from experiences, such as early interactions with caregivers. The notion of a narrative emphasizes a certain holism, and structuredness of one's belief set, especially in its suggestion that there might be core, and, by implication, peripheral beliefs. There may be two kinds of core beliefs, and these may overlap: emotional core beliefs and epistemic core beliefs. Compare my belief that I am a good person with my commitment to the law of non-contradiction. One might be central to my particular conception of myself, and perhaps to my emotional security; the other is a precondition of my ability to make any sense of the world at all. Our narratives are essentially first-personal, not third-personal (although, one can attempt to be more objective or impersonal in one's account of the events in which one features). They attempt to show the connectedness or coherence of the episodes of one's life. One's narrative is a representation to oneself, of oneself, of one's past and projections into one's future.

Wilson's account of narratives raises two questions for us. The first is whether there are any explanations of why it is that we do what we do that go beyond our narratives, which still deal in internal malleable dispositions. The second is whether a narrative is a simple thing, or whether it admits of analysis into parts in some principled way which themselves make up the range of those malleable, yet stable internal conditions which incline us towards our actual volitions and actions. By way of caution, we should worry that people's narratives could prove delusional (a monster may conceive of themselves as being fundamentally decent, for instance) and that they may be rationalizing rather than rational (someone may have done something quite kind for a selfish reason, and convinced themselves that it was because it was kind that they did it).[5] If narratives are to be causally efficacious in general, then they will need to be more than post hoc epiphenomena. Consider the following example of the possibly causally redundant role of the narratives, with which people understand

---

[4] Galen Strawson has criticized the idea that all of us are narrative beings with a need to represent our lives to ourselves as stories, saying it is simply empirically false 'Some of us don't naturally cast or construe our lives as a narrative or story of some sort, and we don't experience parts of our lives in this way either. Nor do we think of ourselves as opposed to our lives in a narrative way' (Strawson 2012).

[5] Delusion can sometimes explain why people do what they do; somebody who is convinced that they are made of glass may be very cautious about being struck by anything, and so one's core narrative explains one's behaviour. Alternatively, it could be a post hoc justification, and so a rationalization rather than causal explanation.

themselves. 'Implicit Bias' is the name given to those biases which we do not know ourselves to have, and which we may even believe ourselves to not have. According to the Stanford School of Medicine's website, social science has shown that, unbeknownst to themselves, people can hold 'a positive or negative mental attitude towards a person, thing or group'. Furthermore, 'our implicit and explicit biases often diverge'.[6]

Learning objectives in schools

Many schools already distinguish learning objectives from learning outcomes, with outcomes cited as evidence of the satisfaction of objectives. It is learning objectives that we are primarily interested in here, for we are interested in what it is in virtue of which people do what they do, not in what they do. The divisions between 'knowledge, understanding, skills and attitudes' form the usual taxonomy of learning objectives. For instance, a lesson might hope to encourage students' knowing the key people, actions and consequences relating to the Holocaust, understanding why the actors did what they did, being able locate and interrogate relevant sources, and their being appalled by the concept of mechanized genocide. These ways of dividing up the respects in which human beings can be formatively influenced are not obviously flawed. They presuppose (and perhaps not wrongly) that knowledge is the only kind of belief which it is worthwhile and acceptable to promote. If Timothy D. Wilson is right, perhaps one might only add the integration of knowledge into stories containing one's own self as an important aspect of formative influence. One might also add the tendency to exercise control by paying relevant attention if John Wilson is right. We might distinguish two senses of 'understanding' and say that a lack of understanding in one of the senses just is a knowledge deficit whereas a lack of understanding in the second sense undermines a precondition of belief. This distinction will become clearer as we proceed. But one is not yet inclined to eliminate any.

Bloom's taxonomy

Benjamin Bloom et al.'s prominent taxonomy of educational objectives divides the range of the learnable into three 'domains', namely the cognitive, affective and

---

6   Stanford School of Medicine, http://med.stanford.edu/diversity/FAQ_REDE.html (accessed 23 June 2015).

psychomotor. Each domain is made up of hierarchically arranged categories, the more sophisticated of which presuppose competence of the less sophisticated parts. The first volume of the taxonomy, on the cognitive domain, was published in 1956, and a second volume, on the affective domain, followed in 1964 (Krathwohl et al. 1964). Bloom projected, but never produced a third volume on the psychomotor domain. Others attempted to fill the gap, but we shall look at the original Bloom handbooks here, and also their more recent development and defence by Anderson and Krathwohl. The original categories to be found in the Bloom handbooks were these:

- The categories of the cognitive domain, from least to most sophisticated, are: knowledge, comprehension, application, analysis, synthesis, and evaluation (Bloom et al. 1956, 18).
- The categories of the affective domain, from least to most sophisticated, are: receiving phenomena, responding to phenomena, valuing, organization (or prioritization), internalizing values (Krathwohl et al. 1964, 35).

The categories of the affective domain are far less plausible than those of the cognitive domain. Their proposed progression seems deeply confused. Surely valuing, which is apparently a higher order skill, is presupposed in receiving and responding to phenomena (which just translate as listening to and engaging with other points of view). Furthermore, the idea that organization (or resolving inconsistencies and tensions, and such like) occurs before internalizing values is absurd: the idea here is that one maps out the values that one ought to have and then uploads the results is manifestly false. It is more often the case that one is challenged about one's behaviour and attitudes, and reflects on them after the fact, perhaps modifying them for the future. Ethical reflection is more often a matter of bringing one's existing commitments into reflective equilibrium rather than deciding which values to internalize in the first place.

The Bloom Taxonomy of cognitive learning defined knowledge as the ability to remember previously learned information. ('Knowledge, as defined here, involves the recall of specifics and universals, the recall of methods and processes, or the recall of a pattern, structure, or setting') (Bloom et al. 1956, 201). Bloom took knowledge to be more basic than understanding, but, as Bernard Williams puts it, 'If you do not know what it is you are believing, how can you be sure that you are believing anything at all?'; that is, belief, and thereby knowledge, presupposes understanding (Williams 2006a, 17). Consider the absurdity of the following reviewer's comment (from an otherwise insightful review):

'Comprehension requires students to understand what they know' (Conklin 2005, 155). Clearly one has to comprehend what one knows, or one would not know what it is that one apparently knows.

These problems might be redressed if we simply recast 'knowledge' as 'memory', for surely someone can remember some string of information without understanding it. Indeed, this change was made by Anderson and Krathwohl (2001). Anderson and Krathwohl also argue that 'the real nature of a synthesis necessitates creating a new product', consequently rebranding 'synthesis' as 'create', modifying its definition, and placing it at the top of the cognitive hierarchy (Conklin 2005, 157). The list of cognitive feats, in order of ascending difficulty, suggested by these authors, is as follows: remembering, understanding, applying, analysing, evaluating, and creating. There does seem to be something right about the idea that synthesis involves evaluation, and that evaluation need not involve synthesis, even though it sets one out on the path to synthesis. However, the idea that creation is the most demanding feat seems doubtful. One can create a new work of art by splashing a bit of paint about, but it is much harder to accurately recreate an old work of art (it may not be worth doing so, but it is a harder task). Indeed, creativity is often a matter of noticing the benefit of some mistake, which is to say, creativity is often serendipitous, rather than deliberate. The sense of 'creativity' that is more deserving of a top spot would be a critical synthesis of existing materials into a coherent whole.

One might say that one need not recollect anything in order to, for instance, be critical of it, or be said to understand it. I have understood many more sentences than I can recollect. And indeed, I could see a sentence for the first time, which I understand, and which I cannot (of course) understand in virtue of recalling it. Indeed, it seems that understanding the sentence 'put the cat on the mat' requires some analysis. Perhaps one might associate it with an action all in one go, without understanding the parts of the sentence, but understanding in general requires some level of analysis due to the compositionality of meaningful sentences from meaningful part (in this case: 'put', 'the cat', 'on' and 'the mat').

In general, the taxonomists want to distinguish between 'higher order' and 'lower order' thinking, the idea being that the higher order processes presupposes competency in lower order processes. We might think of this as being a scale of human cognitive flourishing. But we should just qualify this by saying that mastery of lower levels may produce material of greater worth than mere competence of higher levels of thought. Or one might reasonably suggest that great mastery of the lower levels is redundant (e.g. recalling great sequences of signs, without comprehension, such as recalling the whole of the Yellow Pages, without being able to call a single number in it). It might outline broad categories of phenomena, but it does not help us assess their worthwhileness. Furthermore, it does not help us distinguish between deep and shallow degrees of understanding – we will have to go further and work out what a deep and worthwhile understanding is. I recall Hubert Dreyfus remarking in a lecture that he had taught a course about an aspect of Heidegger's philosophy, and that one of his students had understood it better than he did himself, and, indeed, had understood it better than Heidegger did, as he had proposed more defensible revisions. Here, we see understanding phasing into evaluation and synthesis. We might term this 'deep understanding' and distinguish it from some baser level of comprehension. But it seems that even base level comprehension presupposes something. We also ought to hesitate over the notion that evaluation is a high level activity whereby one who has not evaluated has, in some way, failed relative to someone who has; it might be that withholding judgement is sometimes more rational than passing judgement. I was taken aback when I asked Jonathan Lowe whether he was a theist, agnostic or atheist, as he replied that he had no opinion. It raised the possibility for me that I had rushed to conclusions, when confronted with a much more critically reflective, and informed person who had suspended judgement. Obviously enough though, a deep and worthwhile understanding of a topic will usually require more than an ability to recall strings of symbols.

The idea that evaluating phenomena is a higher order activity is also highly doubtful; people evaluate phenomena instantaneously, and unreflectively. There are more conscious processes where one makes oneself aware of their evaluations, perhaps suspends and informs their judgement and deliberates further on what judgement is best. But simply feeling one way or another about things is part of the most basic processes whereby people are able to survive in hostile environments: infants have pro-attitudes about being nursed that they surely cannot have deliberated on.

Indeed, one might also reasonably seek to blend affective and cognitive domains; Eamonn Callan draws on a distinction between *relational* and *appreciative* understanding. Relational understanding seems to consist in having a mental representation of a thing, and some sense of how it connects with and relates to other things (by similarity, causal chains and what not). Appreciative understanding, however, involves some sense of whether it is good or bad, desirable or undesirable (Callan 2009, 14–15). Michael Hand observes that

> cognition and affect are not at all easy to separate: an integral part of coming to understand the facts, theories, texts and narratives that make up the cognitive content of the curriculum is coming to feel their interest and excitement, their inspiration or disenchantment, their nobility, injustice, comedy or tragedy. (Hand 2011, 330)

The sort of understanding that Hand has in mind here is appreciative, which can be distinguished from more formal and disinterested forms of understanding. For instance, someone may be able to answer questions about the Holocaust correctly, to reason well about it from the evidence, and yet take a disinterested, merely professional view of it. Here, it would seem that there was a major failing in their appreciative understanding, even if their more formal understanding was outstanding.

Anderson and Krathwohl depart from the original, where 'it was assumed that the original Taxonomy represented a cumulative hierarchy; that is, mastery of each simpler category was prerequisite to mastery of the next more complex one' (Krathwohl 2002, 212–13). In their version, some of the skills which exemplify having understood content are considered more complex than some of those that exemplify the ability to apply content (e.g. explaining content versus executing a task) (Krathwohl 2002, 215). They also want to distinguish between the categories' applications to what they call factual, conceptual, procedural and metacognitive knowledge. These do not appear to me to be exhaustive and exclusive categories. They are not clearly related to one another, and they appear somewhat arbitrary. Indeed, Jason Stanley and Timothy Williamson have powerfully challenged the idea that examples of 'knowledge how' cannot be reduced to examples of propositional knowledge (Stanley and Williamson 2001). Indeed, picking out conceptual knowledge and self-knowledge (metacognitive knowledge) from among the contents of things that one can know about might be justified for some practical purposes, but they do not seem to be ontologically special; for instance, self-knowledge is a species of factual knowledge.

In general, the Bloom taxonomy and its revisions provide us with interesting, systematic and recognizable, realist taxonomies of formative influence. The details of the taxonomies at which I have looked seem doubtful, but it is always possible that a much more defensible version will yet be brought to my attention.

E. Jonathan Lowe, belief and desire psychology versus volitionism

According to E. Jonathan Lowe, our actions are sometimes rational, and sometimes non-rational (if still reasonable). Rational actions are those that are performed *for a reason*, and non-rational actions are those that are caused by psychological forces such as combinations of beliefs and desires (Lowe 2008a, 181). (At the same time, in Lowe's own example, unreflectively dodging a piece of falling masonry is reasonable, if not, in this sense, rational.) This view amends the picture of human beings as belief-desire machines, mechanistically determined to act by inner psychological forces over which they have no control (or which comprise them), to allow them the faculty for genuinely free choices or volitions, which are often (although by no means always) part of the explanation of our actions. Indeed, such a psychologically determinist outlook can be seen to be implicit in some of the above accounts if they are taken to be exhaustive accounts of why it is that we do what we do. It would be fair to add here though, that picturing human beings as bystanders to their beliefs and desires, determining their actions in concert, has a false ring to it since human beings may be thought to be largely constituted by their beliefs and desires.

Herbert Kelman on personal identity

Herbert Kelman has written on the extent to which our personal identity can be influenced by others. What he has in mind by 'personal identity' is made up of

> the enduring aspects of a person's definition of her-himself, the conception of who one is and what one is over time and across situations. [Their personal identity] is what individuals bring to the many situations and social interactions in which they become involved as they go through the life cycle and, at any given period of time. (Kelman 1998, 3)

However, as we have seen in our discussion of narrativity, people's self-conceptions can be mistaken: how people think they are, and how they are is different; the latter is more important and encompasses the first, anyway. We could amend this to regard people's actual identity as being constituted by those of their behaviours that *are* 'enduring aspects of a person ... over time and across situations', that they 'bring to the many situations and social interactions' in which they become involved (Kelman 1998, 3). On Kelman's account, those respects in which we can be formatively are our behaviours. However, he makes highly idiosyncratic use of that word (one which seems to include almost every explanatory aspect of behaviour to the exclusion of behaviour itself): 'I use the term behaviour very broadly to include attitudes, opinions, beliefs, values, and action preferences. My model is not concerned with the motor aspects of behavior, but with its evaluative components' (Kelman 1998, 7).

Kelman's list of internal malleable dispositions then, consists of 'attitudes, opinions, beliefs, values, and action preferences', which he terms the 'evaluative components' of behaviour. It seems that the last four of these are all examples of attitudes.

Elmer Thiessen and social grouping

Elmer Thiessen has contributed interestingly (although not explicitly) to this topic in his discussion of the ethics of evangelism. Thiessen glossed 'evangelism' as any 'deliberate attempt … to bring about … a change of a person's belief, behaviour, identity and belonging' (Thiessen 2011, 11).[7] This, it seems, is Thiessen's analysis of the respects in which we might be formatively influenced, with respect to religion. Unfortunately, Thiessen's analysis leaves us wanting a fuller account of 'identity', and although we can form our own plausible conceptions to fit the bill, this does not tell us what Thiessen had in mind. Furthermore, his conception of 'belonging' seems to oscillate between two different senses, namely a 'sense of belonging' (Thiessen 2011, 16) and, more substantively, 're-socialization into an alternative community' (Thiessen 2011, 10); elsewhere, Thiessen even implies identity and belonging to be the same thing: 'A change of identity (belonging)' (Thiessen 2011, 16). Thiessen glosses 'a change of identity' as 'a change of who you are' (Thiessen 2011, 10), which is itself ambiguous. A plausible sense could be 'a significant change of one's character'. More importantly however, and somewhat problematically for me, Thiessen draws attention to influence over social grouping; a respect in which we can be influenced, which does not seem to be anything like a disposition. Grouping people is to put them into groups:

---

[7] Evangelism in this sense may be either religious or non-religious, depending on whether it is religious beliefs, behaviours and identities that one is attempting to inculcate, and religious groups that one is attempting to make people feel part of.

to make them spend time together. It could additionally involve giving them roles within that group and can be more or less coercive. It appears to be a form of behavioural influence then, which will presumably come to have a formative influence. That said, we might take Thiessen to offer the following answers: beliefs, behaviour, character and sense of belonging.

Proposed respects of formative influence

Informed by the accounts that we have considered, I shall now present my account of those respects in which we can be formatively influenced. First though, I want to explain why we should not include behaviour among those respects in which we can be formatively influenced. It is because if one were interested in behaviour, it seems that interest in beliefs, for instance, would be rendered redundant, because it seems that behaviour is to be explained partly in terms of beliefs. Indeed, our behaviour does not count among those things in virtue of which we do what we do; it just is what we do. By way of which sorts of malleable, internal conditions do people do what they do? It is the ethics of our effects on these that we are interested in. I shall now sketch what I take to be the likeliest candidates.

1. One's abilities (or powers) in degree, if not always in kind:[8]

   1.1. One's Mental Abilities:
   These include our abilities to believe certain propositions (via concepts), to perceive things (also via concepts), to refrain from action and to execute an array of mental feats (to be impartial, imagine, remember, direct attention and so on). Anderson and Krathwohl suggested recollection, comprehension, application, analysis, evaluation and creation, and these are also plausible examples.

   1.2. One's Physical Abilities:
   For instance, abilities to perform certain actions such as running, jumping, climbing, chewing, swallowing, reading and so on. Bloom refers to these as 'psychomotor' skills. Such actions as making beds, tying threads and running baths would be too generous a psychomotor ontology, rather what

---

[8] Arguably, we never truly acquire a new power altogether, but only develop those out which we construct more kinds of powers: the power to twist and the power to push down, and the power to rearrange the order in which we execute actions allows us to remove the lids from medicine bottles.

is important is the fine and gross motor skills which are common across all kinds of social activities.

2. One's Concepts:

    One would be unable to decide to perform an action that one does not have the concept of, for instance, somebody from the distant past could not choose to build a nuclear reactor.

3. Those propositions which one understands, and towards which one may have a cognitive or affective attitude:

    Believing or disbelieving that it is true and fearing or hoping that it might come true. Propositions will presumably be composed of concepts.[9] Those propositions which we understand make up the set of those propositions which we may believe, for as we have heard Williams say once already 'If you do not know what it is that you are believing how can you be sure that you are believing anything?' (Williams 2006a, 19). That said, it does seem that we can defer to authorities of both understanding and epistemic warrant, saying: I neither understand nor (for that very reason) believe this proposition, but believe that you both understand it and know it to be true. In this way, we might be committed to a proposition without even understanding it.

4. One's Cognitive Attitudes:

    These attitudes include belief, disbelief and doubt. It seems that the beliefs we have form the framework within which we decide to do what we do: if we decide that we want a stamp and go to get one, where we go will depend on where we believe we can get one, and our decision to go and get one will depend on what sort of thing we think that a stamp is and how it connects with other things that we want to do, such as getting a parcel to a distant friend. Furthermore, insofar as we are rational, our beliefs about what reasons we have to act or believe will also affect what we go on to do.[10] Following Wilson, we might allow the interrelations of these to be a prominent feature. But beliefs have to be interrelated to count as beliefs in the first place it seems. Daniel C. Dennett seems to demonstrate this in a discussion of implanted beliefs. An interesting question is posed by Dennett: 'Suppose we have entered the age of neurocryptography', he says,

---

[9] 'The content of a thought can include only what the content of its constituent concepts (and "logical" syntax) contribute' (Fodor 2001, 6).

[10] For any proposition, a person may take one of the following (mutually exclusive) attitudes: belief, disbelief or agnosticism. They may also take no attitude at all – at least in that case that they are unaware of the proposition.

'and it has become possible for "cognitive micro-neurosurgeon" to do a bit of relevant tinkering and *insert* a belief into a person's brain' (Dennett 2013, 65). Suppose that Tom has the belief: 'I have an older brother living in Cleveland' inserted, and that it is false. This might play out in two ways, says Dennett, one in which Tom's rationality is intact, and one where it is damaged. Were Tom asked whether he has a brother, he would answer that he does, and that he lives in Cleveland. Were he asked anything more about his brother, he might realize that the belief was false and eliminate it (after all, he also believes that he is an only child, and has no recollection of his brother). On the other hand, he might maintain that he has an older brother living in Cleveland ('in the nature of a tick'), and that he is also an only child, in which case 'his frank irrationality would disqualify him as a believer' (Dennett 2013, 66).

5. One's affective attitudes to propositions and objects (such as fearing or hoping that a proposition be true or loving or hating a particular person). They would include Thiessen's example of a 'sense of belonging' to groups. These may be cashed out further, in terms of

   5.1. one's set of wants and their prioritization
   5.2. which stimuli trigger which attitudes (for instance, Nazi propaganda aimed to provoke disgust at the thought of Jews, by associating them with vermin)

Discussion

These might all be described as dispositions, and all perishable dispositions. Indeed, some want to account for beliefs[11] and powers as dispositions. A dispositional analysis of powers might go like this: just in case one wants to do something and wills to do it, they are disposed to do it, whereas, those that aren't able, are not disposed to even if they will to do it (e.g. raising one's arm when under the influence of a powerful sedative). We might think of character and other dispositions more generally being formed by repeated action, sometimes reflective action, so that actions become less reflective and perhaps more

---

[11] Frank Ramsey provides a functionalist account of belief along the following lines. A belief is to be individuated by its causal properties: my believing that the wine is not poisonous will have different causal consequences, all other things being equal, than my not believing it (Ramsey and Moore 1927).

sophisticated. We may be reminded of the following warning about character formation in this regard:

> Mr. Wiseman then cautioned his young friends as to the habits they contracted in early life: 'Whatsoever a man soweth that shall he also reap.' You sow an act, you reap a habit (acts repeated constitute habits); you sow a habit, you reap a character; you sow a character, you reap a destiny. Let them, he said, cultivate habits of industry, application, and order, and they might rely upon it, with God's blessing, they would succeed in life.[12]

Here, actions form dispositions, and so it seems that by encouraging one-off actions, we set off on the journey to forming dispositions.

Where have the other suggestions gone?

We established that Memetics had little to offer us in failing to divide up different sorts of memes. Wilson's narratives, considered as first-person, holistic, belief-structures with cores and peripheries that inform our interpretations and actions were in serious danger of becoming epiphenomenal, and so causally uninteresting. On the other hand, they also had the drawback of failing to discriminate their constituent parts. Their attraction was in offering some degree of structure to constituent parts.

We observed that many schools and curricula distinguish between knowledge, understanding, skills and attitudes as learning objectives. We allowed that beliefs form a broader category than knowledge, without presupposing the value of truth. We allowed also that understanding was ambiguous between being able to entertain the content of a thought and having some appreciation for the value of a thing. We also allowed that understanding could be deeper or shallower to the extent that one recognizes more connections and errors, all of which are items of knowledge. We held that attitudes were a broad enough category to capture belief states. It seemed that integration of knowledge and attitudes into coherent stories containing one's own self might be an extension of this list too, as would 'control by paying relevant attention', in John Wilson's expression (such as when we learn not to look down while rock climbing), that would seem to be an example of developing a habit or eliminating a habit. E. Jonathan Lowe's volitions may well be parts of our mental landscape, but they do not seem to be internally malleable dispositions or, indeed, dispositions at all.

---

[12] Mr. Wiseman quoted in *The Essex Standard* (27 August 1856), p. 2, Column 6.

Kelman's categories of attitudes, opinions, beliefs, values and action preferences were subsumed, it seems. Thiessen's categories of belief and sense of belonging have been accommodated. Behaviour was rejected, as was re-socialization, as not belonging to the category of respects of formative influence. The category of 'identity' is perhaps captured by the taxonomy as a whole. One worry in this line of thinking is that it sets up a false opposition, between individuals in isolation on the one hand, and individuals in situ, on the other. But perhaps there never are thoroughly internal properties that people have; perhaps people's properties are necessarily constituted in part by their surroundings (as Hilary Putnam's belief externalism Twin Earth considerations motivate) (Putnam 1973).

Not all of the ethics of influence is captured with this focus. Indeed, we can influence people to act via coercion, and even if we did not change them much in the above respects, it would seem to be an unethical example of influence (simply playing on what dispositions were already in place).

5

What Forms Can and Should Influence Take?

Introduction

This chapter discusses *means* by which children *can* and *may* be formatively influenced. We begin by trying to make sense of the notion of a 'means' or 'form' of influence by distinguishing between three rival ways of categorizing actions, namely by intentions, processes and outcomes. Three kinds of platforms which influencers can use to amplify or enable their communication acts are then discussed, namely, media used to communicate, the social status of the communicator relative to those communicated with, and the social status of the spaces and occasions in which they occur. An explanation of the differences between directed and undirected, systematic and ad hoc, and rational and non-rational, potentially influential, acts follow. I then develop the notions of rational and non-rational means of influence at length, offering examples of each, before arguing that rational means of influence are morally preferable to non-rational means of influence.

Forms of influence

What forms *can* influence take? We might list all sorts of (potentially or actually) influential activities: propagandizing, journalism, educating, indoctrinating, manipulating, informing, persuading, arguing, recommending, demonstrating, explaining, inspiring, dissuading, impressing, convincing, lying, enculturating, conditioning, training and on and on. But this seems to be a mixed list (i.e. some actions may be counted twice by satisfying more than one member, since the categories cut across each other). For instance, propagandizing, journalism, educating and indoctrinating might all involve persuasion, arguing, inspiring and impressing. Some of its members are to be identified by the effect that they have, since they are (to borrow Gilbert Ryle's expression) *achievement verbs* while other members, namely, *task verbs*, are not to be identified by the effect that they have, but by the effect that they aim to have (Ryle 2000, 49–53). So, while one cannot succeed in impressing without impressing anybody in particular, on the other hand, one can succeed in reporting an event without an audience; for instance, I might report on an event in a private diary, perhaps in a secret cypher. The contents of such a report would remain inert as a potential influence until its code is cracked. Importantly, for each success verb, we may be lacking in a convenient task verb, but there was nonetheless a task conducted to which the success term may be applied retrospectively (with certainty) or prospectively (perhaps with some confidence). For example we may say retrospectively: she has persuaded the audience, or prospectively, that she's persuading the audience as we speak. Alternatively, we might want to say that she is *trying* to persuade the audience, but she might not be trying at all and yet still be engaged in a process which might well have that result. Our task is to specify those discrete kinds of potentially influential acts which may be used to influence people, be they direct or indirect, and which may be employed across various platforms (media, social roles and spaces). We ask: In what principled ways can we distinguish between forms of influence, and what taxonomy of influence is available to us?

There are potentially influential activities which be performed, and it seems that these can be performed on different platforms, changing the probable audiences. For instance, consider the difference between reporting an incident in a private conversation in a private place and reporting it in private conversation in a public place, or reporting it on a popular television show and reporting in a private diary which someone reads. Here, reporting an incident seems to be one sort of communication act, one which may be performed on different platforms, changing the probable audiences. But how exactly are we to specify potentially influential acts, so to avoid mixed lists? It seems that there are three rival ways of categorizing actions, namely, intentions, processes and outcomes.

Intentions, processes and outcomes

We might want to specify potentially influential acts in terms of their intentions, their processes or their outcomes. Impressing, and inspiring seem to specify influential acts by outcome. 'What did the actor do?' one might ask, and an answer might come that 'They inspired me', or 'They impressed me'. On the other hand, we might want to specify potentially influential acts (or activities) in terms of processes; what component actions they involve. This allows that outcomes may vary. Talking, for instance, seems to be very process specific, and nothing to do with outcomes: one can talk without talking to anybody, and without thereby having any particular effect on them. Of course, process and outcomes do have some connection: reporting an episode to somebody (if they believe you to be accurate and sincere) will have the result that they take your word about the episode. Finally, one may intend to affect a certain outcome, act in a way that one thinks will affect it, and yet the chosen act may not affect the intended outcome. While some act terms are tightly connected with the outcomes, such as making an impression or being inspirational, here it seems that we retrospectively characterize the act in terms of the outcome, even though it does not seem essential to its nature. Outcomes are what are desired it seems, and processes are what may be employed to achieve them. Either or both outcomes and processes may form the content of our intentions. We have already argued in Chapter 2 that it is what harm we intend or allow, and what harm we risk (either through indifference or negligence) for which we are morally culpable.

Platforms of influence

There seem to be three sorts of platforms that we might identify for potentially influential acts: media used to communicate (e.g. television), social status of the communicator relative to those communicated with (e.g. a college student's professor), and the social status of the spaces and occasions in which they occur (e.g. during the Royal Society's Christmas lecture).

Media seem to comprise means of recording and/or broadcasting information. Media are means of communicating a message or cultivating a specified outcome (attempting to affect an influence that one can specify in advance). It seems that the printed word, telephones, television, the internet, radio broadcast, all fit on this list. They are all capable of supporting any of the members in the (mixed) opening list of influential activities. Media may make use of different forms of information: images, text, audio recording, and motion pictures (it is less clear how texture, scent, heat and taste, among the forms of data available to other senses may be recorded or broadcast). The internet is a medium that can support any of these forms of information; the printing press can only support the first two; radio can only support audio. One might suggest that a flick book can record motion pictures, and one might admit this (it is not *too far* an artefact from a film reel, which *could* be understood as a motion picture file) but insist on its limitations. One might ask: what about Twitter, and Facebook, and blogs? These are social networks, and, to that extent, they are social spaces comprised of media. They are means of interpersonal communication facilitated by the internet. They are means of exchanging information of the sort listed above. It seems that media are *means* of influence in one distinct sense.

I have said that media are means of recording or broadcasting information. One might wonder whether those things recorded and broadcast can be media as well; whether dance, speech and song might count as media, for instance, or whether a story or play might be a medium. Arguably, all communication is dependent on some medium or other, if only vibrations in the air and language. Here, then, the modifier 'mass' is helpful in distinguishing mass media from more circumscribed media. Media might be thought of as platforms, but not all platforms are media; one might think of public spaces such as soap boxes at Speaker's Corner in London, theatres, cinemas, schools or universities. Any shared space in which one has access to another is a platform for communication; one could list malls in general or particular malls, or crowded streets or places of work. One might also think of social positions as being platforms for influence: being a police officer, a teacher, a doctor, a prime minister, a journalist, a celebrity, are likely examples of individuals whose social status makes a difference to their communicative power. Here, the status of the space and the actor are important because they determine the degree of trust that they will likely be lent by the audience. When an esteemed professor delivers the Royal Society's Christmas lecture, or when a doctor or teacher informs their patient or pupil of a proposition, their audience is often rationally obliged to believe them. (Although discovered abuse of trust can undermine the rationality of investing trust in the future.)

Directed versus undirected communication

One interesting distinction is between knowing and not knowing whom it is that one is addressing. For instance, contrast talking with a dear friend in person with putting a message into a bottle and putting it out to sea. These may be thought of as pure examples of directed and undirected communication, each of which occupy opposite poles of a continuum. Plato voiced a general concern about undirected communication in the *Phaedrus*:[1]

> Once it has been written down, every discourse rolls about everywhere, reaching just as much those with understanding as those who have no business with it, and it does not know to whom it should speak and to whom not. (*Phaedrus*, 275d–e)[2]

Film certification, by such bodies as the British and Irish Boards of Film Classification (the BBFC and IBFC), the establishment of television watersheds, and creation of document passwords somewhat ameliorate this problem. But no content is like Arthur's sword in the stone, presenting itself only to those for whom it is properly suited. I remember admiring the gangsters in *Goodfellas* (dir. Scorsese, 1990) as a teenager, and for that reason it might have been better if the film had known that I was not ready to see it.

Systematic versus ad hoc communication

In conversation, we often tell stories and jokes, to amuse or entertain, or simply to relay something of an interesting experience from our day. These are ad hoc, being told to friends or strangers as we fancy. By contrast, we may assume a slightly more systematic approach: suppose someone says something racist in conversation, we may have developed a strategy for responding to such comments, which may involve either ignoring them, challenging them directly, or dropping hints and problems along the way, for instance commenting, 'Wasn't Martin Luther King a hero?' Or 'isn't Denzel Washington a great actor?' On other hand, as with curricula, we have thoroughly systematic approaches to communicating information. Curricula are systematic programmes for learning.[3]

As we have said, our task is to specify those discrete kinds of potentially influential acts which may be used to influence people (whatever kind of media they assume, directed or undirected, ad hoc or systematic, in various professions and various spaces). We want to know in what principled ways can we divide

---

[1] Cf. Williams (2009).
[2] Trans. Williams (2009, 150).
[3] Curricula can be instantiated across our three kinds of platforms: media, social space and social role.

forms of influence up, what taxonomy of influence is available to us. Rational versus non-rational means of influence is a promising option. But what is this rational/non-rational distinction? Borrowing from Michael Hand's usage, 'held non-rationally' (when said of, for instance, a belief) means held 'without regard for the evidence', thus, 'held rationally' would mean 'held *with* regard for the evidence' (Hand 2002, 545).

Rational versus non-rational influence

Rational influence

One might hope to convince people using *rational methods* that a proposition is true, that an action, attitude or emotion is good or appropriate, or that a habit would be good to cultivate. According to Hand, beliefs can be transmitted in two rational ways. First, 'where beliefs are known to be true, they can be imparted by means of rational demonstration' in which a proposition is proven to enjoy sufficient probative force to make non-belief irrational or at least to make belief rational (Hand 2002, 545). Second, 'other things being equal, when a person perceived by others to be an intellectual authority [on a relevant matter] asserts that a proposition is true, she places them under a rational obligation to accept her assertion. [Insofar as they are rational] she *imparts a belief* to her listeners, and she does so by *appealing to their reason*' (Hand 2002, 551). This is fairly intuitive: belief acquisition can be warranted either by testimony or by acquaintance with the stuff being testified to. Non-rational methods would involve any other means of influencing someone. Perhaps Hand would admit one more form of rational influence, namely, that of providing the conditions within which students might discover the truth of some proposition themselves. This also captures the method of 'steering', which Hand, in turn, glosses as 'guiding participants, by means of strategic prompts, questions, and interjections, toward a predetermined conclusion' (Hand 2013). One might think of such closed-ended exercises as allowing students to conduct experiments to discover facts about the world, as not too dissimilar to steering: after all, when the experiments do not show what they are supposed to, the teacher says, 'we did the experiments wrongly', and not, 'we have made an important discovery'. Are there any other forms of rational influence?

Rational deliberation

In his book, *Redirect*, psychologist Timothy D. Wilson recommends what he calls the 'Pennebaker Technique', in which a writing exercise is set on a topic about which the subject is confused and anxious. The task is to write an account of a traumatic event, say, requiring the subject to contemplate the event until they settle on a telling of the event with which they are content. To this end, Wilson tells us to 'commit to writing about your problem for at least 15 minutes a day for three or four consecutive days – ideally at the end of each day – and [to] write without interruption each time' (Wilson 2011, 72). The technique is, as attested to by robust empirical warrant, apt to markedly reduce confusion and anxiety. The exercise seems somewhat similar to essay writing per se. Indeed, we might observe that writing is a sort of technology, a way of making one's thoughts external. In articulating and externalizing one's thoughts, one is put in a better position to sort through them and, for instance, make them self-consistent (to establish reflective equilibrium among them). However, it is perfectly possible, given the unreliability of memory, that one will, in writing about the incident, reimagine and falsify it. Even so, I suggest that this is a rational exercise. Although no particular conclusion is recommended in setting the exercise, it is recommended that people come to some self-consistent set of opinions on a given topic (a coherent account of it), and a manner of achieving this is recommended also, namely, the writing technique. It is to a large extent a non-directive exercise, allowing for a diversity of acceptable accounts, they are better to the extent that they are self-consistent, comprehensive, simple and detailed.

Two concerns about rational persuasion

There are two concerns that we ought to address before moving on to discuss non-rational influence. First, the limitations of rational persuasion in affecting change and, second, the problems that are inherent in deferring to intellectual authority. Thaler and Sunstein note that 'the evidence does not suggest that education is, in and of itself, an adequate solution' for affecting change; by 'education', they have in mind 'rational influence' in the above sense (Thaler and Sunstein 2009, 121). There seems to be some limits to what rational methods can achieve, the most obvious examples being that phobias, addictions and delusions do not seem to be shaken by the recognition of good reasons or prevent them from being recognized as such. Timothy D. Wilson gives an example of Kurt

Lewin's finding that 'Simply lecturing people about the importance of' eating organ meats during the food shortages of the Second World War 'didn't work'. But women who attended meetings in which 'skilled leaders steered the conversation to the ways in which obstacles to serving organ meats could be overcome ... were much more likely to serve organ meats' (Wilson 2011, 11). This manner of steering can look somewhat underhanded, and, indeed, perhaps we ought to distinguish between rational steering and non-rational steering, which splits in respect of whether or not participants are steered towards influences for which they recognize decisive rational grounds. Albeit, David Bridges (1979) and David E. Cooper (2008) might both very well think that any kind of steering represents an abdication of truthfulness unless it is admitted upfront that this is what one's agenda is.

Michael Hand recommends that we put rationality ahead of autonomy as an educational aim on the grounds that merely being the one whose judgement counts is not always rational; we often do better in deferring to intellectual and moral authorities (i.e. those who are in a proper position to know about something, or tell us what to do) (Hand 2006a). We should usually believe experts and should usually obey police; at least in societies with laws that are (for the most part) just, and police who (for the most part) enforce them justly. Indeed, James Ladyman gives good examples of rational deference to intellectual authority, emphasizing the sheer diversity of deep and narrow epistemic specializations (even within physics) required for undertaking and interpreting data from experiments conducted with the Large Hadron Collider (Ladyman 2014). The complexities of each specialization are such that nobody can be conversant in all forms of expertise, and so not only is the epistemic labour split but so too is any comprehensive and detailed understanding of the enterprise. Each contributor is heavily dependent on deference to the judgement of other colleagues, whose discipline they can understand only dimly by comparison with their own. However, this can sound extremely worrisome in light of reports of German soldiers replying 'I was just following orders' when asked about their role in the Nazi atrocities at concentration camps. In *Obedience to Authority*, Stanley Milgram reports a now infamous experiment in which people defer worryingly to a perceived intellectual cum moral authority. When told by a person in a white lab coat to punish another participant with an electric current which was turned up gradually to what they believed were fatal levels, most subjects obeyed, though they were distressed by doing so.

There are other examples of similar experiments. For instance, C. K. Hofling found that twenty-one out of a sample of twenty-two nurses would have administered a patient with an overdose of medicine when ordered to by unknown doctors in a hospital setting, in spite of official guidelines forbidding giving such a dose (Hofling et al. 1966). One point made by Ladyman is that where doctors abuse their intellectual authority, this undermines the trust people can and should have in their professions. One might suggest that perhaps there is often no good ground to determine who we should defer to and who we should not and it is a case of moral luck as to whether we defer for the best. In these cases, it seems that the participants had good grounds to resist obedience, and yet, obeyed. Similarly, parents are culpable for any harm that befalls their children when they entrust them to 'quacks', but not when they entrust them to medical doctors who then abuse their power and mistreat their patients (a Dr Harold Shipman type, for instance).

Onora O'Neill has argued convincingly that trust ought to be retracted in cases of breach of trust:

> Trust requires an intelligent judgement of trustworthiness. So those who want others' trust have to do two things. First, they have to be trustworthy, which requires competence, honesty and reliability. Second, they have to provide intelligible evidence that they are trustworthy, enabling others to judge intelligently where they should place or refuse their trust. (O'Neill 2013)

If O'Neill's criteria has been satisfied, deference seems to be warranted. There also seems to be a presumption of trustworthiness for qualified doctors so that we would trust them until they prove untrustworthy. But it would be wrong to trust someone who does not have medical training on complex medical matters. In these cases, an institution is being entrusted with selecting competent, honest, reliable professionals, and their trustworthiness is inherited from the institution and its proven track record, one that can be undermined by malpractice by its members. Deference, it seems, is not inherently bad. In some matters, we shouldn't defer to others, with the Milgram experiments chief among them. In the case of Nazi obedience, the consideration of punishment for disobedience was also an important mitigating factor so that one might have known that it is morally best to disobey, and that it might be heroic to do so, but heroism might reasonably be thought to be morally supererogatory. However, what is worrisome is not rationality here, but deference. Deference is sometimes rational, and sometimes not. Contrasting with rational methods of persuasion are non-rational methods of persuasion, which we shall discuss now. Rational methods are to be preferred to non-rational, since they are truth-sensitive, and being able to track the truth seems important to flourishing, as argued in Chapter 2.

Non-rational methods

We have said (following Hand) that using anything but the presentation of, or testifying to their existence of, rationally decisive grounds in order to impart a belief of attitude, belief, policy, etc., makes use of non-rational methods of influence. However, we have allowed that steering and framing discussion and experiments can be utilized as forms of rational influence. It seems fair enough to define non-rational methods by reference to rational methods since, after all, the term non-rational is simply the negation of 'rational'. The range of things that belong to this category may be importantly open-ended. Some prominent examples can be found in contributions to social psychology. Much social psychology seems to be more focused on behavioural influence rather than formative influence. For instance, many of the 'nudges' described by Thaler and Sunstein in *Nudge* and many of Robert Cialdini's mechanisms of persuasion in *Influence* are concerned with what it takes to encourage desired responses and actions on a fairly immediate basis. Nevertheless, there is much which is both interesting and relevant.

Pseudo-rational methods

Leading off from our discussion of rational methods of influence, let us start our discussion of non-rational methods of influence by considering methods of influence that play off of the desirability of rational persuasion and pretend to count as examples of it. These pseudo-rational methods include knowingly presenting fallacious arguments, the motivated provision and concealment of relevant information and arguments, and lying. Feigning intellectual authority and stating something as true without either argument or any intellectual authority seem to count as examples, and so too does reverse psychology. Consider the following illustration of reverse psychology. One man who is unable to walk around easily has a front door that will not close properly unless slammed. He falls out with a visitor, who storms out of the apartment. The immobile man yells after his visitor 'and don't slam the door'. Sure enough, in a bad temper, his visitor slams the door, as per his wishes, but contrary to his request. Hand describes as semi-rational 'Galston's "noble, moralizing history", in which the fine deeds of a mythologized "pantheon of heroes" are rehearsed and celebrated', describing it as 'at once an exercise in emotional manipulation and an attempt to supply pupils with reasons to be patriotic, albeit spurious ones' (Hand 2011, 329). 'Pseudo-rational' might be a more apt description than 'semi-rational', but it is not clear – perhaps aspects of Galston's style of education are genuinely rational, rather than quasi-rational, in that they are scattered among non-rational elements. The difference between quasi-rational and actually rational education might turn on one of two things: whether the teacher offers reasons they believe to be spurious, or which happen to be spurious, despite their own acceptance. After all, it is important to recognize that even experts can be misled by bad arguments, despite paying due diligence.

Motivated acceptance

We can be motivated to believe propositions, and it is easier to believe what we want to believe (what we want to be true), and harder to believe what we don't want to believe (what we don't want to be true). Given this, one may appeal to what people want, in attempting to persuade them.[4] This phenomenon is more commonly termed 'wishful thinking'.

Re-socialization and conformity

It seems that we become more like those around us the longer that we spend time with them. Eamonn Callan terms this 'the magnetic power of conformity' (2014, 160), and Robert Cialdini, 'social proof' (1993). One means we use to determine what is correct is to find out what other people think is correct; we view a behaviour as more correct in a given situation to the degree that we see others performing it (1993, 116).

By way of example, using canned laughter causes audiences 'to laugh longer and more often when humorous material is presented and to rate the material as funnier' (1993, 115). In another example, the 'smoke-filled room study' showed that people were more inclined to stay in a room as it filled with smoke, if stooges remained in the room unperturbed (although that experiment was designed to test whether there was a 'by-stander effect', which lessened people's willingness

---

4   On this matter, see Blackburn (2012, 72).

to raise an alarm than when alone).[5] Here, one's judgements are likely conflicted, the judgement 'I should raise the alarm' conflicts with the judgement 'nobody else thinks that it is appropriate to raise the alarm, so perhaps I am over reacting'. Indeed, the rarity of whistle-blowers may further exemplify this phenomenon. In fact, these social processes may, in fact, be different, but closely related, kinds of phenomena.

Some influences just 'rub off' on us, like a local accent on an extended holiday. We copy one another, and thereby 'fit in' with one another, whether in respect of what we wear, how we speak or even what we believe and value (sometimes more consciously, sometimes less consciously). Becoming self-aware, we might raise our behaviour to the conscious level, and then make a habit of some alternative behaviour in order to have it become a second nature. Lou Reed's lyrics, 'Anything that you might do, I'm gonna do too. You held up a stagecoach in the rain, now I'm doing the same' provide a lively expression of conscious mimicry.[6] One thinks also of a Japanese candid camera show in which hundreds of actors lay face down in the street; when passers-by saw this they lay down on the street also.[7] It seems that intention and consciousness can vary when it comes to conforming with, or mimicking others, just on the grounds of numeracy; one might intentionally emulate another, or one might attempt to keep from emulating another, and yet still do so through unreflective slippage. Finally, one might have no intentions one way or the other, and yet still do so. These are connected with whether or not the emulation is conscious; it seems that intentional acts are necessarily conscious ones.

Because of this feature of human nature, it is possible to influence people by re-socializing them and by setting examples. This might not be considered as a kind of influential act, but rather as an example of determining what we might call 'influence architecture' (borrowing from Thaler and Sunstein's expression 'choice architecture' (2009, 3)). It is not entirely clear if this should be classed as an example of behavioural or formative influence. That is because if we are ever-malleable (or plastic), and able to adapt to conform to new social environments, then we might be tempted to say that we are not formatively influenced but only behaviourally influenced. But still, we can be influenced in those respects in virtue of which we do what we do, even if that is to be explained in terms of a circumstantial fact.

---

[5]   See Latané and Darley (1968); a video of the experiment is available at: https://www.youtube.com/watch?v=KE5YwN4NW5o (accessed 23 June 2015).
[6]   'I'm Sticking With You', performed by the Velvet Underground, lyrics by Lou Reed.
[7]   https://www.youtube.com/watch?v=MQMfiOnVeVo (accessed 23 June 2015).

Consider some other examples of re-socialization. Kilmainham gaol in Dublin, based on Jeremy Bentham's Panopticon design, separates prisoners into individual cells so as to keep them from spreading antisocial behaviours and attitudes.[8] Character reform was sought through separation from bad role models, and being without the privacy to persist in antisocial attitudes and behaviours. Indeed, prison may have the function of a criminal university for convicts. This is well illustrated by a remark of George, the central character of the film *Blow* (dir. Demme, 2001): 'Danbury wasn't a prison, it was a crime school. I went in with a Bachelor of marijuana, came out with a Doctorate of cocaine.' The same worry is put this way in *A Clockwork Orange* (dir. Kubrick, 1971), 'Cram criminals together and what do you get? Concentrated criminality; crime in the midst of punishment.' Indeed, separating friends judged to be a bad influence on one another into separate school classes is also an example of this practice. It is a kind of intervention in people's location and socializing and can sometimes count as an infringement of their rights to freedom of association and self-determination.

Who it is that one emulates can vary. One can emulate some admired individual (as Alexander the Great self-consciously emulated Achilles), some admired class of individuals (as a young boy might emulate his footballing heroes) or the people by whom one is surrounded just in virtue of their being the majority. We may recall Williams' finding obscure the idea of blaming people who do not accept the values by which one judges them wanting, and his interpretation of blame as a pragmatic tool for encouraging people to internalize those values and come to judge themselves by it. For Williams, blame is a 'proleptic mechanism' which depends on the common 'disposition that consists in a desire to be respected by people whom in turn one respects' (Williams 1989, 7).

Herbert Kelman's account of 'identification'

Herbert Kelman's analysis of what he calls 'identification' offers an account of emulation of three sorts distinguished above. For Kelman, 'identification' is a means by which

---

[8] Michel Foucault discusses this design at some length, arguing that the same process of separation and observation is used by modern states in managing and 'improving' their subjects, be they 'a madman, a patient, a condemned man, a worker or a schoolboy' (1991, 200). Sadly Foucault does little to parse rightful and good influence from wrongful and bad.

an individual accepts influence because he wants to establish or maintain a satisfying self-defining relationship to another person or group.

The individual actually believes in the responses which he adopts through identification, but their specific content is more or less irrelevant.

He adopts the induced behaviour because it is associated with the desired relationship. Thus the satisfaction derived from identification is due to the act of conforming as such. (Kelman 1958, 53)

Kelman wants to argue that this kind of process or incitement to an influence is vulnerable to the cessation of the identification. One reservation we might have about Kelman's analysis is that identification might well work the other way around, where one is attracted to a relationship in virtue of the content of a person's memes, and not vice versa. Thus they may lose that attraction if the memes change. Somewhat differently again, some people have converted to a faith in order to forge a relationship, and some have maintained their faith after the relationship has ended. Perhaps this is somewhat similar to those who have moved abroad for the sake of a lover, and at the end of the affair decide to stay on. 'I'm not here for them, I'm here for me', they say to themselves. Kelman identifies 'believing for extrinsic rewards' with 'identification', but presumably belief for extrinsic rewards (we could term this 'motivated belief') can find other motivations than 'identification'. In connection with this, we might be reminded of 'cults of personality', which Wittgenstein's disciples exemplify quite well, as detailed in Ray Monk's biography of Wittgenstein, *The Duty of Genius* (1991). There, students are recounted as having modelled themselves on not just Wittgenstein's philosophical views and methods but also his aesthetic tastes, his style of dress and mannerisms. It seems that we are impressed by the force of personality that some people have, and may, more or less consciously and more or less comprehensively, model ourselves on them.

Timothy D. Wilson's Story Editing techniques

Wilson's 'Story Editing' tools are 'a set of techniques designed to redirect people's narratives' (2011, 11). Wilson counts the 'Pennebaker Technique' that we encountered earlier among these; although, earlier, I argued that setting writing tasks of that sort ought to be classed as an example of rational influence (albeit non-directive). The other techniques that Wilson prescribes are 'Story Prompting', 'Steering' and 'Do Good, Be Good'. Story Prompting 'involves redirecting people down a particular narrative path with subtle prompts' (2011, 14). For example, one might narrate people's actions so that they come to internalize that narrative; in Wilson's example, labelling children as 'helpful people' encourages them to internalize this view of themselves. According to Wilson, 'we have to be more subtle with adults; rather than simply giving them a label for their behaviour, we need to get them to reach that conclusion themselves' (2011, 14). Steering, in Wilson's sense, encourages people to engage in reasoning which presupposes the content that one hopes to transmit (nefarious examples of this technique are Nazi text book maths problems about how to kill Jewish people most efficiently) (2011, 11). One might reasonably describe this as often being pseudo-rational (although perhaps learning to do maths or using proper grammar perfectly innocently requires this sort of instruction). 'Do Good, Be Good' is the name that Wilson uses to describe how 'our narratives will change to match our behaviour' (which will presumably make our behaviour less effortful, or less prompt-dependent, otherwise narratives would appear superfluous) (2011, 17, 74).

Positive and negative reinforcement, and neither

Positive and negative reinforcement are often employed to exercise formative influence. Examples include the following pairings of contrasting concepts: punishment/reward, incentive/disincentive, approval/disapproval, praise/blame, encouragement/discouragement. For each of these pairs, presumably, it is usually possible to do neither and take a neutral stance of neither encouraging nor discouraging whatever respect of influence is in question (a particular attitude, for instance). Likely, there is nothing wrong, per se, with positive and negative reinforcement, but particular examples of it are wrong: humiliation and physical harm (hitting and starving, for instance). However, these look like tools for behavioural influence in the first instance, which may thereby wield a formative influence. They may, for instance, habituate one to certain behaviours through repeated action. One might say that the internal disposition to act in that way is simply the habit (rather than any particular attitudes and beliefs, say).

What forms should influence take?

We have discussed what forms influence can take. Now, we will discuss what forms influence should take. Hand wants to encourage evidence-sensitive belief. This aim seems to be concordant with our conception of well-being detailed in Chapter 3. Hand worries that to influence children by 'appeal to anything other than their reason is to gain their assent by the exercise of psychological power, to charm or intimidate them into belief. It is to implant beliefs in such a way that they are held non-rationally or non-evidentially' (Hand 2003, 95). This is morally wrong, however, because 'insofar as one's beliefs are held non-evidentially … they are highly resistant to rational reassessment. Because they are not founded on evidence, the discovery of counter-evidence has little or no effect on them' (Hand 2003, 95). To the extent that one's beliefs and judgements have been non-rationally imparted in a specific domain, one is prevented from thinking rationally about the content of that domain. One's ability to track the truth is thereby undermined, and so the extrinsic goods of rationality are undercut, and so too is the intrinsic good of being rational.

In his book, *The War for Children's Minds*, Stephen Law observes that 'appealing to someone's power of reason strongly favours beliefs that are true'. He challenges the reader 'to construct a strong, well-reasoned case capable of withstanding critical scrutiny for believing that the Antarctic is populated by crab-people or that the earth's core is made of cheese', and comments dryly, that 'you're not going to find it easy' (Law 2006, 32). For Law,

> reason is a double-edged sword. It cuts both ways. It doesn't automatically favour the teacher's belief over the pupil's. It favours the truth, and so places the teacher and pupil on a level playing field. If as a teacher, you try to use reason to persuade, you may discover that it is actually you, not them, that's mistaken. (Law 2006, 33)

If one thinks that it is important that children become adults whose beliefs track the truth, one should agree with Hand that we ought to equip children to rationally form and revise their judgements, and so worry about anything which damages their ability to do so (Hand 2008). According to Hand, using perceived intellectual authority to convey a false belief 'is a lesser crime than indoctrination' (or 'successful, non-rational influence') on the grounds that rationally imparting and importing beliefs does no damage 'to the child's capacity to make rational judgments … [since their] beliefs are held on the basis of evidence and are open to revision and correction' (Hand 2002, 553). Jim Mackenzie has pointed out that it is an empirical question as to whether teaching a given belief in a particular way will result in the child's being able or unable to revise beliefs on the basis of further reasons and argument. He claims also that it is empirically false. As he sees it, Hand is committed to 'two conditionals: (a) that if a belief is held non-evidentially, then it cannot be modified in the light of evidence or reasons, and (b) that if a belief is held on the basis of evidence, then it can be modified in the light of evidence or reasons' (Mackenzie 2004, 651). As a counterexample to (a), Mackenzie claims that

> we come to beliefs about how to use language (give-gave-given and policeman-policewoman) non-evidentially in childhood, but we can modify these beliefs using reason as adults, and learn to say she where once we said he and police officer unless the officer's gender is relevant. So there are beliefs we came to hold non-evidentially which we can modify by new evidence or arguments. (Mackenzie 2004, 651)

As a counterexample to (b), Mackenzie points out that 'Kelvin did not retract his calculations of the maximum age of the earth even after the discovery of radioactivity invalidated his central assumptions' (Mackenzie 2004, 651).

On the first count, however, as we have seen, Hand takes beliefs imparted on the strength of perceived intellectual authority to be 'held on the basis of evidence' and 'open to revision and correction' (Hand 2002, 553) and since children learn the difference between 'give', 'gave' and 'given' from perceived intellectual authorities, this does not seem to be a counterexample. Furthermore, these are examples of socially constructed truths that are (basically) made true by how people use them, and therefore how people use them *just is* evidence. On the second count, the Kelvin example cannot undermine the belief that 'if a belief is held on the basis of evidence, then it *can* be modified in the light of evidence or reasons', for possibility does not entail actuality; that fact that something *can* happen doesn't entail that it *will*, so it does not matter that Kelvin actually *did* not revise his view in accordance with the evidence, but merely that he *could* have. Indeed, Kelvin might have been well able to revise his views, but unwilling to (and this willingness is something that also ought to be cultivated). Moreover, it seems that what ought to be important is that we do our best to ensure that beliefs be 'open to revision and correction', so the fact that some people who come to their views through the persuasive force of evidence do not revise their views in the light of emergent, contrary evidence at a later time, ought not to persuade against the use of evidence to motivate belief. Indeed, it seems that we ought to maximize the probability of students' being able and willing to revise their beliefs on the basis of further reasons and argument. While it is an empirical question as to what we must do to maximize the chances of this, it does seem likely that presenting reasons or vouching for having seen reasons will facilitate this aim. Indeed, it seems simply to be a matter of initiating them into that practice, and it is hard to see how else they might come to internalize that practice.

Education and indoctrination

Are education and indoctrination to be identified with specific, potentially influential processes? Not if it is to be identified as a success term for acts which happen to bring about intransigent or non-evidential commitment to beliefs as Hand would prefer. However, there are surely practices which will increase the likelihood of this which are morally blameworthy (be they employed misguidedly, maliciously, negligently or indifferently). These practices may reasonably be called indoctrinatory.

Some would prefer to restrict 'indoctrination' to cover only the inculcation, intended inculcation or practices likely to inculcate beliefs such that they will be held non-rationally. They do not want to extend the term to capture the inculcation, intended inculcation or practices likely to inculcate outcomes in other respects of which we can be formatively influenced. For instance, R. S. Peters remarks that 'whatever else "indoctrination" means, it obviously has something to do with doctrines' (Peters 1966, 41). However, it seems that whatever is objectionable about the inculcation, intended inculcation or practices likely to inculcate beliefs such that they will be held non-rationally is equally objectionable about the inculcation, intended inculcation or practices likely to inculcate outcomes in other respects of which we can be formatively influenced.

Stephen Law has offered an interesting list of potentially influential acts and influence architecture which conduce to non-rational formative influence. A communication architect is one who designs the context in which the potentially influential acts take place. He might like to call these indoctrinatory practices and do so because it increases the likelihood of coming to believe X, without having any reason in the normative sense, perhaps even being immunized to reason in respect of that belief. Law's list of 'authoritarian' practices includes the use of punishment, rewards, emotive imagery, social pressure, repetition, control and censorship, isolation, uncertainty and tribalism (Law 2006, 26–30). He describes these as 'essentially manipulative' and observes that 'whether or not the beliefs in question are actually true is completely irrelevant so far as the effectiveness of these methods is concerned' (Law 2006, 31).

In addition to punishing dissent and rewarding assent, one might stigmatize dissent, making it 'seem embarrassing or even shameful', so as to discourage at least overt dissent, if not private belief (Law 2006, 27). It might be well to say, with John Locke, that punishment and such like are hardly likely to encourage internalization of the intended content, but rather public compliance, and indeed, that is a reason not to use such methods if formative influence, as distinct from behavioural influence, is truly one's interest:

> Although the magistrate's opinion in religion be sound ... if I be not thoroughly persuaded thereof in my own mind, there will be no safety for me in following it. No way whatsoever that I shall walk in against the dictates of my conscience will ever bring me to the mansions of the blessed. (Locke 1966, 143)

Effective architecture for non-rational, formative influence includes the use of 'control and censorship', such as that exhibited by totalitarian states which 'eliminate "unhealthy" books from libraries', which can prevent dissent by starving people of the intellectual resources to identify contrary evidence, reasons and arguments (Law 2006, 29). Concordant with destroying cultural resources for dissent, such as books, isolation from dissenting voices can cultivate belief; 'Authoritarians often consider it unwise to allow their own children to mix with unbelievers, from who they pick up unacceptable beliefs' (Law 2006, 29). Three additional devices include the use of emotive imagery, such as 'iconic images of their Authority', to cultivate devotion, 'making people feel vulnerable without the party, church, person or whatever' and taking advantage of people's inclinations towards tribalism: 'Human beings are peculiarly attracted to them-and-us thinking', which he calls 'the twisted looking-glass of tribalism' (Law 2006, 27, 30). Our tribalistic tendencies can be used to secure commitment to content, and not just to one another.

The limits of rational education

Michael Hand tempers his account of the ethics of rational and non-rational influence by allowing that there are 'important and legitimate forms of non-rational influence – the modelling, cajoling and exhorting – by which teachers begin to shape the emotional responses of young children before they are ready to assume responsibility for their own emotional lives' (Hand 2011, 331). Here, though, he adds certain important caveats:

> What I think we can say is that, in so far as we have a fundamental obligation to respect and to develop the rationality of pupils, we must strongly prefer the rational approach to emotional education; and, moreover, that we may consider cultivating non-rationally in younger pupils only such emotional responses and attachments as we are able and entitled to cultivate rationally in older ones. In

other words, unless it is appropriate for us to promote an emotion by rational means, there is certainly no question of it being appropriate to do so by non-rational means. (Hand 2011, 331)

Indeed, champions of autonomy and reason sound more than a little unrealistic in the case of (at least) small children whom they would prefer to be more obedient at following instructions and completing set tasks.[9]

Reliability of influence

Communication acts work on two levels: advocacy and demonstration. For instance, one may act in accordance with some policy, and one may advocate for that policy. Indeed, one's acts and advocacy may contradict one another. The statement 'nobody should speak' when spoken would appear to be self-undermining. In this case, the prospective subject of influence might wonder whether to do as told (and be quiet), or to do as shown (and talk). Even with consistency across the two, there are no guarantees of successfully effecting desired formative influences, whether rational or non-rational methods are used. Methods of influence are, it should be acknowledged, not highly reliable. The processes that one employs may not affect the desired outcome:

> Every historian knows that actions often have unintended and unwanted consequences. It would be perfectly ordinary for a move … to backfire disastrously. (Lewis 2000, 195)

> Events can be the causes of outcomes that they were intended to prevent, and even trigger outcomes that they would normally prevent. (Nolan 2005, 92)

---

[9]   Again, before anyone thinks that children are naturally good, and are poisoned by a corrupt world, one is tempted to point to a brilliant website. http://www.sunnyskyz.com/blog/119/36-Reasons-My-Kid-Is-Crying-Temper-Tantrums-You-Can-t-Help-But-Laugh-At (accessed 23 June 2015).

6

A Theory of Ethical Influence

Introduction

In this chapter, I outline an account of ethical influence quite generally, with little specific reference to religion. Applying the theory to religion will wait until Chapter 9 and will require both a definition of religion and a judgement about its status (to be provided in Chapters 7 and 8, respectively). This first part of our present chapter addresses two questions. Following Michael Hand, call the encouragement or discouragement of children's belief of a given proposition 'directive teaching', and call the facilitation of children's understanding of that proposition 'non-directive teaching'. The first question is: When should influencers teach propositions directively and when should they teach them non-directively?[1] The second question is: Which propositional content should influencers address? When asked of educators in particular, an answer to these questions would amount to what I will call a 'theory of propositional curricula content', by providing both a means for choosing that content and a directive for teaching it. While the answer that I give to the second question is unlikely to prove exhaustive, I still consider that it would form an important part of the answer, bringing us towards a theory of propositional curricula content. In the next part of this chapter, I extend this approach to encompass the determination of non-propositional content. We finish by assessing various objections, including claims that all influence is immoral. But these ethical imperatives can generate a raison d'être for schools as vehicles for delivering curricula.

We begin with an outline and discussion of Michael Hand's 'possibility of truth' argument for compulsory Religious Education (RE), from which the

---

[1] I borrow the terms 'directive and non-directive' from Michael Hand; see especially Hand (2008). Strictly speaking, non-directive teaching would include acquainting students with, and inducting them into assessing the soundness of, arguments for and against propositions, as well as merely understanding them.

theory of propositional curricula content developed here takes its impetus (Hand 2004). We then go on to explain how the theory here developed is a natural extension of Hand's argument. Next, a theory of propositional curricula content is outlined via two steps: (a) outlining a conception of *moment* that motivates a proposition's inclusion on the curriculum, and (b) refining the notion of what degrees of rational support are required to decide between the directive or non-directive teaching of a momentous proposition. We draw on conclusions supported in earlier chapters: (a) the duties of truthfulness that motivate occasions for directive and non-directive teaching, and (b) discussing acceptable means of influencing students' beliefs.

Michael Hand's 'possibility of truth' argument

The theory of propositional curricula content that I want to develop is a natural extension of Michael Hand's 'possibility of truth' argument for compulsory RE. Hand argues that a discrete, compulsory, non-directive subject focused on the critical examination and evaluation of religious beliefs should form part of pupils' education. The argument is this: some religious propositions (about God, salvation, life after death, and so on) (a) 'are sufficiently well supported by evidence and argument, as to merit serious consideration by reasonable people', (b) 'matter, in the sense of making some practical difference to people's lives', and (c) require 'a facility with distinctive kinds of evidence and argument' in order to evaluate their plausibility appropriately. Hand concludes that children are entitled to an education, enabling them to make rational judgements about the truth or falsity of these propositions (Hand 2004). That is to say, the premises motivate a curriculum element whose aim is to enable children to make rational judgements about the truth or falsity of religious propositions, a curriculum being 'a planned programme of learning' (Hand 2010, 49).[2] It is reasonable to think that a planned programme of learning delivered by subject experts is precisely what would be required to enable one to make rational judgements about the truth or falsity of religious propositions. Parents or, more generally,

---

[2] This formulation has the benefit of acknowledging the similarity of all courses of learning, and the similarities between the sorts of ethical considerations that could motivate their existence, whether they be news programmes, programmes of learning for citizenship tests for immigrants, rehabilitation programmes for criminal offenders or educational television series like *Planet Earth* (2006) and *The World at War* (1973). It also acknowledges the variety of vehicles of provision which programmes of learning can be facilitated by.

primary carers could not reasonably be expected to satisfy this entitlement *qua* parents and primary carers. The responsibility would be what I have termed extra-parental in an earlier chapter. Hand calls this the 'possibility of truth argument'. While one might take issue with its premises, I think that the form of the argument is valid, and it is this which I want to build on.[3]

Hand regards this argument as motivating a compulsory, discrete subject for children.[4] I want to observe that the same entitlement would exist for adults as much as for children but admit further that one might reasonably hope to satisfy each person's entitlement during childhood and early adulthood. It is also worth observing that one's entitlement cannot justify one's compulsion to receive that entitlement all by itself (we saw this point argued in Chapter 3). We allowed that whereas it can be reasonable to compel children to undergo formative influence for their own well-being on paternalist grounds, it is not so easy to argue the same for adults. Still, it might be reasonable to urge that, insofar as adults can be said to have an entitlement, they then may thereby have a claim on subsidies in order to avail of it.

Extending Hand's argument

It seems to me that the validity of Hand's possibility of truth argument would imply the validity of what I shall call the 'certainty of truth argument'. Were some religious beliefs certain, as opposed to merely plausible, then this, together with their epistemic distinctiveness and moment, would motivate a discrete, directive (or confessional) and compulsory subject. Let us call propositions that 'matter', in the sense of making some practical difference to people's lives, momentous propositions'. Suppose now that some momentous religious propositions were neither plausible nor certain, and supported by little to no evidence and argument, or even conflict with such evidence and argument that they could not reasonably be believed at all. It seems that educators should include the matter of the truth of such propositions on curricula only on an ad hoc, as opposed to systematic, basis when they have

---

[3]   There are at least two anti-epistemic approaches to challenging Hand's argument. One is to argue with Pascal that we can have non-epistemic motivations to believe that something is true; another is to argue that, for instance, religious language is non-propositional. We can leave the second of these to the next chapter, although I would refer readers to a persuasive critical discussion of both approaches in Mackie (1982).

[4]   It should be said that Hand is non-committal as to which curriculum organizations would best satisfy the educational entitlement, regarding that as a largely contextual matter, but thinks there is as good a case for discrete RE as for any other discrete subject.

reason to think that their students believe such propositions so as to dissuade them, otherwise the curriculum is in danger of becoming a museum of curiosities to the exclusion of plausible and certain momentous propositions (Tillson 2011a).

We should notice that these arguments apply quite generally to any momentous propositions that are susceptible of plausibility or certainty, and not just to religious propositions. We may look on this as the beginnings of a theory of propositional curriculum content. It is important to notice that these argumentative mechanisms can be accepted without accepting Hand's judgements on the plausibility of religious propositions, or indeed any other judgements about the state of knowledge. This should be regarded as one of the strengths of the position. I do not think that if the premises of the arguments from certainty and possibility are met, that their conclusions are guaranteed. Instead, I think of each as defeasible arguments since 'there is always an (open) list of defeating conditions any of which might rule out' their conclusions. Instead the premises are sufficient 'unless some feature is present which overrides or voids them' (Sibley 2001, 7–8). For instance, one shouldn't equip students with criminal modus operandi if the large difference that this information would likely make is the student's committing crimes or bringing harm to others.

The need for intervention

As mentioned, Hand thinks of his argument as justifying a compulsory, discrete subject, and it seems to be his 'distinctive kinds of support' premise which motivates RE being a discrete subject. This is not all the work that the 'distinctiveness' premise does, however. Additionally, it suggests that the intended learning outcome of students being able to understand and evaluate the truth of religious propositions would not be achieved without this intervention; that is to say, the endeavour is not superfluous to, and indeed is the best method of, satisfying its own aim. To a first approximation, what matters for a proposition's inclusion within curricula is that it satisfies of one of the following three sets of predicates:

1. (a) That it is momentous; (b) that it might well not be believed without intervention; (c) that it is certain.
2. (a) That it is momentous; (b) that it might well not be understood and rationally evaluated without intervention; (c) that it is plausible.
3. (a) That it is momentous; (b) that it might well be believed without intervention; (c) that it is false or unfounded.

Where the first set of premises applies to a given proposition, teachers ought to promote students' belief of that proposition. Where the second set of premises applies to a proposition, the teacher ought only to facilitate students' understanding of that proposition and the arguments available for evaluating its truth. Where the third set of premises applies to a proposition, the teacher ought to discourage students' belief of that proposition. It should be noted that a certain value of truthfulness has been presupposed in all of the discussion, and it is this that was defended in Chapter 3. We are now in a position to critically elaborate the notion of momentousness from Hand's suggestive phrase 'making some practical difference to people's lives'.

Moment

For any proposition, a person may take one of the following (mutually exclusive) cognitive attitudes: belief, disbelief or agnosticism. They may also take no cognitive attitude at all (at least where they are unaware of the proposition). In what follows, the key distinction to bear in mind is that distinction between belief and non-belief which captures all the other attitudes and non-attitudes. To determine a proposition's moment, we ask what difference it would likely make if a person failed to believe the truth.

A paradigm example of a highly momentous proposition is that smoking tobacco dramatically increases one's risk of cancer. Knowing this may not stop everyone from starting to smoke, or make all existing smokers give up, but everyone for whom smoking is an available option ought to know it all the same, as it is a consideration that ought to figure into their decision of whether or not to smoke. Indeed, suppose that it were only known by doctors that smoking causes cancer and that a heavy smoker with ailing health goes to see one who, after conducting the relevant tests, informs him that he has lung cancer. Devastated, but also surprised, the man asks how this could be so. In response, the doctor informs him that the cancer is very probably a result of his smoking. Again, the man is surprised: 'But nobody told me smoking causes cancer'; 'you never asked', replies the doctor. The appropriate response is to feel that those in the know were guilty of a moral failing in not spreading the word. Moment, in this case, has to do with the avoidance of one's own serious harm, but this is not the only grounds on which a proposition, if believed, would likely (or should) make a huge difference to the way one will act or live. This example should motivate us to accept that there exists an ethical duty to not only share but volunteer and disseminate information or 'spread the word', in the case of momentous propositions, as well as provide a very striking illustration of a momentous proposition.

What criteria have we for determining a proposition's moment? We ought not to say that 'a proposition is momentous if people would change their lives as a result of knowing it', since clearly the fact that smoking causes cancer is something that the medical profession, at least, has a duty to raise awareness of, and yet many who are made aware do not even try to give up smoking. Alternatively, I could say 'a proposition is momentous if people should change their lives as a result of knowing it'. Alternatively still, I could say that 'a proposition is momentous if it constitutes a reason for people to change their lives'.[5] The point is to equip people with information that is relevant to making decisions that will affect their lives, information that they would likely have wanted to know prior to making decisions. This is likely to include information pertaining to their own well-being, as well as that of others.

Some would point out that information alone is not enough to motivate people to change their lives: meeting people in a cancer ward is more likely to motivate change in addition to information, than information alone. Indeed, simply recognizing that one's phobia is irrational does not make it go away, hence the existence of various kinds of therapies to help do this. This observation should not be seen as an objection to the theory advanced here, rather this consideration should at most be seen as leaving the door open for supplementary, motivational aspects to curricula.

Moment admits of degrees. Of maximal moment, there are eschatological motivations to live in certain ways in the 'here and now' (for fear of damnation, for instance); of minimal moment, there are propositions such that it would make little difference to anyone whether they believed it, disbelieved it, had no opinion on the matter or never even realized there was a matter to have an opinion about. The relevant question here is what difference it would make if someone were not right about a matter, and whether it is worth taking some pains to be right about it.[6] Additionally, the moment of some propositions is

---

[5] For a critical discussion of whether reasons for action ought to be characterized by reference to one's motivational set or by something outside of that, see Finlay and Schroeder (2012). Clearly I am committed to the latter position, given the argument of Chapters 2 and 3.

[6] This matter is often not something that we can determine without knowing the answer. For instance, it would be worth knowing whether things are carcinogenic if they in fact are carcinogenic, and not nearly as worth knowing if they were not. The fact that time and energy invested into some ventures yields information of less value than the resources themselves is a worry faced by researchers and explorers alike.

local, and the moment of others is more ubiquitous: it is quite local that the password to some particular computer network is, say, 'qwerty'. The moment of other propositions is not so local: 'germs cause human illnesses'; 'God exists as described by the Qur'an'; 'human beings are invulnerable'. Finally, there is a contrast between propositions such that it is momentous for everyone that just someone or just a few people should believe them (call this 'specialist moment'), and propositions such that it is momentous for each individual that they should believe them themselves (call this 'general moment'). Consider the proposition that nothing can exceed the speed of light. While it might make some difference to me that physicists know it, it doesn't seem to make much difference to me that I know it. This distinction is an arguable basis for a contrast between general education and specialized education; whereas general curricula would be interested in propositions of momentous importance for each individual to know, more specialized curricula would concern themselves with propositions which is of momentous importance to society that at least some people know.

In this chapter, I will have in mind propositions of ubiquitous, general moment as a factor in determining propositional curriculum content in general, universal education (as opposed to specialist education and locally peculiar education). Some such propositions are supported by such evidence and argument that they cannot be reasonably denied, and others by such evidence and argument that they can reasonably be doubted. Yet others are supported by little to no evidence and argument, or even conflict with such evidence and argument that they cannot reasonably be believed at all. It is here that the duties of truthfulness, discussed in Chapter 3, play their part in determining whether teachers ought to promote students' belief of that content, on the one hand, or just facilitate their understanding of that content, on the other, or discourage students' belief of that content.

It is not the place of this chapter to argue that any particular propositions satisfy the criteria for inclusion within the propositional content addressed by curricula; it is the skeletal theory and not any particular application of that theory that this chapter hopes to recommend. Certainly, the theory could be combined with judgements about the state of knowledge so as to determine propositional content addressed by curricula; indeed, that is what I will attempt to do in the course of the last two chapters. That said, it may be helpful to give a few suggestive lines of thought along which the theory could be applied to contemporary curriculum theory debate, independent to that line of enquiry. As I have said, propositions of ubiquitous, general moment are the stuff of propositional curriculum content in general, universal education (as opposed to specialist education and locally peculiar education). They would comprise, it would seem, a basic curriculum in that they would be propositions which it is everyone's right to be aware of, together, insofar as they are capable of understanding this, with the considerations which grant them their degree of plausibility. It is of ubiquitous, general moment as to what effects politicians' proposed policies are likely to have if adopted, and not limited to liberal democracies. Other likely examples of momentous propositions to constitute a basic curriculum involve information that bears on social conscience (about fair trade and work conditions), and information that bears on personal health and safety (about sexual health, recreational drug and road safety). Clearly, the theory would cash out differently when applied to different contexts; for instance in a land without tobacco, it would not be a momentous proposition that smoking causes cancer. In the next section, I shall attempt to refine the notion of what degrees of rational support are required to decide between the directive and non-directive teaching of a momentous proposition.

Certainty and possibility of truth

Heeding the work of David Hume, Jim Mackenzie has pointed out that law-like statements, such as 'all men are mortal', cannot be verified by any number of observations, since a counterexample could always yet come to light, thus, no amount of evidence could possibly decisively determine their truth (Mackenzie 2004, 649). In the philosophy of science, this is known as the problem of induction since it seems to undermine the evidential authority of law-like scientific theories. On Karl Popper's understanding, such theories are seen as more or less reliable depending on how often they open themselves up to falsification without being falsified.

> On Popper's account scientific theories, since they are not known to be true, cannot be imparted by the presentation of proof or decisive evidence, but to use a form of leverage other than the force of evidence seems to be necessarily indoctrinatory. Perhaps Hand hopes that teaching currently accepted scientific theories can also be justified by using our perceived intellectual authority. (Mackenzie 2004, 649)

It seems that Hand will have to argue that evidence can prove law-like statements (and overcome the age-old problem of induction) or say that we should not teach law-like statements to be true, or argue that they be imparted by perceived intellectual authority. It seems to me that admitting that law-like statements cannot be proved true might be the best option, but to add the challenge 'who wants to bet that the sun will not rise tomorrow?' The idea behind explanatory and predictive science (and probability in general) is to make the best bet, and some bets are clearly much better than others. Thus, we ought to absorb 'best bets' into our taxonomy of education. One could directively teach that 'this theory is our best bet'. If one were very worried about misleading children about the relative certainty of a proposition, they could build some epistemology into the curriculum to discuss the confidence with which different statements can reasonably be invested, given their supporting evidence and argument. Of course, in many cases, a best bet may still not be a strong enough bet to warrant directive teaching, and, in this case, it would instead warrant non-directive teaching. While it would be more correct to switch from describing 'possibility of truth' and 'certainty of truth' arguments to describing 'supported by sufficient probative force to warrant serious consideration' and 'supported by sufficient probative force to make denial irrational' arguments, to avoid clogging my prose with such unwieldy formulations, I have elected to use the former terminology as a *façon de parler*, while asking that the reader bear in mind that it is only that.

The theory

The notions of truthfulness and moment combined in the ways which we have seen above supply a systematic approach to determining which propositional content curricula should contain, and whether teachers ought to promote or demote students' belief of that content, on the one hand, or just facilitate students' understanding of that content, on the other. As we have seen, what matters for a proposition's inclusion on curricula is the applicability of one of the following sets of premises:

1. (a) That it is momentous; (b) that it might well not be believed without intervention; (c) that it is certain.
2. (a) That it is momentous; (b) that it might well not be understood and rationally evaluated without intervention; (c) that it is plausible.
3. (a) That it is momentous; (b) that it might well be believed without intervention; (c) that it is false or unfounded.

Where the first set of premises applies to a given proposition, teachers ought to promote students' belief of that proposition. Where the second set of premises applies to a proposition, the teacher ought only to facilitate students' understanding of that proposition. Where the third set of premises applies to a proposition, the teacher ought to discourage students' belief of that proposition. While it might turn out that this theory is incomplete – since my argument fails to motivate the appearance of a particular proposition on curricula, while a further argument does motivate it – the existence of such arguments will not serve to undermine the theory that I elaborate here, but will serve to supplement it.

The promotional versus non-promotional distinction

One may contrast the educator's aiming to impart something to, or promote or encourage something in, the student, on the one hand (perhaps a belief, a disposition, or an understanding, for instance), with their not aiming to impart something, on the other. This distinction turns on the educator's intention (rather than their methods, or the results of their teaching). As we have seen, Michael Hand tends to talk about directive and non-directive teaching. However, the question 'Should one be directive, yes or no?' gives the impression of an exhaustive and exclusive distinction, since it posits and negates a predicate (namely, directive). But as Hand uses the terms, 'directive' means to encourage belief or disbelief and 'non-directive' means to encourage understanding. Of course, as Hand (2006b) recognizes, they are not exclusive; indeed, he argued in his doctoral thesis and first book that belief could not take place without understanding.

It is better, I submit, to separate out these issues and ask whether we ought to promote or ought not to promote particular formative outcomes in students: first, whether they understand a proposition, for instance, and, second, whether they believe or disbelieve a proposition in addition to understanding it. A given subject matter may be taught with promotional aims in some respects, while being taught with non-promotional aims in others. Thus, an understanding of political ideologies, and an interest in discussing politics might be promoted, while allegiance to a particular ideology is not promoted. At least for my purposes, it will make things more perspicuous. Non-directive education of the proposition that some political theory (PT) is true can be represented in the following table.

Attitude	Promotional	Non-Promotional
Interest in truth of PT	x	
Understanding of PT	x	
Belief that PT		x
Disbelief that PT		x

Extending the theory of ethical influence

I said at the outset that an answer to two questions would amount to what I called a 'theory of propositional curricula content', by providing both a means for choosing content and a directive for teaching that content. The first question was: 'When ought teachers to encourage or discourage students' belief of a given proposition, on the one hand (call this "directive teaching"), and when ought teachers to simply facilitate students' understanding of that proposition, on the other (call this "non-directive teaching")?' The second question was: 'Which propositional content should curricula address?' It seems that we can be more comprehensive by asking: 'When ought teachers to encourage a given formative outcome?' and 'Which potential formative outcomes should curricula address?' These are derivative from the question 'What formative influence (if any) ought we ethically to have?' In Chapter 4, we attempted to give substance to the question by providing an account of those respects in which we can be formatively influenced. The general respects that I suggested were the following:

1. The degrees and kinds of one's physical and mental abilities
2. One's stock of concepts
3. Those propositions which one understands
4. One's cognitive, propositional attitudes, such as belief and disbelief
5. One's affective attitudes to propositions and objects

We may ask what considerations preside over whether and how to impart or promote each of these kinds of formative outcome. Thus far, our discussion has addressed the third and fourth of these formative outcomes, and the first and second in a way that is derivative of them. We shall now expand our discussion to take account of the fifth formative outcome. I have argued that where being wrong about the rationality of a proposition would make a large difference to one's life, and where one is likely to be wrong about its rationality without intervention, that proposition ought to feature on the curriculum. I also argued that where denying that proposition is irrational, it ought to be encouraged;

where affirming it is irrational, it ought to be discouraged; and where affirmation and denial are both rational options, it ought to be taught non-directively. More than merely helping pupils to understand, and believe or disbelieve momentous propositions, I argued that teachers should, insofar as is practicable, aim to acquaint students with arguments for and against them and induct pupils into the practice of assessing the soundness of those arguments. While this version of the framework applies principally to cognitive attitudes, our affective attitudes can be captured by an analogous framework.

We agree with Thomas Nagel that 'there is such a thing, or category of thought, as reason, and that it applies in both theory and practice, in the formation not only of beliefs but of desires, intentions, and decisions as well', and we ask: Is it rational that students should have certain affective attitudes? (Nagel 2001, 6). Where having or failing to have a certain attitude makes a significant difference to students' lives, it ought to be addressed by curricula. Where failing to have the attitude is irrational, this failure ought to be remedied; where having the attitude is irrational, that attitude ought to be discouraged; and where neither having nor failing to have the attitude is irrational, that attitude ought to be introduced and discussed without encouragement or discouragement. Again, teachers should, insofar as is practicable, aim to acquaint students with arguments for and against having these attitudes and induct them into the practice of assessing the soundness of those arguments.

Now it might seem that the question of justification is asymmetrical in the case of cognitive propositional attitudes and affective attitudes, and so it is. But perhaps not in the way one might expect. In the case of cognitive propositional attitudes, one might ask whether there are good epistemic reasons to believe a proposition. In the case of affective attitudes, one might ask whether there are good reasons to have a certain attitude or behaviour. But the question of whether it is good to have a belief is not entirely epistemic. There are theoretical and practical reasons, and since believing is an activity, it is practical reasons that, properly speaking, warrant belief. Insofar as one assumes the policy of believing the truth, then theoretical reasons which track the truth become important. It is true that having a truth-tracking belief set enables world navigation by allowing one to know where one is going, and how one is getting there (both literally and more figuratively, in the case of career ambitions and plans). Thus, one may wonder how the plausibility and mattering clause might be weighed against each other if two contradictory propositions each had a greater value in one respect than the other had.

Something but the truth

Strikingly, Hand allows that there are some occasions where parental discretion on which being known-to-be-true is not a requirement for promoting beliefs. Young children naturally perceive their parents to be intellectual authorities on everything, observes Hand. He continues:

> Insofar as a parent is perceived by her children to be an intellectual authority on religious matters, she is in a position to impart religious beliefs to them by appealing to their reason [without having to demonstrate their truth]. She has no need to resort to indoctrination because her children will be rationally obliged to believe whatever she tells them about religion. (Hand 2002, 552)

One might object that (when done wantonly) this is an abuse of perceived intellectual authority, even if the belief is rationally imparted: using that perception to convey a false confidence in a proposition. When done inadvertently, a charge of negligence might be appropriate, depending on the likelihood and severity of the false impression.[7] Hand pre-empts this, responding that 'most of us, while we recognise that it is *normally* wrong for parents to use their perceived intellectual authority to impart not-known-to-be-true beliefs, are prepared to grant exceptions to this rule when the belief confers a significant benefit on the child' (Hand 2002, 555). Notice that Hand specifies parents in the foregoing remarks, and not teachers or other extra-parental influencers.[8] He gives three examples.

1. Protecting them from physical harm: all wild berries are poisonous
2. Contributing to their emotional security: bad people always go to prison
3. Giving them and their parents pleasure: the tooth fairy will come for your tooth tonight

On the first example, we see a simplified version of the truth, or perhaps a stepping stone towards the truth. And indeed, one hears it remarked by science university students just how crude secondary and primary science education is. Here one

---

[7] Of course, many parents won't be presenting a 'false confidence', but what Hand must consider a misguided confidence, what some might argue to be an immorally unjustified confidence.
[8] Hand has in mind familial benefits, but the thought can generalize to anyone with perceived intellectual authority. Thus, one might think of Plato's noble lie in this connection, a myth which if believed, 'would have a good effect, [in] making [citizens] more inclined to care for the state and one another', *The Republic* (Book 3, 415c–d).

might urge that a lie is not being told, but the nearest approximation of the truth manageable for one's cognitive ability. One might suggest that 'some berries are poisonous, and you don't know which' would have the desired effect, namely, forbearance from eating berries that might, for all they know, be poisonous. Here, an elision is being made between theoretical reason and practical reason; because their practical reason is limited, a noble lie is required to help guide their practical decision-making. It seems then that these are exceptions to the general rule. The second and third are more clearly lies.

Hand then claims that 'there is clearly something in the idea that close social ties, such as those that bind the family, are strengthened by agreement and threatened by disagreement on matters of religion' (Hand 2002, 555). He says this justifies parents' giving their child a false confidence in the truth of their religion, by using their perceived intellectual authority as leverage. It does not justify indoctrination (and thereby damaging students' facility for making rational judgements).[9] Schools (unlike parents), thinks Hand, are not in a position to impart belief without using non-rational methods, and endangering students' recognition of and responsiveness to good reasons. He argues that 'teaching for belief in not-known-to-be-true propositions is, when successful, indoctrinatory, except where teachers are perceived to be intellectual authorities on those propositions' (Hand 2003, 96). He further states that (1) where unsuccessful, that is no vindication, 'teaching which would constitute indoctrination if it were successful is objectionable whether it is successful or not', and (2) 'except perhaps in the earliest years of schooling, pupils … know that their teachers are in no position to testify to the existence of decisive evidence for the truth of religious propositions' (Hand 2003, 98). Granting that in absence of perceived intellectual authority, successfully convincing anybody of the truth of a belief that is not known-to-be-true, the 'teacher must do more than merely present them with the evidence, for the evidence is not decisive' and 'implant beliefs in such a way that they are held non-rationally or non-evidentially' (Hand 2003, 95). But this

---

[9]   For many parents, the perceived intellectual authority and significant benefit clauses are immaterial: they believe that their religion is certainly true, and that its value depends on its truth; Hand's argument can only persuade those who believe that the question of religious truth is genuinely open. Indeed, they may argue that salvation over damnation is a strong enough reason to warrant indoctrination, assuming of course that indoctrination is not incompatible with salvation. In his series 'The Root of all Evil' (Barnes 2006), Richard Dawkins shows rehearsals of a Christian theatre project – 'Hell House' – which is intended to scare children Christian. Its motivation is to save young people from eternal damnation. Dawkins is compelled by the director's argument that given the reality of Hell, it is morally essential to use what he might otherwise term 'child abuse', to persuade them of the reality of hells and perils or ways of living which court going there. Here we must urge epistemic humility in religious belief, so that at the same time as having these beliefs, believers allow that they are not so certain as to warrant passing them on.

seems incompatible with his contention that people may reasonably believe religious propositions: that they have come to believe them without having been indoctrinated, but on the strength of some reasonable interpretation of the evidence. In the same paper, Hand says:

> The truth or falsity of religious propositions is a matter of disagreement among reasonable people. The evidence available is ambiguous. Some people judge that it points in one direction, others that it points in another. (Hand 2003, 93)

All the same, one may argue that it is wrong to teach something that is not known to be true, as true, without its wrongness depending on having relied on non-rational means to impart the belief. It is wrong because tracking the truth is both intrinsically and extrinsically valuable and frustrated by false impressions.

Liberalism versus education

Hand has rejected what he calls 'a behavioural criterion' for teaching controversial issues, in favour of an epistemic one (Hand 2008, 2007). There are two senses in which a matter may, in ordinary parlance, be called controversial, one corresponding to each criterion respectively; a matter may be called controversial in the sense that people disagree about it (especially when they disagree about it passionately), or in the sense that the matter is left unsettled by rational procedures. It may be that a matter has been settled by rational procedures and yet continues to be contested passionately in the public square; take, for instance, the issue of whether the Earth is flat or whether the Holocaust happened. Hand argues that we should use the epistemic criterion to determine what should be taught as a controversial issue, by which he means 'what should be taught non-directively'.

His answer, as we have seen above, would be that we should only teach those matters on which the truth has not been determined by rational procedures in a non-directive manner. This leads us directly into the question of whose determination of the truth ought to count. Some might worry about whose judgement counts when it comes to saying what is known to be true, and what is not. The simple answer would be: the educator. But then there are complications: the employer of the educator (either the parent or the school or the state) may have a contrary opinion about the truth. It would seem as though the educator were being used merely as a tool if their judgement were to be sidelined in favour of their employer's judgement, their teaching would become inauthentic and, usually thereby, lack integrity. Arguably, it is the consensus among intellectual authorities, those familiar with the evidence and arguments relevant to determining a given matter, whose determination of the truth ought to count. But this answer leads us directly into a tension between liberalism and education within Hand's work.

Let us consider Hand's possibility of truth argument with respect to religious belief. Let us suppose that Hand is wrong about the plausibility of religious belief. Let us suppose that religious beliefs have been shown decisively to be mistaken, and yet (for non-rational reasons) they continue to be maintained. On Hand's argument, the educational responsibility of schools is to promote true belief and demote false belief. It would then seem that schools ought to build pupils' resilience to religious belief. However, given the increasingly religiously plural context in which, for example, Irish schooling takes place, caution may be urged to the atheist head teacher who, in the name of education, decides that the role of the school is to build her pupils' resilience to forming religious belief, in case such an enterprise provoked violent reactions from faith communities or had other undesirable consequences in practice. One would likely be the retreat of parents of strong faith from public schooling into home schooling and private schooling in order to protect their faith (a counterproductive outcome for our head teacher). Furthermore, in liberal political theory, seriously respecting the right of citizens to form, revise and pursue their own conceptions of the good, including religious conceptions, is thought by many liberals to properly imply the right of parents to raise their children in their faith. Thus, liberal state education cannot easily defend deliberately eradicating the religious beliefs of children. Considerations such as these will likely temper the implications of any purely epistemic, educational considerations. In this temperance, a tension can be seen to emerge between the proper role of the school, in its educational commitment to promoting truthful belief, on the one hand, and the proper role of a liberal democracy, in its commitment to upholding the peace in spite of what anyone happens to believe, on the other.

One might exclude the dimension of the possible truth of religious claims from schooling altogether by way of compromise (as in France and the United States), instead of building pupils' resilience to religious beliefs or disabusing them of such religious beliefs as they already have. However, this would not seem to be much of a compromise, since the epistemic responsibility of school would seem to have been resigned in such a case. Hand could object that this is not a problem for him at all by pointing out that on his analysis, many religious propositions are plausible. However, he also considers that many religious beliefs *are* implausible: not least, Seventh Day Adventism, and others which take a literal attitude to creation myths, denying evolution. Moreover though, the fact that the system which Hand seems committed to do can yield this problem, just by plugging in different judgements about the state of knowledge, shows that it is a problem with the system, even if the conclusions he derives from it just so happen not to bring this problem to the surface. Indeed, it may be that the state of knowledge would shift, while the state of belief does not, and these problems would emerge.

Religious persecution is indeed a terrible thing. It forced the pilgrims to flee to England, where people were killed on account of the beliefs. America set up a strict(ish) religion/public affairs divide so that each was able to pursue their conception of the good, and not be subject to anybody else's conception of the good. They would not be persecuted for the content of their belief. The idea is that the state ought not to ally itself with, or work under the banner of any particular religious conception of the good. Perhaps there are some which it can reject, such as those with anti-liberal principles. However, the promotion of truth in a non-dogmatic way does not involve persecution, or punishment for false or unfounded beliefs. My contention is that, morally, parents ought not to raise their children in their faith, not that it should be illegal for them to do so, which would be thoroughly illiberal.

Similarly, one might accept that there is a universal educational entitlement to momentous truths and worry that homogeny seems to be a consequence of promoting beliefs of universal, ubiquitous moment. Would such a right correspond to our having a duty to go and colonize distant countries with our superior knowledge? Doesn't that sound impossibly arrogant and colonial; won't it erode cultures to the extent that it is successful? On the other hand, is there something wrong about allowing cultures to live in isolation, as museum pieces, and meticulously avoid intervention? Perhaps there is a happy medium between two extreme policies about how to interact with the other: one that neither aims at intellectual colonization nor forsakes contact altogether, perhaps it consists in opening lines of dialogue and cultural exchange.

Comprehensive and restricted formative influence

At this point, we may introduce the distinction between *comprehensive* and *restricted* formative influence. Granted that we are able to exercise formative influences over one another, the influence that we have may be more or less comprehensive or restricted depending on just how many respects in which we influence one another. One might attempt more or less comprehensive programmes of influence, in attempting to change more or less a person. One might on the one hand, simply want to discourage one particular habit, but, on the other hand, they might want to re-write someone's belief set and simultaneously rearrange their priorities in life. Attending a one-to-one language lesson, or piano lesson, might constitute an example of a relatively restricted, formative influence. What Thiessen meant by 'evangelism' was surely comprehensive formative influence (in addition to socialization; a form of behavioural influence, with formative upshots). Another term one might think of is 'personal transformation'.

An influence is more or less deep depending on what else it *ought* to effect, if accepted. Changing one's religious beliefs usually ought to go deep, as it will have implications for very many aspects of one's life. Providing someone with some fundamental concepts that affect how they perceive the world sounds about as deep as it gets. In connection with this thought, one might bring to mind the notion that two people from two entirely different historic-socio-economic places would be endowed with such different conceptual frameworks that they would see the world very differently. It is interesting to wonder just how fundamentally people are open to influence, and how far their outlooks are intractably hardwired and how universally so, but it is not a question to be explored here. The comprehensiveness of set of influences being imparted raises the moral stakes, and with it, the level of warrant required to assent to be rational.

Is all influence immoral?

How defensible is the idea that all influence is unethical, and that we ought to avoid influencing children (and indeed anyone at all)? There are perhaps more or less defensible versions of this doctrine, and we shall attempt to follow some of the strands of argument that lead to this conclusion that all influence is immoral. First though, we will consider whether a policy of non-intervention is coherent.

Is a policy of non-influence conceivable?

I do not think that it is at all facetious (as some might) to complain that it is not clear what a policy of non-influence would look like. It is fair to say that

I, in particular, have had no influence on Alexander the Great (although notionally, the concept of how subsequent generations might perceive him likely did influence him). The people we can claim most safely that we have had, and risked no influence upon, are those we have had no possibility of contact with at all (even indirectly). However, we do not want to say, in general, that we ought to sacrifice contact with one another in order to avoid influencing one another. We may want to say this about some specific cases. For instance, some parents might rightly think it best to keep their children from having contact with certain people precisely so that they cannot wield any influence over their children. Indeed, children would not grow up at all were it not for their being raised by adults; at best they would be feral, and at worst they would be dead. Whatever points those who oppose influence want to make, they must certainly bear in mind these truisms. However, insofar as it is not possible to avoid influence altogether, it need not entail that there could or should be no ethical prohibitions on influential activities: it might be that we ought to follow the path of minimal influence, for instance. Alternatively, it might be that we ought never to act so as to influence others, but only allow that this is an unfortunate byproduct to be tolerated where we act for other reasons.

Innate teleologies

It seems that in maintaining that influence is immoral one is committed to the notion that children have an innate teleology, and that these may be frustrated. To frustrate the child's innate teleology would be to wrong them. By way of comparison, consider how a seed will grow into a tree if allowed to follow its natural path, but how that innate teleology can be frustrated, for instance, by falling on a road in the baking sun. Indeed, that innate teleology might equally be helped on its path: a seed that falls on a road in the baking sun might be moved to more hospitable surroundings and so be helped to achieve its natural ends.

Let us call the idea that we have within us a perfect way that we could be, Innate Perfectionism. There are two versions of innate perfection, one which allows for influence and one that does not. On the first let us say that a designer made each of us with a perfect form in mind, left to unfold without interference, thus allowing us to fulfil our purpose. Any interference can only pervert the course of reaching our innate perfection. On the second, let us say that a designer made each of us with a form in mind, but that we can be helped to reach that perfection, we can facilitate and cultivate one another's perfect form, and indeed, we can frustrate our own fulfilment. Many people would dissent from the above stories since they do not believe that human beings were designed at all. However, it might be that one can understand the idea of an innate teleology without positing a designer. Indeed, one may wonder what the best way that they themselves could be is: the strongest, smartest, fastest, most caring, and so on. Still others might dissent from the first view since they want to emphasize free will, so that while we might have an innate perfection to fulfil, we will not simply fulfil it if left to get on with it; we may make bad decisions which prevent the fulfilling of our perfect nature. It seems that the second of these ideas is the more plausible, but it already makes room for positive influence. Let us now consider whether the idea of an innate teleology is coherent at all. We begin our next discussion with a poem from the sculptor Michelangelo, which speaks to innate teleologies.

Can we make sense of the idea of an innate teleology?

> The best of artists has that thought alone
> Which is contained within the marble shell;
> The sculptor's hand can only break the spell
> To free the figures slumbering in the stone.

(quoted in Dubos 1972, 10–11)

Michelangelo's poem expresses the idea that he did not create his sculptures. Instead, they resided within the block of marble all along, leaving to him the workman's task of chipping away the marble which obscured them. The thought might bespeak false modesty, since there were likely very many other statues equally contained in the blocks that he worked; many other ways that they could have been chipped away at to produce quite different statues. Of a less creative activity, one might say, 'I did not complete the Sudoku; the Sudoku was complete all along. I just filled in the missing numbers.' Here, the determination of the correct result does nothing to undermine the fact that a process is required to realize it. Even if there were veins running through a block of marble such that no other statue could be produced from that block, but only, say, the David, or a broken David, then it would still take serious skill, insight and effort to bring out the complete and undamaged David. The question here would be: Are children somewhat like the David, or the Sudoku, with an innate perfection, that is to be revealed? (Here we will take it as read that the undamaged David is better than any of the (purportedly) damaged Davids; that the innate teleology does indeed trump its perversions.)

We should be wary of vacuity in the innate/acquired distinction, for if we set the definition too loose, then, granted felicitous circumstance, every feat or trait a person might accomplish or develop would count as innate. For his use of the term, Dylan Evans adds the condition of requiring few special circumstances for a person to develop some skill or trait. Under this use, first-language acquisition counts as innate:

> When I say a trait is 'innate', I mean that it needs very few special conditions for it to develop. In other words, so long as you give a child the basic things it needs to survive such as food, shelter and company, that child will develop all the traits that are innate to humans. Language is innate in this sense; you do not need to provide lots of special instruction materials for a child to acquire a language. All you need to do is bring the child up in a group of other humans who can speak. (Evans 2003, 13)

Evans suggests that on this model innateness should be conceived on a continuum:

> Innateness is not an all-or-nothing thing, but a question of degree. When investigating emotions or any other biological or psychological trait, we should not really ask whether it is innate or not, but rather *how* innate it is. The more 'special conditions' over and above the basic necessities of survival that are required for the development of a trait, the less innate it is. Learning language is less innate than growing legs, since growing legs requires only a normal genome, basic nutrition, and the luck to escape nasty accidents, whereas learning a language requires all these things *plus* interaction with other speaking humans. (Evans 2003, 15)

We should contrast suppressing or not suppressing aspects of children, on the one hand, and encouraging or not encouraging aspects of children, on the other. Some characteristics might develop with encouragement, and atrophy without it, others might develop without encouragement or discouragement, but atrophy with discouragement. Some people might think that how a child grows without either encouragement or discouragement is a way to understand the natural growth path of the child. But why should we suppose that such a path of growth is desirable? Ken Robinson has done well to point out that children have a natural ability to become good pickpockets, but that rather than being something that we ought to encourage, or ignore, ought to be discouraged. Indeed, natural things are not thereby good things. All sorts of things are natural, but not good and ought to be discouraged: it may be more natural to feel jealous of another person's success rather than to take pleasure in it.

While Plato's views shifted throughout his life and are not entirely clear given his tendency to write in dialogue form, in one of his moods Plato held that acquiring knowledge was a matter or recalling a world which one had previously inhabited, but that recollection (or anamnesis) could be brought out through guidance and facilitation (such as Socrates' provocations), as well as through private contemplation. While it is surely wrong to speak of *the* Platonic conception of knowledge, we may construct something we could reasonably call a Platonic conception of the person, and their accumulation of knowledge. We could draw on *The Republic*, particularly the analogy of the Cave, the *Phaedo*, and on the *Meno*. We would see that soul once inhabits a world of forms, which it is taken from to be embodied on earth. Knowledge on earth consists in the recollection of forms. Here, knowledge is transcendentally empirical, since we learnt about the forms through direct acquaintance as souls, but it is present in us from birth in human form and so also innate. In the *Meno*, Socrates leads a slave boy to demonstrate Pythagoras' theorem by asking a series of questions to tease it out of him, and indeed, Socrates thought of himself as a midwife, teasing knowledge out of other people, and this would be a paradigmatic example of him doing so.

Certain sorts of true beliefs do not fit this form so well; the fact that I am an embodied person does not seem as good an example of a form as, say, the shape of a triangle. However, it is undeniably a fact, and no more illusory than the shape of the perfect triangle, and arguably less so. It could have been a form perhaps, but then human history would appear to exist predetermined in the realm of the forms. Perhaps we could say that the realm of the forms consists of all truths from all time, simultaneously, and perhaps that is a coherent idea, but it is a huge departure from common sense and under-motivated as a departure from simplicity. Indeed, it seems simpler to suggest that human beings perceive their existence, rather than recall it. To the extent that Plato insisted knowledge to be only about that which was changeless, such as mathematical truths, we may caution that this was also unmotivated. Facts may *be* states of affairs, or true statements *about* states of affairs. States of affairs themselves can come into existence and make certain statements about them true. Those states of affairs that come into existence may be contingent, and so too may be the truth of propositions about them, and they may only be true once they have materialized (if irreversibly so). For instance, it may not be true today that Arsenal football club will win tomorrow, even if come tomorrow Arsenal really do win. Mathematical ideas are among those about which Platonism is most plausible.

Let us accept this for the sake of argument that mathematical advances take place by recollection, rather than by discovery. This would be an example of innate perfectionism. It does not follow that mathematics is best pursued in isolation. Without interventions, people may misremember and instead they may be able to help each other remember. While one might worry that they will recall a false story between them, falsely believing themselves to have remembered something when reminded by someone else, it is not quite like this in the case of mathematics, since the beliefs, such as 2 + 2 = 4, are supposed to be self-evident. It cannot but be true, and one cannot understand that at the same time as not believing it, to entertain it is to be convinced of its truth. Indeed, Plato favoured education as a process which leads people to recollect the forms, and live in their light. Let us now consider the case that valuing 'independent mindedness' conflicts with the exercise of influence.

Independent mindedness as a virtue

There is a virtue of independent mindedness which is contrasted with being sheep-like, following the crowd, and with deference to an authority. Similarly, people are chastised for being gullible. At the same time, we should remind ourselves that we don't praise people for recalcitrance or excessive scepticism (to believe as little as possible is not the best policy); indeed we praise open-mindedness and chastise closed-mindedness. The comic Tim Minchin qualifies this with the warning, 'If you open your mind too much, your brain will fall out' (Minchin 2009). The close-minded person will not admit (even to themselves) that they are wrong; they are dyed in the wool and intransigent. The open-minded person can entertain doubts, they can assume things for the sake of argument, they can be taught new ideas, and can let go of old ideas.

Michael Hand has observed that rationality and heteronomy are not proper contrasts. Whereas autonomy contrasts with heteronomy, rationality contrasts with irrationality (Hand 2006a). Autonomy means doing what one thinks is best or believing what one would estimate to be true, heteronomy means deferring to some other in this respect. Hand points out that, in some circumstances, we might judge something to be best or true, but be in such a weak position to judge, and rationally ought to defer to those better placed to judge; for instance, the claims of qualified doctors are often better than those of those without medical training. By way of hesitation, we may consider the following entreatment from Michael Mann's film adaptation of the novel *The Last of the Mohicans* (1992).

> Well, then, Cora. In my heart I know, once we're joined … we'll be the most marvellous couple in London. I'm certain of that. So why not let those whom you trust, your father, help settle what's best for you? In view of your indecision, you should rely on their judgment. And mine. Will you consider that? Please consider that.

The theme of his film and the novel is that Cora ought to have followed her heart rather than the reasonable-sounding supplications of someone of whom she was fond, but about whom she was not impassioned. It is perhaps not always obvious as to when deference or insistence is most rational.

Impartial surveys of possibilities

One (fairly weak) version of the idea that all influence is immoral might be the following: that we ought to broaden the possibilities available to those that we influence, and not to narrow them. On this understanding, it is acceptable to tell people about a range of competing conceptions of the true and good, but never to promote anything in particular as true or good. Such an endeavour might be an example of what Hand calls non-directive education. An advocate of such a conception of education might deny that directive education is ever acceptable, although they must accept that some influence is being sought: at least one's understanding is being adjusted (and some beliefs) in broadening the range of possibilities that one has available. Thus, one is brought to understand a proposition, if not to believe or disbelieve or suspend judgement over its truth value. Or, one is brought to understand, and be capable of an action, practice or way of life, if not fully initiated into it or encouraged to identify with it. The objective would be to inform decisions without commending any.

It seems that some values will be in evidence (modelled, and thereby potentially transmitted) in what one frames as being a domain of options, and what one offers as being a consideration in its favour. Indeed, one might argue that employing the policy of global non-direction, amounts to directively recommending it. Where the question of how education ought to proceed is discussed (perhaps in teacher training colleges), the lecturer might take a non-directive approach again, allowing general directivity to be a reasonable option, but insofar as they do not take directivity, one might suggest, again, that in employing non-directivity, they are taking a directive attitude about it. This seems false. There seems to be scope for commitment without advocacy, even if one's commitment is manifest.

The problem with taking a permissive attitude is not incoherence, but undue reticence. Some might accept the theory of formative influence advocated earlier but claim that nothing is so well justified as to be deserving of directive teaching. However, this seems much too sceptical. Students ought to be taught directively, because the history of free enquiry has accumulated a wealth of wisdom. It seems unduly sceptical that school students should start from scratch; that they should have to reinvent wheels, re-falsify dead theories or, worse, remain captured by them (one recalls the words of Newton: 'If I have seen further than others, it is because I was standing on the shoulders of giants'). It seems unduly sceptical that the four humours theory should be considered as equally credible as modern medicine in a science classroom.

Thiessen on Foss and Griffin

By way of defending the possibility of religious evangelism being an ethical endeavour, Elmer Thiessen critiques Sonja Foss and Cindy Griffin's (1995) paper, 'Beyond Persuasion: A Proposal for Invitational Rhetoric', in which it is lamented that 'most traditional rhetorical theories reflect a patriarchal bias in the positive value they accord to changing and thus dominating others' (Foss and Griffin 1995, 2). Foss and Griffin worry that 'embedded in efforts to change others is a desire for control and domination, for the act of changing another establishes the power of the change agent over that other' which simultaneously 'devalues the lives and perspectives of these others' (Foss and Griffin 1995, 3). Thiessen neglects to allow that Foss and Griffin do not rule out the use of persuasion entirely. In their own words, 'We believe that persuasion is often necessary' (Foss and Griffin 1995, 5). Instead, they argue that 'an alternative exists that may be used in instances when changing and controlling others is not the rhetor's goal', calling this an 'invitational rhetoric' (Foss and Griffin 1995, 5). They conclude that 'invitational rhetoric is one of many useful and legitimate rhetorics, including persuasion, in which rhetors will want to be skilled' (Foss and Griffin 1995, 17). Here, rhetors will 'recognize situations in which they seek not to persuade others but simply to create an environment that facilitates understanding, accords value and respect to others' perspectives, and contributes to the development of relationships of equality' (Foss and Griffin 1995, 17).

It seems that Foss and Griffin provide us with reasons to reject persuasion wholesale, and no reason to entertain it as a reasonable endeavour for rhetors. One wonders what it is that might 'necessitate' persuasion, if it is merely an expression of a will to dominate. It is not clear how the will to dominate can legitimate a form of rhetoric; it might be desirable by some, but it does not seem to be justified. However, it does not seem at all fair to say that the will to persuade is thereby a will to dominate. Indeed, it is not just changing others for its own sake that is usually desired but changing others in desirable ways. Indeed, by the same token, those that wield influence ought to accept that they too might be improved or benefitted and thereby be open to the prospect without shame. Thiessen offers examples of morally unexceptionable persuasion: 'A mother persuades her child to tie her shoe laces. A father his teenage daughter to consider attending college' (Thiessen 2011, 56). Consider additionally a negotiator persuading a suicidal person not to jump, or a terrorist to release their hostages? Thiessen's cases seem unobjectionable, and in the cases that I suggest it seems morally obligatory for the negotiator to exercise persuasion.

Thiessen objects further that 'none of us are quite as independent as we would like to think we are'; in particular, many of our beliefs and values are acquired from those around us: 'most (maybe even 95%) of the beliefs that we hold are a result of persuasion' (Thiessen 2011, 56). Thiessen emphasizes 'an inescapable degree of human interdependence' (Thiessen 2011, 57). This might be so, but as we have observed earlier, it might be that we ought to follow the path of minimal influence. It might be that we ought never act so as to influence others, but only allow that this is an unfortunate byproduct to be tolerated. Foss and Griffin can reasonably complain that we live in a poor moral climate. And similar responses can be made to Thiessen's complaint that 'the purpose of argumentation, scholarship, and indeed the educational enterprise generally, is precisely to persuade and alter beliefs' since it is not as though this is essential to scholarship: one can assert one's beliefs, and the reasons for them without trying to persuade (Thiessen 2011, 58). Thiessen might then observe believing testimony is desirable, for without it, our knowledge base would be much smaller. But Foss and Griffin can agree with this also, and advise: we ought not to persuade, but share what we take to be the case, and often we will do well to learn from one another in doing so.

Thiessen might suggest that Foss and Griffin's writing amounts to a performative contradiction: 'But look', he might say, 'you yourself are writing to persuade.' And if indeed they are, they are doing wrong on their own account, but that does not mean that what they are doing is not wrong. A more compelling objection seems to be that Foss and Griffin do not seem to be providing an alternative to persuasion in the form of invitational rhetoric. It seems as if they are trying to soften persuasion by calling it 'invitational rhetoric', but 'a rose by any other name is still a rose', as Thiessen says. Does Foss and Griffin's thesis amount to, in David Lewis' (1994, 41) memorable dismissal of rebranding materialism and 'physicalism', 'a *tacky marketing ploy*, akin to *British Rail*'s decree that *second class* passengers shall now be called "standard class passengers"'? Understanding ought not to be the preserve of those who communicate for purposes other than persuasion. It seems that persuasion is justified only where one understands the position that they are recommending, and the position they are criticizing. Indeed, it seems that one ought always to be open to the possibility of being proven wrong, if believing the truth, and doing the good really are what one is concerned with. One might suggest that the difference turns on the difference between invitation and insistence. But Thiessen does not advocate for insistence in evangelism: 'The requirement that there needs to be an invitation to persuade is too strong. … It is when permission to persuade is denied … that it is immoral to continue to try to persuade' (Thiessen 2011, 59). However, they might perhaps claim that they are not writing to persuade, but merely to record their thoughts. In doing so they would be saying: I think the following, because *x*, *y* and *z* – I might be wrong. In doing so, one wonders where the meaningful difference lies between this and persuasion. Perhaps it just amounts to fallibilistic, open-minded, rational persuasion. It might also simply amount to a difference of intention, of whether one speaks in order to persuade, or speaks in order to report one's thought or perhaps to invite criticism.

Notwithstanding Thiessen's hesitancy, there are perhaps occasions where insistence might be warranted, with the only misgiving being its practicability; intransigence is not likely to be swayed with insistence (one may worry that insistence is a symptom of intransigence, but it need not be). We might find persuasive consequentialist arguments to favour bypassing rationality on some occasions. Consider whether there are any conditions under which one ought to slip another human being a conversion pill, a pill which will instantaneously change their beliefs, attitudes and projects to what one desires. A plausible example might be that the British Special Operations Executive would have been justified in slipping such pills to leading Nazis, so as to avert the Holocaust or the Second World War (Tillson 2013, 248).

Not all influence is immoral

In sum, Foss and Griffin's alternative to persuasion seems doubtfully genuine, and their arguments against persuasion rather weak, too. However, children's ideal futures are under-determined by their genetic endowment: one cannot read off from their genome how things ought to go for them ideally. While I am happy enough to defend a conception of well-being as an approximation of Godliness (as I have in Chapter 2), I do not think that there is one goal towards which we should bring children which is their fullest and most ideal development, or that we could easily imagine what that would be. Thus, different upbringings and different goals can be of equal worth within this conception. Furthermore, even if there were some latent perfection, it is far from obvious that scrupulously avoiding both encouragement and discouragement of those things which we admire and disapprove respectively is apt to lead them there. It seems that we often have good reason to encourage certain formative outcomes and discourage others.

7

The Nature of Religion

Introduction

We want to know how (if at all) children may be ethically influenced, with respect to religions. To reach that point, we will have to try to answer the prior question 'what is it that we mean by "religions"?' Some objects of study routinely appear in religious studies courses and books: the Abrahamic faiths, Judaism, Christianity and Islam (from oldest to youngest); and the non-Abrahamic faiths, such as Buddhism, Hinduism and Sikhism. Other objects of study, such as Scientology, Marxism and Secular Humanism, have appeared less routinely, alternatively referred to as cults, ideologies and world views. But how are we to discern between religion and non-religion? A good illustration of the problem is given by Timothy Fitzgerald, who points out that in

> denying the legitimacy of an overall theoretical structure [of religion], on the grounds that the 'conceptual geography' of the concept is too rich and complex, the editor [of a book on religion] seems to have deprived himself of any principles for controlling what does and what does not get included in the book. (Fitzgerald 1996, 226)

After sketching a number of ways of approaching this question, including, by stipulation, identifying family resemblance, and proceeding with examples in mind, I defend taking an essentialist approach. Ultimately, I defend an essentialist definition of religion, namely, that a religion is anything which essentially requires (a) belief in superbeings and (b) submission to them as having rightful dominion.

Essentialism

Jonathan Lowe (2008b) distinguishes between two kinds of essences: those conditions in virtue of which something qualifies as a particular *kind* of thing, and those (identity) conditions in virtue of which something at an earlier time (T1) qualifies as one and the same thing as something at a later time (T2). The kind of essence that we are interested in here is the essence of kinds, rather than the essence of individuals. Essentialists venture to identify criteria which are individually necessary and jointly sufficient for something to count as an instance of a kind. They interpret the question 'What is it that we mean by "religion"?' in the following way: What are the constitutive features of religions, those features of a phenomenon in virtue of which it is a religion? Some concepts are seemingly exceptions in that they seem to be incapable of such analysis, we might call these atomic, or basic concepts, in that they are too basic to be so analysed but may be drawn on in other such analyses: arguably the notions of action, belief, cause, knowledge, person, substance, time and truth are such concepts. Indeed, analysis works by way of cashing out some concept in terms of others, and analysis has to stop somewhere.

Consider the matter of what is to count as breaking the 100 metre world record, a feat accomplished by Usain Bolt. To achieve this, it is necessary to run 100 metres, but not sufficient. Conversely, it is sufficient to run that distance a whole second faster than anyone previously, but not necessary. It is both necessary and sufficient for breaking the 100 metre world record that one run that distance faster than anyone has done previously.[1] This is an essentialist definition of that phenomenon.

We ought to distinguish now between words and their objects, between signifiers and things signified. So we can ask both whether some things in themselves have essences, and whether words used to refer to them have essences of application. It is at the level of things in themselves that I am looking for an essence of religion. But this is to be found by starting at the linguistic level, with common usage: by picking paradigmatic examples of religion and seeking an essence which they share. That said, we should be wary of undue deference to common usage since it may create false or otherwise bad nominal unities: 'We cannot ignore everyday usage in trying to analyse such a concept [as seeing], but we must be ready to criticise and refine that usage where it is confused or vague' (Lowe 2000, 3). We must not be afraid of revision at the linguistic and conceptual level if we care about tracking truths about phenomena.

---

[1] This is probably not quite precise; it will likely also be necessary to run that distance in gravitationally similar conditions to those that we currently enjoy on Earth, on a straight course with a 0-degree gradient.

We also ought to acknowledge that words can have distinct senses. Consider the homonyms in the sentences 'hear the dog's bark' and 'feel the tree's bark'. We would be foolish to seek a single set of necessary and sufficient conditions in the application of the word 'bark'; given the differences of sense, it is more reasonable to seek them for each case. It is less obvious that words such as 'meaning', 'health', 'art' and 'religion' might be such cases, but we should be prepared to allow that they are.

Another possibility is that there are separate senses of 'religion', which have common core. Christopher Shields refers to this as 'core-dependent homonymy'; it is used by Aristotle to explain the relationship between the senses of the word 'healthy' in the expressions 'Socrates is healthy', 'Socrates' exercise regimen is healthy', and 'Socrates' complexion is healthy'.

> First, they are non-univocal, since the second is paraphraseable roughly as *promotes health* and the third as *is indicative of health*, whereas the first means, rather, something more fundamental, like *is sound of body* or *is functioning well*. Hence, *healthy* is non-univocal. Second, even so, the last two predications rely upon the first for their elucidations: each appeals to health in its core sense in an asymmetrical way. That is, any account of each of the latter two predications *must* allude to the first, whereas an account of the first makes no reference to the second or third in its account. So, suggests Aristotle, *health* is not only a homonym, but a *core-dependent homonym*: while not univocal neither is it a case of rank multivocity. (Shields 2014)

The natural kinds of the mind-independent world are perhaps more likely to be defined by necessary and sufficient features, that is, by essences, rather than as cultural concepts. To put it differently, the mind-independent world of such things as the periodic table elements, species and natural laws, rather than the social or mind-dependent and culturally constructed world consisting of artefacts and institutions, seems more likely to consist in essences. We could think of 'water is H_2O' as being a paradigm example of a natural kind having an (identifiable) essence. But while we might seek necessary sufficient conditions, they may not be available for mind-dependent concepts. On the other hand, some sort of public consistency, and correctability seems to be required for words to have a shared meaning. Words cannot mean whatever we want them to mean, as Humpty Dumpty wanted in Lewis Carroll's *Alice in Wonderland*, otherwise they would mean nothing at all, since they would fail to communicate anything. But perhaps this consistency need not consist in necessary and sufficient conditions.

Functional analyses

Brian and Beverly Clack (1998, 2) suggest that *substantive* and *functionalist* approaches have been the two main ways of defining religion. While E. B. Tylor's (1871, 424) 'belief in spiritual beings' and 'super-empirical beings' are offered as examples of substantive analyses, the functionalist, we are told, 'lays stress on the functions rather than the content of religion' (Clack and Clack 1998, 4). However, I want to suggest that these are less fundamental than the distinction between essential and non-essential analyses since one might say that the sort of essence we should be looking for, with respect to religion, is a functional one. There is a large body of literature in the sociology of religion from Durkheim to present, both defending and criticizing functionalist definitions of religion (Durkheim: reinforces social norms; Marx: the opiate of the masses; Freud: a crutch for the weak in the face of death). The functional analyses above will likely be disputed by religious people, but we should not class any of these functions as the essence of religions, even if they were true. Even if they were all true – and all religions fitted them – they would still hardly be sufficient. Other things might satisfy those functions also (comedian Bill Hicks suggested that the television program American Gladiators constitutes an opiate of the masses). What alternatives are there to essentialist analyses of religion (whether substantive or non-substantive, or some combination)?

Five alternatives to essentialism

One might abandon looking for an essentialist definition of religion, either because it is too difficult to do so or because it is not, in principle, possible or because it is both unnecessary and undesirable. A range of alternatives may be available: one might stipulate a definition; one might appeal to sufficient, but not necessary conditions; following Wittgenstein, one might appeal to a loose unity of family resemblances; one might simply proceed with 'excellent examples'. In the next five sections, I shall explain and evaluate each of these strategies in turn.

Stipulation

'A stipulative definition imparts a meaning to the defined term, and involves no commitment that the assigned meaning agrees with prior uses (if any) of the term', says Anil Gupta (2014). Stipulation usually dictates a definition for a word in terms of necessary and sufficient conditions. While one might quite innocuously baptise a previously unnamed concept, used as an alternative to analysing some prior use of a word, stipulation looks suspect. It becomes a blatant misappropriation of word and multiplies senses beyond necessity. One concept becomes proxy for another under the name of the original, risking intellectual oscillation between them, total conflation or substitution to the neglect of the concept originally of interest. One does better to invent a term, rather than arrogate it from common usage, but then it is plain that one has neglected the concept that had originally been of interest. While we might provide an essentialist analysis of some concept which does act well as proxy for religion in one or other of its senses, it is more appropriate not to call it religion. Besides, we cannot be sure just how far it does become proxy for religion without an essential characterization of that concept. It seems to me, then, that stipulation is not a promising alternative to seeking out an essence of an interesting concept.

Merely sufficient conditions

Despairing of finding 'a single principle or essence' (James 2008, 23), one might produce a definition of how they shall use the term that is rightly, but not exclusively deserving of it; something that is religious *if anything is*. That is, they might offer some conditions sufficient for religion, but not essential to it. This seems to be essentialist in its commitments, but to take the essentialist's task is to be practically overambitious and unnecessary for its purposes. Should they be available while necessary and sufficient conditions are not, that may be the best that we can do, and represent an acceptable fall-back position.

One sense among many

In *The Varieties of Religious Experience*, William James seems to suggest that an essentialist definition cannot, in principle, be provided to capture the range of phenomena that are claimed to be religious:

> The very fact that there are so many [definitions] and [that they are] so different from one another is enough to prove that the word 'religion' cannot stand for any single principle or essence, but is rather a collective name. … Let us not fall immediately into a one-sided view of our subject, but let us rather admit freely

at the outset that we may very likely find no one essence, but many characters which may alternately be equally important in religion. (James 2008, 23)

It is not clear what he can mean by 'collective name'. 'Triangle' might constitute a collective name, in that it names a kind to which many instances belong. But here, an essentialist analysis is obviously forthcoming for its members. Alternatively, James might be taken to anticipate the existence of a plethora of homonyms, but in that case his collapsing them together in the expression 'equally important in religion' is clearly illicit. Indeed, as we have seen above, it is no skin off of the essentialist's nose to say that religion is one word with many meanings: the essentialist can readily admit that homonyms exist. If that is the case with 'religion', one should begin to differentiate them and specify the sense at issue. Indeed, the various senses of 'religion' could prove to be *core-dependent homonyms*.

James gives 'a narrow view' 'for the purpose of these lectures', 'out of the many meanings of the word ... choosing one meaning in which I wish to interest you particularly' (James 2008, 25). The single sense that James delineates is this:

> Religion, therefore, as I now ask you arbitrarily to take it, shall mean for us *the feelings, acts and experiences of individual men* [sic] *in their solitude, so far as they apprehend themselves to stand in relation to whatever they consider to be the divine.* (James 2008, 26)

The expression 'arbitrarily to take it', suggests that James' use is stipulative, with no reference to common usage. On the other hand, 'choosing one meaning' from 'the many meanings of the word' suggests the contrary. I suggest that James is best read as delineating a single sense, which has no natural priority (for instance, it is not the core on which its homonyms are dependent). It will be well now to evaluate this definition.

The word 'divine' is cashed out as 'denoting any object that is godlike, whether it be a concrete deity or not' (James 2008, 28). 'Godlike' is glossed in turn as what is 'most primal and enveloping and deeply true', and, in particular, only 'such a primal reality as the individual feels impelled to respond to solemnly and gravely, and neither by curse or jest' (James 2008, 31). Ironically, this understanding of 'godlike' does not seem to capture gods. Gods are (as we shall argue later) super-powerful rational agents; they are not propositions and so cannot be true. He also says (which sounds different again) that 'a man's religion might thus be identified with his attitude, whatever it might be, towards what he felt to be primal truth' (James 2008, 28–9). This would seem to suggest that to believe that there is a 'primal truth' is to have a religion, namely whatever one takes to be primal truth, and would abandon James' stipulation that one's response to it need be solemn. I would suggest that people would have an easier time saying whether they were religious (perhaps confusedly) than whether they took anything to be primally true. I would also suggest that, to the extent that I can make sense of it, nihilists would then count as being religious in saying that the universe is basically meaningless, as would materialists in saying that nothing exists but matter and its relations. These both seem to be putative examples of primal truths about the universe if anything does.

It is interesting as to why James mentions 'individual men *in their solitude*'. Arguably, it is to isolate belief from social reinforcement to the furthest extent possible so that it is what one thinks really, rather than what one merely 'goes along with'. Contra James, Durkheim has argued that religion is essentially social. But while religion can be learnt from others, one could subsequently become a Robinson Crusoe, who retains his or her religion. Moreover, it seems that a Robinson Crusoe might invent a religion or a religious ceremony. It might be thought unlikely, but Durkheim's intuition is not one that I want to preserve or dismiss in advance of presenting a definition. I want to say that since human beings are social creatures, it is not surprising that their beliefs spread and are reinforced and developed and acted upon in a social way. Indeed, one cannot understand religion *as it actually exists* without employing social concepts. However, it does not follow from religion's being social *in practice*, that religion must be social *in essence*.

Excellent examples

Alvin Plantinga (2014) suggests that while it is 'extremely difficult to give (informative) necessary and sufficient conditions for either science or religion', 'we do have many excellent examples of each' and suggests tentatively that 'perhaps that will suffice for our inquiry'. (His inquiry is not ours, but is to determine whether the relation between religion and science is 'characterized by *conflict* or by *concord*'. Still, our projects share a concern about the demarcation of religion.) Scott A. Davison seems to concur with Plantinga's approach: 'In general', says Davison, 'it seems doubtful whether we need criteria to decide whether or not something falls under a given concept. We may be aware of paradigm cases, for instance, without being aware of criteria' (Davison 2012, 34). Sven Hansson (2008) dissents from this view:

It is in a sense paradoxical that so much agreement has been reached in particular issues in spite of almost complete disagreement on the general criteria that these judgments should presumably be based upon. This puzzle is a sure indication that there is still much important philosophical work to be done on the demarcation between science and pseudoscience.

Indeed, one may know the paradigm examples, but one cannot read off from these what else falls under the concepts; to see whether some other thing is a religion, you have to ask how similar is it to our excellent examples (paradigm cases), which would require specifying which aspects of the examples they ought to be similar to, which is the same thing as to determine criteria. Bearing in mind these misgivings, we shall now evaluate Wittgenstein's contention that excellent examples are not only enough to get by with, but that they are sometimes (perhaps often) all that are available.

Family resemblance analyses

In his later work, Wittgenstein was to deny that there must be an essential feature common to all the correct uses of a given word. In the *Philosophical Investigations*, Wittgenstein maintains that there need be no essence to any common noun, not even core-dependent homonymy. To elucidate how we apply words without their objects sharing an essence, Wittgenstein discusses the concept of games. An imaginary interlocutor suggests that 'a game consists in moving objects about on a board according to certain rules', but is corrected: 'You seem to be thinking of board games, but there are others' (PI, §3). Wittgenstein suggests that we should not assume that there are necessary and sufficient criteria available at the outset of our task (*PI*, §66). He then reminds us of the variety of things that we call games and suggests that while many may share all sorts of similarities, no combination of these are common and exclusive to all. He suggests that in the case of 'games', the best that our actual investigations can afford are what he calls 'family resemblances' (*PI*, §67): 'A complicated network of similarities overlapping and criss-crossing: sometimes overall similarities, sometimes similarities of detail' (*PI*, §66). This is so much as to say that concepts do not need necessary and sufficient concepts to be applied. Religion may prove to be a family resemblance kind; what Christopher Shields amusingly calls a 'motley kind'.

Given Wittgenstein's account of 'games', how, then, might we challenge him on the question of whether games are distinguishable from things which are not games? What is it that makes the concept of a game usable? Wittgenstein's response comes in two parts. He first characterizes the various similarities as 'family resemblances': 'For the resemblances between members of a family … overlap and criss-cross in exactly the same way' and games, he says, 'form a family' (*PI*, §66). It is these resemblances that distinguish the word's correct application. Wittgenstein then further justifies his idea by saying a concept does not need to have distinct frontiers in order to function. 'What still counts as a game and what no longer does? Can you give the boundary? No. You can draw one for none has been drawn. ("But that never bothered you before when you used the word 'game'")' (*PI*, §68). That is, common nouns like 'game' do not suddenly become unusable simply because we do not like what constrains their proper use. Perhaps more likely we could say that the word 'game' is applicable in virtue of sharing some (but not complete) similarity with one species or sense of 'game', and then we have a sort of initially loose or metaphorical application, which comes to forge a new literal application, and thereby a new sense.

Indeed, the *Philosophical Investigations* convinced many people that 'game' failed to have necessary and sufficient conditions. Applying this Wittgensteinian understanding, Peter Byrne (1988), Benson Saler (1993) and Ninian Smart (1973) have all attempted to give family resemblance analyses of 'religion' (Fitzgerald 1996, 234). Timothy Fitzgerald acknowledges that while any 'essentialist definition of religion such as "belief in God or gods" must be "too parochially tied to Judaeo-Christian theistic origins of the word"', a Wittgensteinian family resemblance analysis promises 'a distinctive role for religion as a universally applicable analytical concept' (Fitzgerald 1996, 215). However, he objects that on such an analysis 'the "religion" family and other neighbouring families such as ideologies, worldviews, values or symbolic systems … becomes so indefinite that the word ceases to pick out any distinctive aspect of human culture' (Fitzgerald 1996, 215). He recommends that we do away with the term religion and look to other, more universal anthropological categories. The term while perhaps alright for everyday purposes is no good for academic uses, and according to him, it is too imprecise, and confused. It seems to me however, that a decent essentialist definition may still be forthcoming. Which essentialist definition shall we accept, or which back up shall we revert to? It is ultimately Michael Hand's that I shall employ, amend and defend.

Before discussing Hand's essentialism, I want quickly to make a comment about the importance (or unimportance) of self-identification in identifying religious people. There is a difference between self-identification, and identification. That an insane person might not self-identify as insane does nothing to imply that they are sane. Sometimes, self-identification is a necessary condition, of belonging to a category, but not always. It is never sufficient however; indeed, it makes little sense to think of the set which that would imply – the set of all people who claim to be part of that set.

Hand's essentialism

I want to defend a slightly modified version of Michael Hand's essentialist definition. Hand does not investigate the word 'religion', but the word 'religious', and claims that to be religious one must believe that there exists at least one god who makes a positive difference to one's life. Granting this, perhaps a religion would be, in essence, a body of beliefs central among which is a belief in the existence of at least one god who makes a positive difference to the lives of at least some believers. Additional aspects of particular religions, such as institutional form, rituals and what not would be incidental at least *qua* religion, if not *qua* the particular religion that they are.

For Hand, to be religious, one must hold 'beliefs about a god or gods'; in particular, presumably, one must most fundamentally believe that they exist (Hand 2006b, 95). Immediately, we think of the common objection raised, for instance, by Clack and Clack: 'To deny that Buddhism counts as a religion … would surely be a bizarre consequence' (1998, 3). However, if Buddhism is presented as a counterexample, Hand is prepared to respond convincingly that, first, 'it is not unusual to hear people deny that Buddhism is a religion and describe it instead as a philosophy or a way of life, precisely because they take the crucial element of belief in a divine being to be missing', and second,

> a great many Buddhists manifestly *do* believe in gods or something very like them. For schools of Buddhism in the Mahayana tradition, the heavens are richly populated with Buddhas and Bodhisattvas, ready to help human beings along the Eightfold Path to Enlightenment. (Hand 2006b, 96)

He concludes that 'Buddhism is a philosophy in some of its forms, and a religion in others' (Hand 2006b, 96). While I should not like to drive a wedge between 'religions' and 'philosophy', for it seems reasonable that something could be a religious philosophy, I would accept that Buddhism is a religion in some of its forms and not a religion in its other forms, while perhaps being a philosophy in all of its forms.

The Clacks, Hand and Plantinga all agree that belief in god(s) alone is insufficient. Clack and Clack state: 'Religion is certainly more than cool adherence to a rather bizarre belief or system of beliefs' (1998, 3). Hand observes: 'A person may hold beliefs about gods and yet be utterly indifferent to them. She may regard the existence as one more fact about the world which has no relevance to her life' (Hand 2006b, 96–7). Plantinga (2014) conjectures:

> The truth here, perhaps, is that a belief isn't religious *just in itself*. The property of being religious isn't intrinsic to a belief; it is rather one a belief acquires when it functions in a certain way in the life of a given person or community. To be a religious belief, the belief in question would have to be appropriately connected with characteristically religious attitudes on the part of the believer, such attitudes as worship, love, commitment, awe, and the like.

Indeed, 'For Kierkegaard Christian faith is not a matter of regurgitating church dogma. It is a matter of individual subjective passion' (McDonald 2012).

While John Wilson suggested that, additionally, a person 'must adopt a moral code for reasons connected with her beliefs about gods', Hand suggests, instead, that though sufficient, this would not be necessary 'since people who worship and revere the gods they believe in, or supplicate their gods for assistance in times of need, certainly have a religion, even if their religious beliefs have no influence on their moral principles and judgements' (Hand 2006b, 97). Instead, Hand suggests that 'a person must hold the gods she believes in to have *some positive relevance to her life*' (e.g. 'Worthy of worship', 'receptive to supplication' or 'moral authorities'), 'any of them is sufficient' (Hand 2006b, 98–9).

This has the benefit of leaving out those whose attitudes to gods seem unreligious. Hand's example is Ivan, of Dostoyevsky's *The Brothers Karamazov*, who is contemptuous of God, whom he regards as morally repugnant on account of the suffering He allows (Hand 2006b, 98). Plantinga has added that devils believe in God and yet, in their antipathy to God, are not religious: 'According to the New Testament book of James, "the devils believe [that God exists] and tremble"; the devils' beliefs, presumably, aren't religious' (Plantinga 2014). Perhaps devils *should* regard God as having some positive relevance to their lives – perhaps their souls can be redeemed – but the crucial point is whether or not they *do* regard God as having some positive relevance. Furthermore, perhaps this positive relevance should not just be seen as some sort of silver lining to an otherwise grey cloud, where one makes the best of a generally bad thing (e.g.

finding solidarity in opposition to the bad thing; perhaps as opponents of animal cruelty or torture do).

Instead of Hand's criterion of 'holding gods to have *some positive relevance to her life*', I would suggest that Plantinga's understanding of religion requiring certain attitudes would be better; having some positive and invitational attitudes to the god, or gods, rather than merely a belief that they have some positive relevance (that one benefits from their existence). Christians might petition God through prayer for intervention in worldly matters, but they additionally defer to God as being the authority on moral matters; both in respect of knowledge and motivation, they defer to Him willingly. On the other hand, one might petition some god without thinking that they are a rightful ruler, and yet believe the god to have some positive bearing on their lives. One might like to construct the counterexample of an individual being specially favoured by a god who they regard as a fool, and so take to be a positive relevance without having the slightest respect for them, but on the definition of 'god' that I shall defend, this will not be possible; a god is one who excels us in every respect, and with whom we have no chance of competing successfully. A demigod is one who we may have some (however small) chance of beating (more on gods later). Despite having this counterexample unavailable, I hope that I have said enough to convince that 'positive relevance' is insufficient as a necessary condition. One could anyway imagine a case of someone who (wrongly) believed that they could 'get one over' on a god, perhaps planning to deceive their way into paradise. They might then regard the god as having some positive relevance to their life but would not thereby be religious.

I would suggest that the characteristic attitude is one of willing deference. Possible attitudes to gods include contented and discontented subordination, and (futile) overt dissent. Discontented subordination includes resentfully placating powerful gods. Overt dissent is exemplified by Ivan, in *The Brothers Karamazov*. It is interesting to think of dissent and discontented subordination in relation to gods' powers and desires, since the dynamic is like that of an omnipotent Orwellian Thought Police. Of course, George Orwell's Thought Police (from his novel *1984*) attempted to engineer willing subordination, not being satisfied with discontented subordination, and hoping to undermine the possibility of dissent in the style of Ivan. I will suggest that willing, as opposed to engineered, subordination is the religious attitude. The criterion of regarding gods to have rightful dominion may exclude those that worshipped the gods of the Parthenon as people who deferred to the gods more through expedience than through what they considered rightful (where what is considered right is not constituted by the arbitrary or self-interested preferences of the mighty, which is anyway just to erode the concept of right), but I do not take this to be problematic.

Gods

For Hand, a 'god is a transcendent or superhuman person, a person who transcends or exceeds the ordinary limits of human personhood' (Hand 2006b, 107). I take it that Hand offers two ways of characterizing an identical property, that a transcendent person and a superhuman person are the same thing. DC Comics' Superman is a superhuman or transcendent person, in the sense that he is much like ordinary people except that his powers far exceed those of humans in degree and also in kind.

It is interesting to wonder whether the degree of superability necessary to qualify a being for godhood is absolute or indexical. Is there some absolute standard which constitutes godly levels of superhuman power, or is it that having greater powers than some group makes one a god relative to them? One may think of a group of aliens having regular powers relative to one another, but much greater powers than human beings (the species of which Superman was a member, for instance), and so be gods relative to us. Alternatively, Anselm's monotheistic definition of a god as 'that than which nothing greater can be conceived' might help us anchor an absolute notion of a god as having maximal powers.

However, I think that an indexical concept of gods is all that we require: a god is one who excels us in every respect, and with whom we have no chance of competing successfully. A demigod, on the other hand, is one who we may have some (small) chance of beating. For instance, Hector was powerful man, but not sufficiently powerful to be a demigod, and Achilles was also a powerful man, but not powerful enough to be considered a god; Achilles' being half human and half god explains his limitations rather than defines them.

It is interesting to consider how Jesus maps onto our definition of a god. Jesus' Incarnation, it is said, 'does not mean that Jesus Christ is part God and part man, nor does it imply that he is the result of a confused mixture of the divine and the human. He became truly man while remaining truly God. Jesus Christ is true God and true man' (*Catechism of the Catholic Church*, §464). It is regarded as something of a mystery or paradox as to how this is conceivable, and so, if Jesus fails to fit our definition of a god it may do little damage to our definition. It was thought to be a paradox that Jesus could have both died on the cross and been a god. It was thought by some to be an outright incoherence.[2] It was also thought to be a paradox or outright incoherence that a god could have been born to a human being. But our definition has not committed itself to whether gods must be immortal, uncreated or creators. This openness allows that a god could perhaps come into and go out of existence, could have been created, and could fail to have created anything. I have said that one god is relative to another, where their powers exceed the possibility of being beaten at any task. It seems that Jesus could be beaten, since he was crucified, and so was not a god, but it seems that he allowed himself to be beaten. It was not against his will, and perhaps he could not be willingly beaten. Indeed, it also seems logically if not empirically possible that a human being could be a god relative to other humans in that they belong to the species but are endowed with such incredible powers that they cannot be beaten by other human beings.

It will be well now to see whether the definitions can withstand objections that I myself haven't suggested.

McKinney's critique

Hand's definition has been critiqued in a review by McKinney (2011). In this section, I shall quote five challenges made by McKinney, and defend Hand's thesis against them.

1. It is questionable whether his [Hand's] sketchy account of the concept of god ... adequately reflects the centuries of scholarly debate on this concept. (McKinney 2011, 164)

The term 'sketchy account' seems more name-calling than critique. In providing analyses, simplicity is desirable (although not to the point of oversimplification: while there is sometimes a trade-off between explanatory power and simplicity, other things being equal, simplicity is in itself a theoretical virtue). Furthermore, 'an adequate reflection of the centuries of scholarly debate on this concept' is not required for a satisfactory definition. Indeed, it is only those considerations which threaten to undercut Hand's definition which are relevant to his project. Should we know of any, we ought then to challenge Hand with them rather than

---

[2] Tertullian remarks in *De Carne Christi*, '*Et mortuus est dei filius; credibile prorsus est, quia ineptum est*,' 'The Son of God died: it is *immediately* credible – because it is silly,' where 'silly' is meant in the sense of the ridiculous which is properly contrasted with the sublime (Tertullian 1956, Chapter 5, Vol. 4).

chide him for failing to scour centuries' worth of texts to find them; it is quite enough to pick up on the key discussions in contemporary texts.

2. It is further questionable if he really acknowledges, never mind addresses, the tension that arises for contemporary philosophy from the obfuscation of the delineation of the relationship between the god of philosophy and the god of revealed religion as exemplified in the sourcing of texts (e.g. scripture) from revealed religion as evidence of the nature of this god. (McKinney 2011, 164)

It is hard to know what the accusation is here. If it is that there is a difference between the god of philosophers and the god of revealed religion, and that Hand neglects the latter, I want to say that that is a poor objection. There is no such thing as 'the god of philosophers'; either philosophers want to characterize something more general than the god of revelation (if indeed there is just one god of revelation at all), or they do not. If they do, then it is not a problem that they do not refer to *just* the god of revelation. If they want to characterize the god of revelation in particular, they can. Richard Swinburne wants to do so when he talks of 'a person without a body (i.e. a spirit) who is eternal, free, able to do anything, knows everything, is perfectly good, is the proper object of human worship and obedience, the creator and sustainer of the universe' (Swinburne 1989, 1). Hand's definition does capture the god of revelation, if that means 'the god, or gods who appear in the Abrahamic scriptures', but aims to capture, and quite rightly, *more* than just the god of revelation. On the other hand, if the accusation is that the Bible cannot be used to provide evidence for a definition of the God of philosophers, then again this seems to be mistaken. Again, while there is no god of the philosophers, one may define a more general concept of god which contains the god of revelation, but other gods also. In this case, it is perfectly proper to use the god of revelation as a constraint on one's definition of gods; if a paradigmatic example of a god (namely, 'the god of revealed religion') does not fit within one's definition, then so much the worse for one's definition.

3. Is it not problematic for the philosopher to be building logical structures connected to *inexact* concepts? (McKinney 2011, 164).

McKinney makes a good point here. Indeed, Aristotle makes a similar point apparently about ethics along these lines: we want exactness and clarity in our thought, but not more exactness and clarity than the object of our thought allows. Aristotle claims that 'it is the mark of an educated man to look for precision in each class of things just so far as the nature of the subject admits'

(*Nicomachean Ethics*, I, III). 'Now fine and just actions, which political science investigates, admit of much variety and fluctuation of opinion, so that they may be thought to exist only by convention, and not by nature', says Aristotle. Admitting 'ambiguous cases' is even among the *desiderata* that Eshleman (2008, 4) places on an adequate definition of religion.

Timothy Fitzgerald complains that 'analysis of "religion" texts shows that the word is used in such a large range of contexts that it is devoid of analytical value' (1996, 215). The pendulum might seem to have swung too far in the opposite direction with too precise a definition. If the term is inherently vague, though, it may be so vague as to be useless in this context. Neither of the problems appear to me to be material, however. It seems to me that Hand makes the concept no more definite than it already is; he just makes it clear to us where its exactnesses and vaguenesses lie, or, rather, our modification of Hand does that. One question will be whether the concept is too narrow, whether it presides over the range of phenomena that we might want it to in order to keep it from being too parochial (the second prong of the dilemma which Fitzgerald uses to challenge the efficacy of the academic usefulness of the term 'religion'). This concern will be addressed in the next chapter.

4.   Is religion necessarily some form of collective enterprise? If the person is part of a collective enterprise, she would believe that her gods have some relevance for the lives of others within her group. Further, it could be argued that the collective enterprise believes that it contributes positively to society. This may, of course, take the form of the religion being critical of society and the values of society. If it is the case that religion is a form of collective enterprise and believes it contributes positively to society, perhaps a third point can be added: (3) she believes this religion will have a positive influence on others in her group and on society. Clearly this argument rests on the idea that religion is a collective enterprise and others may quibble with, or refute, this phraseology and statement, but this example is used to illustrate the complexity of this *inexact* concept of religion and suggest that perhaps philosophers such as Hand need to explore this concept more deeply and draw on a greater range of sources to inform their thinking. (McKinney 2011, 163–4)

McKinney asks whether religion is essentially social in nature, and suggests that if it were, a further constraint on the definition of religion ought to be that any putative religion should regard itself as being a good for society. I do not think that that conclusion follows: one could conceivably have a corporate religion which was ego-centric, so that a society considered that it ought to sacrifice its own good for someone they considered to be divine, or divinely favoured (one may think of the Egyptian pharaohs as being in this vein). Still, I do not think that religion is essentially social in nature; instead, it seems that a person could have a private religion (or to the extent that they could not, it is no different from any other aspect of human belief, understanding and activity, and so a trivial thesis).

I want to suggest that it is not at all surprising that 'religions', in a derivative sense of the word, have social structures; religions in one sense of the word *are* social structures, but they are social structures constructed around religion in a primary sense. A religion is anything which essentially requires (a) belief in superbeings and (b) submission to them as having rightful dominion. There exist social structures which may be called 'religions', in a derivative sense, in that they are built around this primary sense of the word. A person is religious if and only if they believe in super-powerful beings that they submit to, regarding them to have rightful dominion. A social group is religious if and only if they share a belief in super-powerful beings that they submit to, regarding them to have rightful dominion.

There is an interesting relationship between societies or clubs and doctrines. A cycling club usually will not consist of people who believe a certain set of propositions; they will consist of people that want to ride bicycles together. Here, there is an emphasis on belonging, rather than believing (although obviously some, rather common beliefs will need to be shared for that to be possible). A political society will, on the other hand, be a group of people who gather, perhaps to advance certain causes in light of certain shared beliefs, and perhaps to debate the finer points and applications of their basic, shared beliefs. Here, there is a case of belonging *and* believing – indeed, it is belief that motivates belonging. Grace Davie (1994) has argued that in the later part of the twentieth century, Britain became a more privately religious society (which is not to say that beliefs could not be expressed or acted on in the public space, but that people did not form congregations on the basis of their beliefs but maintained them individualistically).

5. How are philosophers, for example, to respond to the contemporary reshaping of the landscape of religion? The nomenclature can be a little confusing but 'new age religions' and 'new age spiritualities', so easily dismissed and ridiculed, have, in fact, been the subject of serious academic study and debate and, crucially, have proved to be the catalyst for a

> revision of the (always porous) boundaries of the sociological concept of
> religion. What are the implications of this for the philosophical concept of
> religion? What are the implications for the distinction between religious
> and non-religious people? This is a new challenge for the philosophers
> who engage in discussion of religion (possibly the result of the insufficient
> philosophical focus on this *inexact* concept) and philosophers have an
> important role in the contemporary clarification of the concept of religion.
> (McKinney 2011, 164)

Philosophers ought to respond to the new, putative cases of religion by seeing
whether they fit with a definition; this would seem to be Hand's ready response.
Being a subject of serious academic study is no criterion of religion, and indeed
something need not be the least bit plausible to reward study in a sociological
sense. Indeed, mental illness is worthy of study without being desirable, in part
to help cure it.

McKinney claims that the so-called new religions 'have proved to be the
catalyst for a revision of the (always porous) boundaries of the sociological
concept of religion'. One may worry with Fitzgerald that the boundaries are
so vague that the concept does not yield enough determinations as to whether
something is or is not a religion; it is quiet on too many cases, and is hence
useless or useless for some practical purposes (such as an academic field of study
with a specific remit).

Religions and propositional content (or truth-claims)

One of the biggest questions that we face in trying to understand what a religion
is, that we face in the light of the discussions of Wittgensteinians (such as D.
Z. Philips), is: How important are doctrines for religions (sufficient, necessary,
necessary and sufficient, irrelevant, or incompatible)? It seems that religious
people express propositional attitudes or make truth-claims; the propositions
asserted are commonly called 'doctrines'. Indeed, the first of the five pillars of
Islam (found in the Hadith of Gabriel) focuses on belief content: *Shahadah*,
the declaration that there is no god except Allah, and that Muhammad is
his Messenger. The Nicene Creed, professed in mass by Christians of several
churches, appears to consist of a set of propositions, which are asserted to be
true in the profession. Indeed, St Paul writes to the Corinthians that 'if Christ
be not risen, then is our preaching vain, and your faith is also vain' (1 Cor. 15.14,

King James Version). However, Paul does not say that Christ's having risen is to be taken literally, and if he did, he may still have been speaking non-literally (e.g. metaphorically, ironically or exaggeratingly).

On my own definition of religion (namely 'a doctrine which claims the existence and rightful dominion of one or more gods, and requires submission to them') and doctrines (namely 'there exist one or more gods, who have rightful dominion') are essential. However, the aforementioned Wittgensteinians deny that religious claims are meant literally (or at least claim that many are not). They have one of two options open to them: global and local non-literalism. The global non-literalist says that not only are religious propositions not meant literally but there is no such thing as literal language for them to be contrasted with. The local non-literalist says that religious propositions are not meant literally, that they might be meant as exaggerations, or metaphors or some other non-literal thing. J. L. Mackie (1982, chapter 12) suggests that Philips was hoping to carve out an understanding of religious claims such that they would fall somewhere between literal statements and non-literal statements (a clearly impossible task). Certainly, Jesus is reported in the Gospels as making frequent use of non-literal language, like allegorical tales. But it seems that he literally made frequent use of them.

There is a large literature on what can be meant by religious language. Proponents of the via negativa seem to deny that it has any meaning to humans. It is possible for sentences to have meaning that is not appreciated by the speaker, as when I phonetically pass on a message sent by someone else in a language that I do not understand. On the other hand, it must mean something to someone to be meaningful, and, if it means nothing to me, it is hard to see how I could believe it since, as Bernard Williams (2006a, 19) puts it, 'If you do not know what it is you are believing on faith, how can you be sure that you are believing anything?'

We may ask, are propositions involved, and what would these matter? What are their truth conditions? Are they the same as the truth conditions of their statements literally construed, and what literal sentences would share their truth conditions? Is there anything that secularists could reject?

Tim Crane suggests that 'a lot of humanists treat religion as if it were simply a kind of rival cosmological hypothesis, and that this is all it is. My view is that to the extent that religions are cosmological hypotheses, this is not the only important thing about them' (Crane 2012). What if they all turned out to be false, would this matter? Wittgenstein wants to say 'no':

Queer as it sounds: The historical accounts in the Gospels might, historically speaking, be demonstrably false and yet belief would lose nothing by this: *not*, however because it concerns 'universal truths of reason'! Rather because historical proof (the historical proof-game) is irrelevant to belief. This message (the Gospels) is seized on by men believingly (i.e. lovingly). *That* is the certainty characterizing this particular acceptance-as-true, not something *else*.

A believer's relation to these narratives is *neither* the relation to historical truth (probability), *nor yet* that to a theory consisting of 'truths of reason'. (1984, 37e–38e)

It would not only be conceivable but also amusing to think that the utterances of people who regarded them as in some way less than literal turned out to be literally true, as many regard them to be (many philosophers of religion at least; Alvin Plantinga, Richard Swinburne, William Lane Craig and others give impressive defences of literal belief). Non-literalists should not be regarded as being religious in my view, but as quasi-religious at most.

As we have seen, Jonathan Lowe distinguishes between two kinds of essences; those conditions in virtue of which something qualifies as a particular *kind* of thing, and identity conditions in virtue of which something at T1 and again at T2 qualifies as one and the same thing. In connection with this, Lowe considers that 'it is *metaphysically* possible – even if not *biologically* or *physically* possible – for any individual cat to survive "radical" metamorphosis, by becoming a member of *another* natural kind of living organism' (Lowe 2008b). In connection with Lowe's suggestion, it might be possible for an individual tradition to pass between being a religion and no longer being a religion. Suppose that a tradition needs to affirm belief in a god to be a religion, and that a tradition used to do so in its past but does not any longer, it may be that an individual tradition has passed from the kind of religion into another kind, a non-religious ideology or society, perhaps.

I do not want to say that religions consist of truth-claims that have no evaluative dimensions, and that have no social dimension of membership. The Nicene Creed opens (in English) with the words 'we believe in one God'. That utterance may be distinguished from 'we believe that there exists only one God', meaning instead that they obey or trust one particular god. It seems to mean a combination of these interpretations that (a) there is only one god, and (b) they obey and trust in Him. Professing 'belief in' a subject or ideal is additionally relational and may contribute to one's being so related to that subject or ideal. As J. L. Austin (1962) famously noted in his William James lectures, words can be deeds, as when one says 'I do' at a wedding service or signs a name on a contract. While I do not wish to deny that there are important, performative dimensions to professing the Nicene Creed, they should not be seen as ruling out the presence of propositional content; content which is required for their identification *as* religions.

Is faith accidental or essential to religion?

Suppose that a group of scientists working on the Large Hadron Collider discovered (however that might be) that God existed, and that historians converged on the consensus of the historical veracity of the Bible, or something near enough to it, and that they did so because it was supported by, among other things, archaeological discoveries. Would these scholars have faith and would what they have be a religion? It is fair to say, though, that one's attitudes to the impersonal discoveries of history and science are not dictated by those disciplines, so that one could perhaps find the truth of some doctrines about God to be true, and yet not be inclined to willing subordination, and so not be religious. Suppose also that they regarded God to be worthy of worship, due to sound arguments and submitted themselves to his will accordingly. Again, would these scholars have faith and would what they have be a religion? They would have reasonable belief and not faith in the sense 'belief without evidential or argumentative grounds'.[3] Admittedly, it has been that the best justified theories have turned out false (Newtonian physics being the paradigm example), and so it might turn out that orthodox learned opinion could yet be false, and reason could yet emerge for people to reject it. So too, it seems that these scientists, unless they had discovered some logically incontrovertible evidence, might too have to abandon their beliefs, even though it seems to me that faith is accidental rather than essential to religion and that while these scientists and historians do believe in the existence and rightful dominion of God, and accordingly submit to Him, they are thereby religious.

In opposition, one might urge that the nature of true faith is that one never gives up one's beliefs (and holds their beliefs independently of the shifting sands of evidence).[4] Certainly, Kierkegaard emphasized leaps of faith: '*Without risk*

---

[3] This distinction is a bit quick: there are very arguably 'properly basic beliefs', to use Alvin Plantinga's expression; beliefs which are not based on evidence and argument, but that are still reasonable, and indeed, that are presupposed in other arguments.

[4] Alternatively, it could be that private revelation cuts decisively through the public evidential record.

there is no faith. Faith is precisely the contradiction between the infinite passion of the individual's inwardness and the objective uncertainty' (Kierkegaard 1941, 182). It might seem to the extent that a religion's doctrines constitute a compellingly supported hypothesis (so that nobody could reasonably deny it), what we have is no longer a religion.

Certainly, *never gives up one's faith* seems too strong a criterion for religion: people have converted from one religion to another, part of which involved a change of beliefs. While it might seem strange to think that a phenomenon depends for its nature on how it was arrived at, the notion of a scientific view certainly has that built into it. Newton's ideas would not have been scientific if (a) they were not reasoned towards and (b) they were not applied at the risk of falsification. A definition of science is at least a difficult as a definition of religion (I would suggest even more difficult), but we can have a sense that how an idea is reached (via a scientific method, perhaps) and how it is treated subsequently (through experimentation) makes it scientific rather than some intrinsic property of the idea.

Arguments for the existence of God, for the coherence of theism, and more generally, for the reasonableness of religious doctrines have existed for a very long time. Certainly, Thomas Aquinas offered a very sophisticated defence of Christian Theism, and more recently, so too has Richard Swinburne. It would seem bizarre to deny that these were religious thinkers. Indeed, the tradition known as fideism, which this thought dovetails with, has consistently been rejected by the Catholic Church, which is surely a paradigm example of a religious institution (Sauvage 1909).

8

The Status of Religion

Introduction

We want to know how children ought to be formatively influenced with respect to religions (to religious beliefs and attitudes, and to beliefs about and attitudes to religion). With a definition of religion in hand, we now ask what the value (or normative status) of religion is. Religion has at least two kinds of status: a social status and a normative status. Its social status consists in whether people think it is true or good, and its normative status consists in whether it is in fact true or good. It is the latter, and whether this can be established well enough to justify either discouraging religion or encouraging religion that is important for answering our primary question.

As we saw in Chapter 6, ethically speaking, whether a given formative property should be encouraged turns (in part) on its theoretical and practical rationality, on whether it is rational to have that formative property. Where the having or not having of a certain attitude makes a significant difference to students' lives, and requires some systematic, professionally led education for its effective encouragement or discouragement, it ought to be addressed by curricula. Where that attitude requires only informal, minimally systematic encouragement or discouragement, the educative role falls to parents. Where not having that attitude is irrational, it ought to be encouraged; where having it is irrational, it ought to be discouraged; where having or not having it are both rational options, it ought to be taught non-directively. Again, teachers and parents should, insofar as it is practicable, aim to acquaint children with arguments for and against having these attitudes and initiate them into the practice of assessing the soundness of those arguments.

Notice that we have been discussing religion in essence, and not any one in particular. It could well be that religion in essence is true, because some particular manifestation is correct; perhaps Roman Catholicism, for instance, is broadly correct about what is true and good. Just because religion in essence is true, it would not follow that every religion is true in essence, since the essence of each particular religion may be more expansive than the essence of religion per se. For instance, the figures of Jesus and Muhammed play no role in the essence of religion but are plausibly essential to the essence of Christianity and Islam respectively. That said, establishing just that religion is true in essence can lend support to every particular religion. Indeed, for religious pluralists establishing such a conclusion would do rather more. Religious pluralists (notably John Hick) argue that there are no fundamentally important differences between religions, and so to establish religion in essence is to establish all that is most important about all the particular religions. However, I take it that pluralism is one more form of exclusivism alongside all the others. Indeed, the truth of religious pluralism entails the falsehood of any other claim to exclusive truth.

This chapter cannot attempt detailed treatment of the rich and multifarious defences of particular religions (e.g. via evaluating the historical credibility of particular religious texts). Such texts are too numerous, are open to diverse interpretations, and leave ample room for what is sometimes, unfairly, called 'cherry-picking', insofar as adherents do not accept texts to be inerrant, but instead to be variously flawed relayed messages from a divine source. Given these complexities, what can we reasonably hope to achieve in this chapter? One thing we might do is look at arguments that could be used in support of any of the various particular superbeings that people think it proper to submit themselves to.[1] We could look at arguments about whether or not a superbeing worthy of deference exists, or ones that establish at least part of that claim. Additionally, we could consider some arguments to the effect that religion is inherently good, or inherently bad, and then consider that the problem of evil gives a significant problem to theists, and that in the absence of a critical, open institutional network such as is used to warrant scientific theories, which then subjects beliefs to systematic scrutiny in the pursuit of rational consensus, religious belief is not rationally compelling.

---

[1] The various arguments for the existence of a god are just such arguments, employed equally by Muslims, Christians and Jews. Some might like to urge the self-same identity of these three gods, but this seems a dubious move. That is because we need to fix a referent of which the various accounts are supposed to be accounts. Thus, various biographers might write radically different accounts of Tony Blair, but we can fix the referent of the biographies independently of the accounts (it is not just whatever the account is an account of). In the case of God, three people who accept each of the rival accounts would need to have another way of fixing the referent than their accounts, perhaps a shared revelation or a mystical experience.

Religion is not inherently good or bad

We ought to distinguish between religions as practised, and religions as prescribed by their own canonical texts. Arguments can be made that various religions are more objectionable if taken at a textual level than they are as practised, and vice versa, that religion would be better if the texts were more closely observed than those who profess to follow in its footsteps. So, for instance, if Christians stoned people, for the various reasons they are told to in Leviticus, morally, they would be the worse for doing so. On the other hand, if Christians really all did love others as they love themselves, morally, they would be the better for doing so. Concordantly, there are two modes of defence (tending in different directions) available to the religious apologist:

1. It's not the religion in essence that's at fault when people enact perversions of the text, since the real religion is that prescribed by its canonical texts.
2. It's not the religion that's at fault when the texts make immoral and unjust pronouncements, since real religion is lived religion.

It seems that religion has scope to be horrendous if, for instance, people believe a superbeing exists, whose word ought to be deferred to, and take that being to require things which are in fact deeply unjust and immoral. Examples abound through history, with human sacrifice being common. The recent examples of 9/11, the Charlie Hebdo massacre and the atrocities of the Islamic State in some countries help illustrate the point.

In a public debate on the question of whether the world would be better or worse without religion, Tony Blair has attempted to answer the criticism of textual religious evil, admitting that it is a hard criticism to answer. His response comes in two parts. First, that the spirit of the text is different from the prima facie literal readings, and that spirit is not one which recommends evil acts (Blair and Hitchens 2012). Second, believers must interpret scripture in a way that makes sense to people in the modern world, seemingly suggesting that, seen in their contexts, the (by modern lights) horrendous prescriptions of ancient texts are less horrendous, and even thoroughly admirable (Blair and Hitchens 2012). It might be that it is our modern liberal standards that are at fault if these views do come into conflict (and that we are misled by our bias of presentism – that the most recent developments are just fashions and not improvements), or it might be that moral truth changes over time. Neither seems plausible in the case of Leviticus. Instead, it is better to suggest that religious texts are fallible.

Indeed, the idea that revelation is inerrant, un-updatable and entirely perspicuous is unsustainable given developments in scientific understanding and the sheer variety of interpretations of religious texts. Indeed, there is something odd about the notion that there exists a text in which nothing is certain except that it is correct so that, if what we took it to mean turns out to be false, we must simply have misread it. There is more integrity in the approach of geologist Kurt Wise, who found that the Bible would be revised beyond recognition if updated by modern science, and so rejected modern science: 'If all the evidence in the universe turns against creationism, I would be the first to admit it, but I would still be a creationist because that is what the Word of God seems to indicate' (Wise 2001).

To the extent that religious people object by denying that religion really is represented in these examples, one must reply that such denial amounts to whitewashing religion, by sweeping any inconvenient examples under the carpet. Attempts to do so merely exemplify what Anthony Flew has termed the 'no true Scotsman fallacy', an (underhanded or misguided) argumentative manoeuvre in which one denies that bad examples of a phenomenon are really examples at all, so as to insulate it from criticism. Consider the following example from Flew:

> Imagine Hamish McDonald, a Scotsman, sitting down with his *Glasgow Morning Herald* and seeing an article about how the 'Brighton (England) Sex Maniac Strikes Again'. Hamish is shocked and declares that 'No Scotsman would do such a thing'. The next day he sits down to read his *Glasgow Morning Herald* again; and, this time, finds an article about an Aberdeen (Scotland) man whose brutal actions make the Brighton sex maniac seem almost gentlemanly. This fact shows that Hamish was wrong in his opinion, but is he going to admit this? Not likely. This time he says: 'No *true* Scotsman would do such a thing'. (Flew 1975, 47)

Lest we make a similar mistake, bearing in mind our definition of religion, it seems amply possible that religions may be both false and harmful. Whether one is religious in a good way seems somewhat hostage to the fortune of what they take the content of their god's edicts to be. It can be that what one takes to be the possible range of god's edicts can be limited by what they take to be the content of morality. As an illustration of this case, take Kant's assessment of the situation in which Abraham found himself when God purportedly asked him to sacrifice Isaac:

> For if God should really speak to a human being, the latter could still never know that it was God speaking. It is quite impossible for a human being to apprehend the infinite by his senses, distinguish it from sensible beings, and be acquainted with it as such. – But in some cases the human being can be sure that the voice

he hears is not God's; for if the voice commands him to do something contrary to moral law, then no matter how majestic the apparition may be, and no matter how it may seem to surpass the whole of nature, he must consider it an illusion. (Kant 1996, 7:63)

However, our discussion ought to focus on religion at its best, as much as on religion at its worst. If we are to encourage belief of the true, and emulation of the good, it might be that acceptance of some particular religion ought to be encouraged, while some others ought to be discouraged. All the same, it may be that the essence of religion is true; that there really is a superbeing to whom we ought to defer, and that we ought to orientate ourselves accordingly, irrespective of how much wrong is falsely done in their name.

The normative status of religion

Is religion, at its best, true or good? It might be that one religion or another is actually true and, perhaps unsurprisingly, cultivates goodness and gives purpose (perhaps it is more surprising that other religions might do so as well) and it might be that religion is in some way good without being true. Consider two ways in which this could be so:

1. Religion (at its best) is a scaffold that cultivates goodness better than its absence; for instance, religion is a noble lie, a necessary tool for paternalist elites to manipulate ignorant masses for their own good.
2. There are no atheists in fox holes, as they say, because a life without religion is impossibly bleak and death terrifying.

We shall consider whether these two considerations bear critical scrutiny before considering whether there is good reason to think that religion is in essence true (that there exists a superbeing to whom we ought to defer).

Practical reason and the utility of religion

In this section, we shall consider the utility of religion, apart from the question of whether it is true, whether practical reason decides in its favour, irrespective of theoretical reason. We will discuss whether religion (at its best) is a scaffold that cultivates goodness or whether life without religion is impossibly bleak and death terrifying. I argue that the existence of God is tangential both to the content and existence of morality and also to the objective meaning of our lives.

Religion and moral goodness

Some say that religion is of negative value, some that it is worthless, others say that it is highly valuable, and yet others say that it is a mixed bag. Sam Harris thinks that religion is very bad indeed:

> If I could wave a magic wand and get rid of either rape or religion, I would not hesitate to get rid of religion. I think more people are dying as a result of our religious myths than as a result of any other ideology. I would not say that all human conflict is born of religion or religious differences, but for the human community to be fractured on the basis of religious doctrines that are fundamentally incompatible, in an age when nuclear weapons are proliferating, is a terrifying scenario. (Saltman 2006)

There is a case to be made (and it frequently is) that religion is a terrible affliction on human beings; much evil has been, and still is, done in the name of religion. However, one might just as well run a parallel case with an assessment of the value of science, which more obviously shows the inadequacy of the argument:

> At a 2011 conference, another colleague summed up what she thought was the mixed legacy of science: the eradication of smallpox on the one hand; the Tuskegee syphilis study on the other. (In that study, another bloody shirt in the standard narrative about the evils of science, public-health researchers beginning in 1932 tracked the progression of untreated, latent syphilis in a sample of impoverished African Americans.) The comparison is obtuse. It assumes that the study was the unavoidable dark side of scientific progress as opposed to a universally deplored breach, and it compares a one-time failure to prevent harm to a few dozen people with the prevention of hundreds of millions of deaths per century, in perpetuity. (Pinker 2013)

Atrocity seems to be an accidental property of religion. It is not religion per se that is at fault when people commit atrocities on religious grounds. If Harris were to have his wand and wave it, we might reasonably worry that a baby would be thrown out with the bath water here. Daniel C. Dennett's more sympathetic account of religion is that it has good aspects and bad aspects, but that what is essential to religion is false, and we can salvage the good parts in other ways, that religion is not essential to them (Dennett 2011). Indeed, Dennett has presented an interesting case in which he hopes to 'salvage' the good of religions from the bad. What he takes to be the bad is basically that all religions are false: that no superbeings exist, and therefore no superbeings exist that deserve our deference. All the same, religions do have much positive value when considered in terms of their utility, but that a noble lie is not necessary for accessing those incidental goods. Christopher Hitchens (Blair and Hitchens 2012) asks what good a religious person can do that a non-religious person cannot or would not. This challenge, if it cannot be met, suggests that religion is incidental to doing the good.

One may think that our question is whether the world would be the worse, the better or much the same for lacking religion to be relevant, that whether getting rid of religion would mean getting rid of evil or whether getting rid of religion would mean getting rid of good are the questions on which our decision must turn. Perhaps they are, but neither answer seems plausible. Weakened versions of those contentions would also seem relevant, namely, that to promote religion is in effect to promote evil, or to decrease religion, is in effect to undermine the good. It seems that religions, *qua* religion (identified on our rationale from Chapter 6), may just as likely promote evil as it does good. 'Religion' is not an unqualified force for good nor an unqualified force for evil. People may want to distinguish between good and bad religion.

It seems that there is no necessary connection between being religious and valuing the good and the just. The eponymous character of Plato's dialogue, *Euthyphro*, suggested that piety is what is pleasing to the gods (6e–7a). But, as Socrates presses, there exists a question as to whether it is pious just because it pleases the gods, or whether it pleases the gods because it is pious. In the first case, the pious is arbitrary; in the second the pious is quite independent of the gods. It is a partly empirical question as to whether what particular religions encourage are good works. One needs a conception of the good, and to compare this to what it is that particular religions promote. The concept of the good that I am working with has been elaborated on in Chapter 3. On that conception of the good, it is evident that much that is unethical and much that is ethical have at different times and places been encouraged by religions. I cannot plausibly attempt to survey and estimate the extent of the good or ill encouraged by each, or indeed any, particular religion (indeed, ring fencing a particular religion for such an assessment might prove enough of a challenge). And indeed, such analyses may be relevant to judging the ethical utility of particular religions.

It does not seem, then, that religion is a necessary tool for paternalist elites to manipulate ignorant masses for the general good. Is it (at its best) a scaffold that cultivates goodness better than its absence? In the absence of evidence either way, it is best to suspend judgement on this point. However, one practical reason can be given for not connecting the teaching of morality with religion, and that is that (even putting the Euthyphro considerations aside) there is a danger that where children lose their religious faith, they may also lose their moral commitments if they consider the latter to be dependent on the former.

Having discussed whether religion (at its best) is a scaffold that cultivates goodness, we now move on to consider whether life without religion is impossibly bleak. I argue that just as the existence of God is tangential to the content and existence of morality, so it is also to the objective meaning of our lives.

Religion and lives worth living

Timothy D. Wilson (2011, 40) has argued that people benefit from having a strong sense of purpose, and that this purpose is often religious. Some may take false comfort from such passages as Psalm 23; false, that is, if Christianity were not true. It is not obvious, however, that false comfort is undesirable, or less desirable than, say, a properly appreciative terror at death or a sense of emptiness in a world without meaning. Insofar as life does not seem impossibly bleak to unbelievers, this might be because they are not honestly confronting the prospect but deluding themselves. This is the worry that in the absence of religion, nihilism must be true.

> Psalm 23 A psalm of David
>
> Even though I walk
> through the darkest valley,
> I will fear no evil,
> for you are with me;
> your rod and your staff,
> they comfort me.

One metric of meaningfulness might be whether one's beliefs are capable of inspiring great art. It might be worried that there is little of inspiration in a godless world and that atheism is incapable of inspiring art worth seeing or music worth hearing. Disenchantment is all that is left. There is nothing to marvel at, no glory to reflect without God. There is indeed a preponderance of religious art works, but there are non-religious ones too. It might reasonably be expected that there would be, since religion has been around for a very long time, and atheism seems to have been a rather more marginal position throughout history. Furthermore, the explanation for why there are such wonderful religious works of art is not that religion is necessary for the production of great art, but that religious institutions had the money to commission it. We do not need to be religious to benefit from religious works of art, but we will not benefit from them in the same way that a religious person will take themselves to benefit from it, by, for instance, coming to better appreciate the person of god or the sacrifice of Jesus.

With or without God, the level of objective meaning in our lives seems the same. The question is sometimes put to atheists as to what the meaning of life would be without a God. The question is usually put on the assumption that either God gives us our meaning or we have no meaning at all. Atheists might hope to correct this assumption, arguing instead that either God gives us our purpose or else we have only whatever meaning we make for ourselves. William Lane Craig argues that 'whatever meaning we make for ourselves' boils down to 'no meaning at all', and while one might construct some sort of meaning as an atheist, it will be merely an illusory, subjective meaning. Meaning in theism, by contrast, is objective, in deriving from God. One may live one's life with meaning 'as an illusion' in the absence of absolute value, but it is still ultimately meaningless (Craig and Hitchens 2014). Interestingly, contra Craig, Bernard Williams (2006b) points out that if there is no perspective from which one can identify absolute importance or meaning (as Craig claims of the atheist world view), then there is no perspective which can deny our importance or meaning:

> If there is no such thing as the cosmic point of view, if the idea of absolute importance in the scheme of things is an illusion … then there is no other point of view except ours in which our activities can have or lack significance. (2006b, 137)

I side with neither Williams nor Craig; contra Williams, there are facts of value (both of goodness and meaning), and, contra Craig, whether or not God exists makes no difference to whether or not there are facts of value. The import of Euthyphro's dilemma ('is the pious loved by the gods because it is pious, or is it pious because it is loved by the gods?') can be made relevant just by swapping 'pious' for 'meaningful'. God doesn't add anything 'objective' to the picture: either God's judgements about how we are to live, what counts as valuable and what the best investment of our time is are just one more opinion or they defer to a standard that we would have anyway. Now, if God exists, it might be true that he created us with a specific purpose in mind. This purpose does not limit our meaningful possibilities, however. Even if this were determinate as the purpose of a knife is fairly determinate, we could still find other remarkable employments; the given one is not the only one (consider using the knife as a screw driver or lever). Some people suppose that life without an eternal afterlife is meaningless, and that life with such an afterlife is, for that very reason, meaningful. Wittgenstein points out that the problem is not resolved; it just applies for longer.

It is true, however, that we may have to count God into our practical deliberations if he does exist. But that does not affect the point that God makes no difference to the objectivity of meaning. For instance, in our practical deliberations, we may have to factor in that God can totally satisfy all of the people all of the time, and we might want to commit ourselves to this satisfaction. Craig says that the point of life is to 'give glory to God and enjoy him', and this might prove satisfying. On the other hand, while a world with God might be preferable to one without, in being more godlike, we ought to acknowledge and make the best of the world we have, rather than live with the illusion of greater meaning. Alex Miller tells us that, for Brian Leiter,

> the central features of religious practice and belief ... are that religious obligations are experienced as trumping all other considerations, that religious beliefs don't aspire to answer to empirical evidence and that religious beliefs provide 'existential consolation' in that they 'render intelligible and tolerable the basic existential facts about human life, such as suffering and death'. (Miller 2013, 11)

Miller demurs, 'In one respect Leiter is perhaps over-generous to religion', for 'while he agrees that many fundamental religious beliefs are false, his talk of religion as "rendering intelligible" important facets of existence should perhaps be replaced by talk of its apparently rendering such facets intelligible'. Miller observes that 'given the falsity of fundamental religious beliefs, the "existential consolation" it provides is akin to consolation provided by a drug, which is why Marx described it as the "opium of the people"' (Miller 2013, 11). Richard Dawkins refers to this sort of view as patronizing and condescending, that while intellectuals might do alright without religion, 'you hoi polloi, you ordinary people down there, you need religion' (Dawkins 2013). Dawkins is more optimistic about the prospects of people to reconciling themselves to living in a universe without God.

How rational is religious belief (at best)?

We now turn to assessing the theoretical rationality of religions. We have two questions to answer here. First, should we assess religious belief by the standards of theoretical reason? Second, if we should assess religious belief by the standards of theoretical rationality, how do they fare by those standards (i.e. what is the state of religious apology and natural theology)? There are at least three strands of argument suggesting that we need not to assess religious beliefs by the standards of theoretical rationality: Pascal's Wager, Alvin Plantinga's instance on 'properly basic belief', and various versions of Wittgensteinian Fideism.

Pascal's Wager

Pascal argues that where theoretical reason cannot decide the matter of whether or not God exists, practical considerations give us reason to cultivate belief in God (Pascal 1925, Section III, §233). He reasons that rationally, we ought to minimize our potential losses in deciding whether or not to believe in God. If we believe in God where he does not exist, we lose relatively little, whereas if we fail to believe in God where he does exist, we lose out on eternal bliss to eternal damnation. This argument only gets off the ground if theoretical reason is, in fact, unable to determine whether or not to believe in God, which is what is in question. Moreover, though, Pascal only addresses his considerations to deciding between the existence and non-existence of one particular God (one who punishes disbelief with torment, and rewards belief with paradise). But the range of options is not so narrow: 'another possibility is that there might be a god who looked with more favour on honest doubters or atheists … than on mercenary manipulators of their own understandings' (Mackie 1982, 203). But deciding between which of these two gods, with their contradictory attitudes to your potential decision, cuts away any practical reason to believe in one rather than the other, since the odds of benefitting or suffering from either decision are equal.

Properly basic belief

According to Alvin Plantinga, it is 'entirely right, rational, reasonable, and proper to believe in God without any evidence or argument at all' (Plantinga 1991, 17). All arguments require premises, and some premises are 'properly basic', requiring no further validation. Among those beliefs which require no further validation is belief in God. The warrant for our beliefs may properly be provided by perception or memory, for instance, and neither perception nor memory need further support, otherwise justification would set out on an infinite regress. Belief in God is properly basic, Plantinga says, requiring no further argument. Some human beings, he contends, have been graced with a *sensus divinitatis* which equips them with knowledge of God just as perception equips us with knowledge of our environment (Plantinga 2000, 214). Thomas Nagel (2012) responds to this contention by remarking that

> if I ever found myself flooded with the conviction that what the Nicene Creed says is true, the most likely explanation would be that I was losing my mind, not that I was being granted the gift of faith. From Plantinga's point of view, by contrast, I suffer from a kind of spiritual blindness from which I am unwilling to be cured.

Plantinga and Nagel need not reach an impasse, however. Each properly basic kind of warrant is defeasible and can be proven unreliable by further investigation; perceptual illusions are possible after all. Perhaps Nagel has scope to persuade Plantinga by pointing out the inconsistencies of the import of Plantinga's *sensus divinitatis* with the deliverances of his other senses. One method by which this could be done is by appeal to the problem of evil.

Kinds of fideism which may call themselves Wittgensteinian

Ludwig Wittgenstein never advocated a position which he called 'fideism', but the following are four positions drawing inspiration from his writing which may be so called (although the second pair may have a low fidelity):

1. In *Lectures and Conversations*, Wittgenstein seemed to regard religious claims as different in kind from historical and scientific claims:

   > Suppose, for instance, we knew people who foresaw the future; make forecasts for years and years ahead; and they described some sort of Judgement Day. Queerly enough, even if there were such a thing, and even if it were more convincing than I have described, belief in this happening wouldn't be at all religious belief. (Wittgenstein 2010b, 56)

   Wittgenstein suggests that such a forecast would not make us change the way we live, but this is doubtful, as people adjust their lives to all sorts of new information insofar as they are rational. Wittgenstein then offers an example of something that he does take to be a religious forecast: whereas some particular individual would not be foolish enough to say 'I had a dream that it will rain tomorrow, therefore it will', they would say 'I had a dream of the last judgement coming, therefore we can expect that'.

These sorts of things can change the way you live, he suggests. So the sort of fideism which may be encouraged here is a sort of anti-realism, to be contrasted to the realism of science and history; religious statements don't say things which have much to do with science or history.

2. Wittgenstein observes in the *Philosophical Investigations* that explanations, reasons and justifications must come to an end somewhere: 'Explanations come to an end somewhere' (*PI*, §1), 'the chain of reasons has an end' (*PI*, §326) and 'justification comes to an end' (Wittgenstein 1969, §192). One stops somewhere and cannot go on defending their views ad infinitum. One might be inclined to suggest that it is the language community that cooperatively (and perhaps unconsciously) decide where justifications are to come to an end. This could allow for some religious beliefs being incorporated at that level.

3. Also, in the *Philosophical Investigations*, Wittgenstein comments that 'the meaning of a word is its use in the language' (though he goes on to say that this is true only of 'a *large* class of cases') (*PI*, §4). Richard Rorty takes this to mean that 'no linguistic items represent any non-linguistic items' (Rorty 1991, 2). This creates a sort of parity between science, religion, mathematics, psychoanalysis and so on: none can be said to be 'picturing', 'mirroring' or 'capturing' the world, so none can be said to be the way the world is really. Language is kept 'in touch' with reality by being a useful tool: like saying 'ouch' when our feet hurt, or expressing disapproval with rude gestures (although even the ideas 'reality' and 'language' are meant to be linguistic constructions). One then need only say that people speak in religious ways as one form of world-coping, which is no more accurate or inaccurate than any other. One might attempt to insulate it from external criticism by saying that it shares nothing with other ways of speaking, such as scientific ways. This sort of story requires that I do not say: all religious remarks are ethical and aesthetic ones, because that would mean they are not logically unique. Instead one would have to insist that they are without non-religious synonyms.

4. John McDowell uses a kind of parity argument to defend ethical realism: the idea that ethics is just as much part of the world as scientific laws (McDowell 1983). This argument can be used for apologetics. McDowell say that there is no objective way of seeing the world from which point of view we can say what is and is not a part of the world *really*. This seems to be the sort of argument one can use to defend religious beliefs: there's no way of seeing what the world contains really, we have only the things we

say about the world to go on and so long as religion isn't just bad science, the things it describes are as much a part of the world as ethics and the laws of physics.

These forms are not satisfying, however. In the first position, it sounds like Wittgenstein is employing a principle of charity, as if to say: this is so absurd, it cannot be of the same kind as sober science and history, or no sane person could possibly believe it; but this is exactly what is in question and cannot count as a reason. Indeed, if Jesus were to return, this would have nothing to do with Christianity as Wittgenstein understands it and this is too counterintuitive a result; that it would surprise Christians if this were to happen and that it would have nothing to do with the Christian faith. One might deny that this objection could not sensibly be raised since there is no difference between 'Jesus will return to judge us' and 'Jesus will really return to judge us', since they are both a part of the religious language game. But we clearly can make sense of them as having cognitive and non-cognitive senses (e.g. one being a prediction and one being a false story that one acts 'as if' true in order to regulate their behaviour).

Against the second and third strand, there are two arguments I'd raise. The first is due to Bernard Williams: if we take religion to be true in a non-universal way and not true in the way that science is true, then the claims of religions are weakened to mean something other than intended (Williams and Magee 2001). This applies also to the first form. The second is that conceptualism (the idea that reality is in some way dependent on the concepts that we use) is self-defeating, since it fails to

> accommodate *thinkers*, their *thoughts*, and the *concepts* that they deploy ... because concepts themselves are either *something* or else *nothing* – they either exist or they do not. If they don't, then conceptualism is out of business. But if they do, then they themselves have an essence [which cannot itself be constituted by concepts]. (Lowe 2008c, 84)

Against the fourth variant, we should defend the possibility of an absolute conception, since denying the existence of such a conception undermines itself by denying that we can describe mind-independent reality at all:

> [Since] if nothing about the structure of mind independent reality is accessible to us then, by the same token, nothing about the structure of our own thought is accessible to us either – for in the relevant sense of 'mind-independent', our thought itself is nothing if not part of mind-independent reality. (Lowe 2002, 8–9)

The state of religious apology and natural theology

Michael Hand comments on the state of religious apology, saying:

> the most even-handed view of the arguments [in support of religious propositions] is that they have some, but not decisive, rational force. They do not place one under a rational obligation to accept their conclusions, but they carry enough weight to make those conclusions rationally credible. (2004, 162)

Michael Hand then answers 'no' to both of our questions: failing to believe in and submit to a superbeing is not irrational, and belief in and submission to a superbeing is not irrational. We first want to ask what constitutes a rational belief, and what constitutes an irrational belief. We then want to ask whether belief in superbeings to whom one submits on account of their rightful dominion is rational. Rational belief, at a minimum, requires that the content of one's belief is coherent, that is, that it has content and is not self-defeating. More than that, though, it requires that one have reasons for one's belief that show it to be more probable than not, and more probable than its contraries. We may also require that they be capable of falsification. For, if they are consistent with all the possible data, they seem not to be genuinely contentful at all, if they are genuinely contentful at all. To be a genuinely reasonable hypothesis they will need to generate predictions that might turn out to conflict with contingent data, but happen to be confirmed by it, and will need to be the simplest explanation of the data that we have. It ought to be acknowledged that these standards cannot apply to all beliefs, and some, as Plantinga has convincingly argued, must be properly basic, requiring no further justification. But again, even these such beliefs are not thereby infallible but are defeasible.

Roughly though, there are two main kinds of arguments which can be appealed to: *a priori* arguments, and *a posteriori* arguments; the former hope to be true without the need to consult evidence and the latter hope to be true given the available evidence. It is only the ontological arguments which claim to be the former, the others all claim to be the latter.[2] The ontological argument claims that God's existence is necessary, since existence is built into the very concept of God. In the simplest version of the argument you are asked to imagine something than which nothing greater can be conceived. What you are imagining must have *every* kind of perfection, otherwise something yet greater

---

[2]   Three notable versions of the argument were developed by St Anselm (1903), Descartes (1968) and Plantinga (1974).

could be conceived in having one extra kind of perfection, and that would mean that you weren't thinking of that than which nothing greater can be conceived. Existence, it is said, is more perfect than non-existence, and thus the greatest conceivable thing must also exist. However, it was convincingly objected by Immanuel Kant (1933) that existence is not a property that something can have or lack. As Peter Hacker (2011, 8) has pointed out, 'the verb "to exist" looks no different from such verbs as "to eat" or "to drink"', but while 'it makes sense to ask how many people in College don't eat meat or drink wine, it makes no sense to ask how many people in College don't exist'.

The arguments *a posteriori* are arguments to the best explanation of some contingent facts about the world. Wherefore life on earth, wherefore rationality, wherefore the character of human consciousness, what best explains these? Richard Swinburne suggests that we would expect these features of the universe if god existed and would not expect them if God did not exist. Since they exist, it is more likely that God exists than does not (Swinburne 2004). They also include arguments from some basic principles of rationality plus general features of experience, such as the arguments from contingency to necessity, arguments from motion, and causation, for instance: explanation has to terminate somewhere and cannot go on ad infinitum; there exist contingent beings, objects in motion and events which are caused and these must terminate in a necessary being, an unmoved mover and an uncaused causer, respectively. All of the arguments from contingency to necessity, from motion, and causation could go through and converge on a single, necessary unmoved and uncaused causer, but they would not establish the existence of an agent, let alone a super-agent, or one to whom we should defer.

Moreover, though, the argument to necessity from contingency doesn't go through. The principle of sufficient reason suggests that for each contingent being, there must be a sufficient explanation for its existence, and then again it must be asked what the explanation for the existence of that contingent being is. Such a regress can only terminate in a necessary being, it is thought. But it seems that the principle of sufficient reason is not a principle that we may fairly apply in this way. It is a prejudice to expect that there is a sufficient reason for everything; it seems just as likely that some contingent aspects of reality are inexplicable.

Some insist that the principle of sufficient reason demands that there be some sufficient cause for the world's existence. Some (notably William Lane Craig) suggest that God is the most parsimonious explanation that we have. A god being a simple entity made of no parts, but capable of acting and creating is the simplest explanation for the existence of something rather than nothing, and God being necessary (and ontologically simple, made of no parts) requires no explanation himself. Apart from this use of the principle of sufficient reason, we should respond with Dennett by asking: 'How could postulating something supernatural and incomprehensible be parsimonious?' It should strike us as 'the height of extravagance', as it strikes him (Dennett 2013, 39).

The problem of evil

As we have already noted in Chapter 2, the problem of evil challenges theists by asking why it is, if God is able to prevent suffering, knows about the existence of suffering, and is morally good, that suffering persists. Anselm's definition casts God as that of which no greater can be conceived, others as an omniscient, omnipotent and omnibenevolent agent composed of no parts. Obviously such beings would qualify as gods, and ones to whom it is right to defer, but suppose a being existed except that it did not know exactly one thing, and that no other similar being existed. It would seem odd to deny their being God, especially if that being played the role that is traditionally thought to have been played by Yahweh or Allah. In Chapter 6, I defended the view that a god is one who excels us in every respect, and with whom we have no chance of competing successfully. This allows that for us, mortal, fallible and flawed human beings, God need not be that than which no greater can be conceived, and so the problem of evil poses less of a threat to religion. The sort of god required for religion is one to whom we ought to defer. We ought to defer to being where they know the good and recommend the good to us. Still all that is required for the problem is that God is supposed to know about human suffering, care about it and be able to stop it, while, as a matter of fact, suffering persists.

Again, as noted in Chapter 2, the apologist's usual responses is that (a) suffering is a consequence of allowing free will and (b) suffering allows for moral growth. These arguments are susceptible to very reasonable counterarguments: free will does not account for natural evil, and natural evil can do as much to diminish moral growth and makes unfair use of some people. We might add another: God is knowledgeable, powerful and good enough to be beyond human rivalry, but not knowledgeable, powerful and good enough to prevent human suffering. Indeed, they may know and recommend the good to us, but be weak-willed themselves (if less so than we human beings), and sometimes fail to live up to it. Still, the problem poses enough of a threat to suggest that denying religious belief is not irrational. It seems to be a discussion on which reasonable arguments and interpretations can be made by both sides.

Socially embodied rationality

We can, each of us, evaluate arguments for ourselves, but it may be well to defer in part to the judgement of others, for unless we can convince others that we are right, we may have reason for hesitancy. It is possible to be the lone bastion of truth in a population of ignorance, but if one seems unable to persuade others who patiently listen to our arguments, we may suspect that we may not have certain knowledge. Let us say, with James Ladyman, that science progresses with the benefit of argument and evidence (they are what it is hoped will persuade people), but also relies on certain features of social organization (Ladyman 2014). Certain social organizations allow open-minded people to come together and present possibly true claims. They then attempt to offer evidence and argument in support of these claims. Others are then able to look for evidence that would be consistent or inconsistent with it. Those which are best supported will, by and large, be accepted by the group. The group's aggregate belief set is more likely to track the truth than the belief set of any particular member. It would have to be those that are familiar with the relevant arguments, and have some talent at assessing them, whose opinions would be of interest, and not just anybody's.

Have we any such social organization in academic philosophy? The survey of philosophers' opinions conducted by Bourget and Chalmers (2013) show 72.8 per cent of respondents embrace atheism, 14.6 per cent embrace theism and 12.6 per cent embrace neither. The clear majority of respondents, then, consider themselves to be atheists. However, it might not be in their professional capacity that they hold this view; it might not be that those asked were expert enough to have a properly informed view; not being philosophers of religion but, for instance, ethicists. There might be a selection bias in asking philosophers of religion or theologians for their opinions; they might have gotten into philosophy of religion in order to justify their views, and so not be good, impartial judges of the success or failure of their arguments. On the other hand, those outside of these fields might be insufficiently familiar with the arguments to have given them a fair hearing.

It is highly doubtful that the survey should be taken as an indicative that denying atheism is irrational, and indeed it was not intended to show any such thing, but merely to give philosophers some basis for making statements about which theories are so common as to warrant being called 'the orthodox view', or 'the official doctrine'. There may be ways to systematize academic philosophy such that the majority opinion among experts cannot rationally be rejected by non-experts. However, unlike science, it seems that it is in no such state at present. Still, perhaps in the absence of a critical, open, institutional network which subjects beliefs to systematic scrutiny in the pursuit of rational consensus, religious belief is not rationally compelling.

9

How Children Ought to Be Formatively Influenced, with Respect to Religion(s)

Introduction

It is now high time to consider what implications our foregoing chapters have for the question of how (if at all) we may ethically influence children, with respect to religion(s). In our first chapter, we identified seven sub-questions, the answers to which put us in a position to answer the primary question. These seven questions were:

1. What are the sources of responsibility? (Chapter 2)
2. What is the content of responsibility? (Chapter 3)
3. In what respects are we apt to be formatively influenced? (Chapter 4)
4. What means of formative influence are available? (Chapter 5)
5. What ethical obligations and restrictions are there on the means by which and the ends towards which we formatively influence children? (Chapter 6)
6. What is a religion? (Chapter 7)
7. How rational is religious belief? (Chapter 8)

In this concluding chapter we will briefly review the findings of our enquiry so far, and explain what import, taken together, they have for answering our primary question that we set out in our first chapter.

Ethical foundations

Over Chapters 2 and 3, I unfolded what I took to be the ethical foundations pre-requisite for any answer to our primary question. That involved answering the following questions:

1. What sorts of beneficiaries *can* we be morally responsible for?
2. In virtue of what is it that people are responsible for averting harms to and ensuring benefits for any such beneficiaries?
3. What counts as a harm or benefit for human beings?

In answer to the first, I argued that what we *can be* morally responsible for is those of our actions and omissions which bear on the well-being of intrinsically valuable objects, such as human beings. In answer to the second, I concluded that the best person for the (ethical) job is responsible for making sure that it is done, and argued that this principle is able to ground both parental and extra-parental responsibility to children. From this, I concluded that, ethically speaking, some primary care giver (usually a biological parent or biological parents, in virtue of their usually being best able to satisfy the role) is responsible for ensuring basic benefits for children, and averting harms to them. Additionally, we saw that some extra-parental responsibilities are generated by children's welfare needs (by their harm benefit profiles) which out-strips what parents are able to provide (at least *qua* parents). In answer to the third question, I defended the view that the nearer an act brings us towards becoming like God, the better it is for us, and the more it keeps us from becoming like God, the more it harms us.

Respects in which we can be formatively influenced

As we have frequently reminded ourselves, it is the ethics of deliberate, formative influence that I am interested in here, rather than behavioural influences. I have distinguished formative influences from behavioural influences, claiming that whereas behavioural influences make a difference to what people do, formative influences make a difference to those of their internal malleable characteristics in virtue of which they are apt to do what they do. But in virtue of which characteristics is it that people are apt to do what they do? In Chapter 4, I argued that we can be formatively influenced in the following five respects:

1. The degrees and kinds of one's physical and mental abilities
2. One's stock of concepts
3. Those propositions which one understands
4. One's cognitive attitudes, such as belief and disbelief, to those propositions
5. One's affective attitudes to those propositions and to other objects

Ethical means and ends of formative influence

In Chapter 5, I argued that, morally, influence should take a basically rational form so far as that is practicable, but that non-rational means could be used where people, such as small children, are insufficiently rational to benefit from rational influence. The import of Chapter 3 was that people are better off the more rational they are (i.e. the more competent and inclined they are to apportion belief to the evidence, and to seek evidence and suspend judgement where they lack evidence).[1] In particular, we should equip children to be in a position to rationally form and revise opinions about those matters which are momentous to their lives. In Chapter 6, we saw that for each prospective formative influence which a child could adopt, influencers may ignore it, promote it, demote it or draw attention to it as something worthy of consideration to adopt. The theory of ethical influence that I developed was the following: that for each prospective formative influence, it ought to be promoted, floated or demoted respectively, according to the following three sets of criteria, and where none of these apply, it might be fairly ignored:

1. (a) It is momentous; (b) it might well not be adopted without intervention; (c) failing to have it is irrational.
2. (a) It is momentous; (b) it might well not be understood and rationally evaluated without intervention; (c) neither having nor failing to have it is irrational.
3. (a) It is momentous; (b) it might well be adopted without intervention; (c) having it is irrational.

In Chapter 6, we also saw that the influences which may be had may be more or less comprehensive or restricted, depending on just how many respects it is in which we influence one another. We argued that the comprehensiveness of a set of influences being imparted raises the moral stakes. Furthermore, while it might be alright morally, on some occasions, to favour the practical rationality of the beliefs that one imparts over their theoretical rationality, insofar as those beliefs are highly comprehensive, it becomes significantly immoral to sacrifice theoretical rationality in formative influence.

---

[1] Evidence is not always necessary or relevant to establishing the truth of claims, it seems. There are some things which are (quite properly) immune from evidential refutation: seemingly basic truths of maths and logic, as these are prior to evidence. Furthermore, it seems that some (defeasible) warrants for belief require no further justification, on pain of infinite regress, warrants such as memory and perception.

These same considerations were seen to preside over both formal educators, and informal educator, such as caregivers. Also, in Chapter 6, it was shown how the above theory of ethical influence could be used to select curricula content where a planned programme of learning delivered by subject experts is the sort of intervention that would be required to rationally encourage and discourage them in children, or to enable children to better judge their rationality. Since parents or, more generally, primary carers could not reasonably be expected to satisfy this entitlement *qua* parents and primary carers, the responsibility would be on what I termed 'extra-parental' in Chapter 3. However, we admitted that even to the extent that we are equipped with such evidence to warrant being directive, we ought still to emphasize fallibility and deference to reasons rather than commitment to conclusions, and to the extent that we are not so equipped, we ought to encourage interest, and rational deliberation but stop short of promoting or undermining particular views. This, then, amounted to our theory of ethical influence. Chapters 7 and 8 began to lay the foundations to apply this theory of ethical influence to religion.

Application to religion

To give content to the question of how children ought to be influenced with respect to religions, we have had to explain what sorts of things religions are. Our answer was that religions are those things that essentially require (a) belief in superbeings and (b) and submission to them as having rightful dominion. As became apparent in Chapter 6, the key questions for whether religious initiation is ethically acceptable were these:

1. Are the content of one's beliefs about, and attitudes to, religion momentous?
2. How rational is religious belief?
   2.1. Is failing to believe in and submit to a superbeing irrational?
   2.2. Is belief in and submission to a superbeing irrational?

3. Does correct belief require intervention, or is it likely to occur without intervention?
4. Is religious belief more comprehensive or more restricted in its effects on those respects in which we can be formatively influenced?

Both by providing some fresh considerations, and by drawing on the import of Chapter 8, we shall turn now to answering these questions.

Does is it matter whether one is religious?

Some might like to suggest that religion is essentially idle, an epiphenomenon that it is causally impotent. Arguing along those lines, they may suggest that the world would be much the same with or without religion. But it seems that religious beliefs and beliefs about religions do motivate actions, and so this is not true.

It is instructive to consider Pascal's Wager here (Pascal 1925, Section III, §233). Either there is a superbeing to which one should be oriented in a certain way or there is no such being, and no such orientation is possible. As we have seen, Pascal observes that there is less of a cost in living as though there is such a being when there is not than in living as though there is not such a being when there is. Whether one is religious matters more if religion is true than if it is false, then, but it does still matter. Non-religious people would be less inclined to evangelize against religion if being religious was only significant for religious people. To the extent that being religious is of public significance in what they consider to be bad ways (to take an extreme example, bombing abortion clinics), they will be inclined to evangelize against it. While I accept that Socrates' response to Euthyphro's dilemma rules out the possibility of superbeings' judgements about goodness being moral truth-makers, others do not. Furthermore, one may allow that superbeings are better placed to track moral truths, even if they do not invent them. And so the believer will defer to the god about what they ought to do, what is good, what is important and what is best, all of which makes a convincing case that it matters whether one is religious or not. Without knowing in advance whether or not it is true that a god exists and that we should defer to them, it is at least pragmatically significant whether or not there is such a being.

How rational is religious belief?

Is failing to believe in and submit to a superbeing irrational? Is belief in and submission to a superbeing irrational? Or are neither irrational? In Chapter 8, we discussed whether religion, in essence, was inherently good or bad, and it seemed to be neither. We then evaluated two utilitarian arguments to encourage religious belief, namely that religion (at its best) is a scaffold that cultivates goodness or that life without religion is impossibly bleak and death terrifying. I argued that the existence of God is tangential both to the content and existence of morality and also to the objective meaning of our lives. Finally, we discussed whether there were good theoretical reasons for religious belief. We found that there may be scope for some people to believe rationally, insofar as (a) they already take god to exist as basic datum and (b) other basic beliefs do not conflict with it. However, the problem of evil poses enough of a threat to the existence of god that one cannot think it unreasonable to deny religious belief. From this necessarily brief overview of the relevant arguments, it seems that I must agree with Hand that failing to believe in and submit to a superbeing is not (always) irrational, and neither is a belief in and submission to a superbeing (always) irrational.

Does rational evaluation of religion require intervention?

An intervention is an action which aims to make a difference to a state of affairs, so that a different outcome obtains than it would in its absence. It seems that interventions are required to cultivate rationality, with respect to religious beliefs and attitudes, and beliefs and attitudes about religions. Whereas many things come naturally to most children, such as swallowing, speaking, walking and playing, it seems that critical reflection on prospective respects of formative influence does not. Furthermore, a planned programme of learning delivered by subject experts is precisely what would be required to enable one to make rational judgements about the truth or falsity of religious propositions. Parents or, more generally, primary carers could not reasonably be expected to satisfy this entitlement *qua* parents and primary carers.

Does religious initiation amount to a comprehensive set of formative influences?

Michael Hand observes that 'most of us, while we recognise that it is *normally* wrong for parents to use their perceived intellectual authority to impart not-known-to-be-true beliefs, are prepared to grant exceptions to this rule when the belief confers a significant benefit on the child' (Hand 2002, 555). He gives as an example telling one's children that 'the tooth fairy will come for your tooth tonight' (Hand 2002, 555). However, there seems to be a significant difference between this belief and religious belief, namely that the latter is very much more comprehensive. The enabling reasons as to why it might be alright to tell children to believe in tooth fairies and Santa Claus are that the falsehoods propagated are (a) fairly narrow and (b) come with a somewhat limited lifespan. All the same, it still carries underappreciated epistemic costs.

Some might like to say that children do not really believe in Santa, or that it would merely count as make-believe to pretend that he exists, and not as lying. However, I think that these claims are both false: children do believe in Santa, and to the extent that we sustain their belief in Santa, we often lie, conceal information and otherwise mislead them. Belief is to be distinguished from make-believe (certainly on their part). Make-believe involves at once being aware of the falsehood of propositions, and yet playing along 'as if' they were true; when children act in plays, they do not confuse their part for real life. Allow me to cite two personal experiences by way of illustration. As I saw it, my toy was delivered down the wrong chimney by Santa, and the neighbouring family unjustly kept it from me, which was as good as stealing, for I had requested that very toy of Santa, while my neighbour had not. Indeed, when I mentioned the problem to my neighbour's parents, they laughed about it. The point to notice is that I drew well-reasoned inferences on the basis of false beliefs.

How far does one go in sustaining the belief if it is questioned? One might have to make fake reports. Sometime later, while still at primary school, I tried to disabuse another child of her belief in Santa, and she was, in the moment at least, devastated. With tears streaming from her eyes, she listed her evidence for her belief in Santa: she had written letters to him, and had received replies, had heard sleigh bells, and her parents had testified to his existence. I told her that the evidence was easily faked, she might have fooled herself and that her parents could well be lying. She insisted that she would have recognized her parents' and neighbour's handwriting, and that her parents would not lie to her. Loss of trust is one reason why you would want to avoid being caught out as a liar. But most parent–child relationships are not too damaged by children realizing that their parents lied to them about Santa. Indeed, coming to see through the lie can be seen as a positive experience of coming of age, of leaving one's childish state. However, to the extent that this girl had been robustly initiated into a comprehensive set of false beliefs there was a significant chance of residual epistemic collateral damage once she had been disabused of the central beliefs. As I have emphasized, truth is unitary, and to the extent that one successfully and comprehensively integrates false belief into one's belief set, residual damage can be left when the central beliefs are eliminated.[2] The worry is that a narrow set of beliefs (about Santa) may sprawl to affect other beliefs, in light of the unity of truth. Consider the following questions that might be posed, and to which

---

[2]   At best, one might compartmentalize their belief sets, giving truth a duality, as in George Orwell's novel *1984*, in which it is allowed that two and two always makes a four in weapons development, but makes a five in politics.

answers would further elaborate and damage the accuracy of one's belief set and, perhaps, one's ability to form and rationally revise beliefs. What has Jesus to do with Santa? How can Santa do the things he does? How old is Santa and can he die? Where does he live? Can we visit him? The more inquisitive the child is, the more elaborate the stories have to become and the more danger there is that they will cultivate a systematically false belief set, leaving residual damage when the principle beliefs are gone. John Broome (2008) gives an example of this working at a simple level: 'I look out of the window and see that it is raining, and immediately believe it is raining. Sometime later I look up and see that it has stopped raining, and no longer believe that it is raining. The initial belief is immediately erased.'

However, it is not at all likely that all beliefs will be amended to fit together and less likely the more comprehensive and fundamental the beliefs are. In contrast to a belief in Santa and the tooth fairy, it seems that religions are comprehensive, and it is their very comprehensiveness that makes them morally special: 'Religious traditions are so comprehensive and all-encompassing in their claims that almost every domain of philosophy may be drawn upon in the philosophical investigation of their coherence, justification, and value' (Taliaferro 2013).

Religions are doctrinally totalizing, that is to say that they are often close to a theory of everything. The same might be said of some scientific theories; however, religions are usually more comprehensive in this way than is any single theory in, say, physics, and with far less warrant than, say, Einstein's theories of general and special relativity. Religions often have cosmological hypotheses, but they also make prescriptions and evaluations (they, in Hand's phrase, 'recommend patterns of life'). They have readymade answers to lots of questions that are to be accepted wholesale. That would be fine if they were well justified to make denial irrational, but as we saw in Chapter 8, it seems that they are not. It is not just religions that have this feature; indeed, Daniel C. Dennett's physicalism is similarly comprehensive, as are humanism and dialectical materialism. In Chapter 8, I argued that no religion has sufficient support to warrant its directive teaching to young people, that is, to warrant religious initiation. At the same time, it seems entirely possible that some children do already believe rationally, and while promoting rational belief is a desirable aim, and thereby so too is promoting critical scrutiny, going further and making it an aim to disabuse children of their religious beliefs carte blanche is also not acceptable, for they are not all obviously irrational in their beliefs.

Should religious initiation be optional for children?

What is the range of choices possible regarding one's potential initiation? One may, by default, have been either 'opted in' or 'opted out' of some initiatory process. One may have been opted in, with the option to leave, or opted in with no option to leave. Alternatively, one may have been opted out with the option to enter, or without the option to enter. These four options can be represented in the following figure:

Originally opted in

Subsequently able to opt out	1
Not subsequently able to opt out	2

Originally opted out

Subsequently able to opt in	3
Not subsequently able to opt in	4

From our discussion of basic goods and paternalist duties to ensure that they be satisfied in Chapter 3, it seems that if a child would like to start riding horses at no particular cost (e.g. financial) that would be alright, and if a child wanted to stop riding horses at no particular cost (e.g. being a worse huntsman in a hunting community) that too would be alright. Neither a system in which children were initiated into horse riding, with the option to stop doing so, nor one in which they were initiated into riding horses only if they opted in, is objectionable. In the absence of any significant drawbacks to those that cannot ride horses (or to others dependent on their being so able), a system which insisted on children's learning to ride horses (opting them in without the choice to opt out) would seem unduly coercive. It would then seem appropriate to say that horse riding was being unfairly forced on children. On the other hand, there are some activities that we do not think we ought to initiate children into at all. Gambling, drinking alcohol, sexual intercourse and blood sport are perhaps strong examples.[3] Here, neither do we opt children in, nor do we allow children to opt in. Conversely, there are some forms of initiation which we do not think that children ought to

---

[3]   Actually a more nuanced position might think that forms of initiation into safe forms of alcohol consumption, and harmless gambling, or even sexuality (cf. John Wilson (2003) on sexual initiation among children, who emphasizes role play and fiction) might be reasonable.

be able to opt out of, and which they ought to be opted into by default. Moral development, numeracy, literacy, language development and leading a healthy life style are perhaps strong examples here.

Where should the various ways in which one can be formatively influenced, with respect to religion, fit on this fourfold array of choices? It seems that being initiated into a religion should be a matter of total option for adults – where one must opt in, and where one has the ability to opt out at any point – but what about children? At what age should people be allowed to 'opt in' to religion? Should, for example, the Catholic Church address children as potential converts? I argue not. Instead, the Catholic Church ought to recognize that even though it takes faith to be true and of maximal significance, there is a plurality of other options which are at least as reasonable, and that it is not so well supported by evidence and argument to make its denial irrational, which, as we saw in Chapter 6, is what is required for the encouragement of a formative influence in children to be warranted; this is all the more important when the set of formative influences in question is so comprehensive as religious belief. Equally, however, we saw in Chapter 8 that religious belief can be rational and so it is not thereby irrational to deny that atheism is true, and so morally wrong to encourage atheism, even if children ought to be encouraged to reflect critically on religious doctrines and practices.

None of this is to urge that students ought to be insulated from religious belief and beliefs about religion, or that they should not be able to discuss any that they themselves may have acquired or developed. Indeed, in line with Chapter 6, we should inform children about religions, and facilitate their ability to evaluate religious claims and attitudes, and attitudes to and claims about religion. Indeed, it seems that learning about religions (among other forms of diversity, theories of meaning and ethical systems) is neither a matter for opting in or out where children are concerned. Before concluding this chapter, I must address an objection commonly posed to the kind of position I advance here.

Some are wont to respond that there are no neutral forms of initiation (e.g. Trevor Cooling, Anne Hession and Elmer J. Thiessen).[4] Instead, they regard the failure to initiate children into a religious perspective as initiating them into a substantive, non-religious perspective. I want now to discuss some terms that are often used as if they were interchangeable, but which ought to be distinguished. I have in mind the concepts of neutrality, impartiality,

---

[4]   Trevor Cooling (2012), Anne Hession (2015) and Elmer John Thiessen (1993).

objectivity, unbiasedness and balance. What have these concepts to do with one another? First, we should distinguish between their being used to characterize (a) methods of inquiry, (b) the presentation of issues and (c) the state of one's opinions or allegiances. Methods of inquiry are procedures which one uses to come to one's decisions. The presentation of issues is to be understood as, for instance, how journalists report on, or how teachers teach topics, events and disputes (in particular, whether they are taught directively or non-directively). The state of one's opinions or allegiances is made up of one's propositional attitudes and relational attitudes and behaviour. Let us start by discussing the term 'neutrality', and which terms are in fact interchangeable with it.

The nature of neutrality

The word 'neutrality' may be used to characterize one's opinions and allegiances, but also how issues are presented – that is, to whether issues are taught 'directively' or 'non-directively' (cf. Hand 2007, 2008). It is better, I think, to use the terms 'directive' and 'non-directive' to refer to how topics are taught than the term 'neutral', since those terms apply to how topics are taught. It is better, too, to reserve the term 'neutral' for characterizing the state of one's opinions, and that is the sense in which I shall use it beneath. This sense of the term is interchangeable with 'non-partisan', which is to be contrasted with 'partisan'. It is also interchangeable with 'uncommitted', which is to be contrasted with 'committed'.

Some people claim that neutrality is impossible. However, I take neutrality to be a state of indecision between options, and it would be absurd to say that indecision was a decisive state. Hess and McAvoy claim that '[educational] aims are never neutral' (2014, 76). While it is true that aims, and people, cannot be neutral tout court, or neutral about everything, they can be neutral on particular matters, or neutral between other states. And, once this is admitted, it must be acknowledged that questions, aims and people can be neutral on some matters (even while they cannot be neutral on all matters).

Why might neutrality be unattainable? One might say 'whoever is not for us is against us', and conclude that someone neutral between, say, the Allied and the Axis forces, such as Switzerland, was thereby an enemy. But this is also absurd: an enemy opposes one's ends, rather than simply fails to support them. One might suggest that neutrality is a commitment in itself, that it is a position (that neutrality is itself not neutral, and so is a self-defeating concept). In the case of Switzerland's role in the Second World War (or lack of it), we can reasonably say that Swiss state took a policy: that of refusing to take sides. In this case, they were committed to non-commitment to both the Allied and Axis forces. That is to say, their commitment was of a second-order kind. While this preserves the notion of neutrality, second-order commitment is not required to understand the notion of neutrality. As an illustration of this, we may regard Burden's ass as being neutral on which bale of hay to eat from first, on account of simple indecision between those options, not because it prefers not to commit to either option. Whether due to a decisive refusal, or a state of indecision, neutrality is clearly possible, meaning either a failure or refusal to take sides. We might thus say that there are two kinds of neutrality: decisive and indecisive neutrality. A refusal to take sides seems more specific to practical courses of action, or siding with disputants, than to resolving theoretical questions about whether or not a proposition is true. Indecisive neutrality seems equally applicable to siding with one or another disputant and coming to an intellectual decision.

Bearing these distinctions in mind, let us consider the question of the existence of God. The attitudinal options are often presented as being just three: God exists; God does not exist; I am unsure whether or not God exists. One might allow that degrees of confidence can be had, but basically one must be a little inclined to bet for or against the existence of God, and where they are unable to decide which of the ontological options (namely of God's existence of non-existence) to bet on, they can be said to be *neutral*, non-committal or non-partisan between those options.

It is true that these options exhaust that question, but that's epistemological stances regarding not where neutrality & normativity comes in.

The nature of impartiality

I take it that the following contrasts are identical in meaning: impartial/partial, unbiased/biased, unprejudiced/prejudiced and disinterested/interested. These concepts (and their various markers) apply in the first instance to methods of inquiry and decision-making procedures. Only in the second instance do they characterize states of opinions which were formed in these ways. How are we to understand 'impartiality' in this sense? In Kant's aesthetics, the distinction between interestedness and disinterestedness plays the following role: one is

The normativity comes to play at the level of which questions you ask in the first place. There are many questions you could ask, and whether these questions are in play is the question of neutrality.

a better judge of an object's aesthetic value insofar as one has no irrelevant interest in the object being appraised. For instance, an art auctioneer interested in selling a painting of two young sweethearts for the highest amount possible may judge it mainly in terms of its monetary value, the father of the painter may be unduly proud of the work, and perhaps a bitter, aged bachelor may be unable to appreciate its value: some facts about our experience, character and desires may be irrelevant to making aesthetic judgements, and ought to be bracketed in making them. But what are we describing here if not biases, or prejudices that warp one's judgement? So too may we describe one's partiality as a factor which warps one's judgement beyond the domain of aesthetics; for instance, one may be less capable of adjudicating well between two disputants if one of the disputants is one's own child and the other is a stranger, perhaps with an annoying voice.

[handwritten annotation: not just about questions being in play, disinterested / interested. uninterested without there]

What has neutrality to do with impartiality?

As we have said, one use of the term 'impartiality' characterizes a method of inquiry; other than that, the term may be used to characterize the state of one's opinions or attitudes, and here it can have two distinct senses: one in which it means those attitudes or opinions were arrived at through an impartial process, and one in which it means that one's attitudes or opinions are neutral. To save confusion, I think that it is best to use the terms impartial and partial to characterize methods of enquiry and decision-making procedures, and to talk about the opinions arrived at as being neutral or non-neutral in some regard.

Thus, the question of whether one is neutral about some matter is quite distinct from the question of whether one got there impartially. For instance, one could come to take a neutral stance *because* of a bias (i.e. due to their partiality). Imagine someone who regards both the potential existence of God, and the potential non-existence of God as being decisively unattractive because of, say, the prospect of no afterlife and the prospect of being judged respectively. Because of these biases, they may irrationally be neutral between these options as to which of them is true. Indeed, impartial inquiry often leads to substantive conclusions and not neutrality: perhaps impartial inquiry might lead to neutrality about the cause of the extinction of the dinosaurs, but it does not lead to neutrality on the question of whether the Earth is only thousands of years old.

Two conceptions of balance

The concept of balance applies to the presentation of issues (e.g. by journalists and teachers in reports and lessons). While the BBC makes it policy to frame the arguments of disputants without taking sides, and calls this impartiality, actually it is neutral presentation, and may not be the result of impartial methods of investigation. The BBC might have a fair claim to offer 'balanced' reporting, but 'balanced' is too vague to be a worthy value. It is important to ask: how do they balance their reporting? If they balance it in such a way that each disputant or opinion is given equal coverage, then that is balance in a certain sense, but it is unbalanced in another; sometimes such coverage gives credence to the incredible, whereas it ought to correspond to credibility. On the question of whether or not the Earth is flat, it would seem absurd to favour a neutral report. Indeed, it is sometimes held that in forming a more defensible opinion, one does well to take a thesis, consider its antithesis, and somehow merge the two to form a third view which is more defensible than either of the others. But we should not assume that such a procedure is rational; one position may have an outright victory over the other, with no room for rational synthesis.

According to Michael Hand, one can be directive or non-directive. I have already said that I think this terminology can be improved on; we should distinguish between each of those things that one hopes to promote, demote, or neither promote or demote but merely introduce, rather than collapse them together. However, let us use it for the moment for the sake of convenience. One might think of directive teaching as being unbalanced and non-directive teaching as being balanced. However, that is only so in the sense of balance which considers that equal time for each disputant is required, no matter what the deliverances of impartial inquiry. If one thinks that the presentation of topics ought to be balanced according to the deliverances of impartial inquiry, it might be that directive teaching is balanced and that non-directive teaching unbalanced; teaching creationism versus evolution as an open-ended debate (non-directively), say, is unbalanced, in failing to reflect the actual weight of evidence. I think that we can do well to stop talking about 'balance' and talk instead about justification of steering, and relatedly of disclosing one's own views. Still, some might doubt the coherence or practicality of non-directive teaching, especially if the teacher is not neutral between the options themselves.

The possibility non-promotional commitment

I contend that teachers (and parents) can have an opinion about something without either wanting or trying to steer their pupils (or children) towards sharing that opinion. Indeed, one might even think that they ought not to steer children towards that opinion. Some people contend that this is either impossible in practice because one cannot bracket all of one's opinions away (especially in framing issues for discussion) or they believe that it is undesirable to do so. These are the sorts of considerations cited in its favour. For instance, it might be thought that an educator cannot guard against steering pupils towards such an opinion.

As argued above, we ought to concede that global neutrality is indeed impossible for rational agents. It is almost inconceivable that there should be a conscious person with no attitudes or beliefs. Nor do I think it is desirable that there should be. There are many beliefs and other kinds of attitudes which it is rational or at least not irrational to have. However, it does not follow from having an attitude or belief that one should systematically promote it in others. Nor does it follow from having a belief that one must either withhold or disclose it. Indeed, it is often hard for pupils to tell where teachers sit on certain issues, partly because teachers are capable of playing roles, such as devil's advocate; they can simulate having certain views for pedagogical purposes.

A quite different worry is whether disclosing one's belief is ever compatible with non-directive teaching, for, arguably, announcing one's views *just is* a form of steering.[5] Sometimes, the teacher's disclosure seems equivalent to directive education; consider the teacher's endorsing views or asserting those views. In particular, consider their using universal and prescriptive language such as 'we believe that' and 'it is true that' or 'certainly', or failing to qualify assertions, for example, by not adding 'Catholics, like me, believe that' to the claims like 'Jesus died for our sins'. Alternatively, however, they could stress their own subjectivity in confessing/disclosing their personal views, namely by stating: 'I believe that', or 'it seems to me that'. One can also use less emphatic language: 'it seems that', or 'arguably', or 'one reason to think x is that'. On topics that one aims to teach non-directively, when, if ever, should teachers withhold or disclose their views?

I agree that one's actions will sometimes reveal one's attitudes; training children to swim shows at least that I think it worth my while teaching swimming to children, and doing so unenthusiastically may reveal the opposite. It may also indicate that I value swimming itself and think that it's worth the children's time.

---

[5] I borrow the terms 'withholding' and 'disclosing' from Hess and McAvoy (2014).

However, it is often possible and desirable to withhold one's views, and often possible and desirable to reveal one's views. Disclosing one's views need not entail any more than that; by simply disclosing them, for instance, one need not state one's reasons for belief and one need not defend one's view against objections, and certainly one need not allow one's view to become the focus of the class. To the extent that children neither opted in, nor can opt out of such a class, this could be reasonably described as forcing one's private views on pupils, especially to the extent that one denies children scope for dissent. Indeed, the privileged position of the teacher can in itself make dissent less easily voiced anyway. In the case of spending time doing something, it must be admitted that one cannot live and yet not spend time doing anything. And in the case of doing worthwhile things, religiously committed educators must promote activities which are considered worthwhile within one's religious outlook, but not for religious reasons per se, nor as a form of initiation into their religion. In the case of belief about whether or not a proposition is true, one can be neutral; one can genuinely not have an opinion on the matter. That may amount to living as though there were a negative answer to the question, but c'est la vie, that's the way the cookie crumbles, rather than a reason to initiate children into a faith. There is still room for commitment without advocacy. I now propose to critically discuss the aim of 'learning *from* religion', much emphasized in religious education literature, policy documents and teaching materials.

Against learning *from*, in favour of learning *about* religion

How can we make sense of the expressions 'learning about' and 'learning from'? We can learn from (among other things) our mistakes, the past and other people. It seems that to learn 'from X' is to identify X as the *source* of our learning. We can learn about (among other things) books, other people and the past. It seems that to 'learn about X' is to identify X as the *object* of our learning. But clearly in religious education, it is important to learn about religion; in fact, it would seem to be the very raison d'être of such a subject. It can comprehensibly be urged that to deserve the name of 'religious education', religion might not be the *object* of understanding at all, but perhaps the student, or the world in general, should be. Instead, religion would be the source of knowledge, shedding light on the student, and upon the world in general. However, that presupposes religions to be a source of knowledge on these things, but that seems too epistemically contentious to presuppose in a learning objective (as the combination of our findings in Chapters 6 and 8 has shown). As to which sources we should learn about religion from, that seems to be a further, albeit very important, matter that in no way conflicts with what the subject matter of religious education is. One might reasonably suggest that children should learn about religion(s) from religion(s), on the grounds that each religion is *an* authority on itself. There is no guarantee that religions are the *best* authorities on themselves, but it seems reasonable to suggest that particular religions should be able to speak for themselves where they are the object of learning (even if they are not presumed to have the final word on themselves).

When we speak of learning from religion in the sense of learning from a religious source, we still need to specify what lessons should be taught. It is not enough to say that children should learn from religion. It is important to specify *what it is* that children should learn from religion. Should the various religions teach children about the world as they see it, or should they merely teach children about how they see the world (together, perhaps, with what are their aspirations and practices)? For instance, should children learn from Christians that Christ died for their sins, or should they learn that Christians think that someone special was born (whom they call the Christ) who died for mankind's sins? This latter option seems less contentious where it is admitted that the epistemic credentials of religion are less than intellectually compelling (as Chapter 8 argued). During a public panel discussion entitled 'What is the Place of Faith in Schools?', Richard Dawkins contended that people have nothing to learn from religion(s).[6] That is to say, according to Dawkins, any uniquely religious content is false. While you can learn kindness from religious sources, you can learn kindness from non-religious sources. While you can learn what Christians believe from Christians, you can learn this from non-Christian sources. While it is admitted that good and true things can be learned from religions, Dawkins contends that all of the teachings *specific* to each religion are false. If Jesus *did in fact* rise from the dead on the third day subsequent to his execution, *you could learn this* from Christianity, but (again, according to Dawkins) he did not, and so you cannot. On this view, it is a mistake to suppose that religions are to be learnt from in the respects that they are unique. One need not hold that every religion's teachings are demonstrably false to share Dawkins' reservations. Instead, it is enough to hold that none of that content which is specific to religions is so well demonstrated that we may presume to promote

---

[6] 'What's the Place of Faith in Schools?' Westminster Faith Debates, featuring James Conroy, John Pritchard, Richard Dawkins and Robert Jackson, 22 February 2012. AHRC/ESRC Religion & Society Programme.

its belief among children. It ought not to be an educational aim that children should come to assent to any specifically religious content (even if it may not be an educational failure if they did come to do so).

How to understand religion

If the import of Chapters 6 and 8 are right, then it seems that Michael Hand (2004) is right in arguing that children have the right to an education enabling them to make rational judgements about the truth or falsity of religious propositions. And if the arguments in favour of paternalism in Chapter 3 are correct, it ought to be compulsory for children. But being able to recall information about religions is hopelessly superficial for this purpose (not least since one may not have even understood it at all). Furthermore, learning about religions in a deep way involves not just being presented with information and being able to recall it, but understanding that information through having it explained. Moreover, in addition to explanation, existential engagement and imaginative identification might well be required, but again this is not best termed 'learning from' religion. Instead, it is better marked out with the terms 'personal' and 'impersonal' understanding. John Lippitt explains the role that Kierkegaard gives to the terms 'objective' and 'subjective' understanding well: 'To relate oneself appropriately to certain ideas means to relate to them *in the first person*. Ethical and religious concerns, Kierkegaard insists, fall into this category' (Lippitt 2003, 8). Again:

> To certain ideas – a mathematical proof for instance – I can relate myself, entirely appropriately, in a disengaged, impersonal manner. But to certain other ideas – such as what kind of person I ought to become, or the fact that I will shortly die – such a disengaged reaction would be entirely inappropriate … [perhaps] a way of evading the significance my death has for me. (Lippitt 2003, 8)

I would recommend the use of the terms 'impersonal' and 'personal' over 'objective' and 'subjective', since that latter pair is already quite equivocal enough.

A political rather than moral right to religious upbringing

Many defend religious initiation according to parental preferences (through denominational schooling). It is important to make clear that a political liberty right is not a moral claim right; just because, politically speaking, nobody should stop you from doing something, that is not enough to say that it's morally incumbent upon you to do it, or even morally alright for you to do it, and certainly not that anybody ought to facilitate you in doing it. However, as I have emphasized throughout, my question is how children ought morally to be influenced, with respect to religions. In this particular case, it takes the form of whether it matters morally if we initiate children into religious beliefs or refrain from doing so. It is true that children benefit from feeling a sense of belonging, indeed, think of the converse: exclusion, isolation and its high risk of loneliness and alienation. However, being a member of a community (belonging) does not presuppose being initiated into a set of beliefs (believing). We must be careful to say that we can agree that belonging is important, without thinking that believing is necessary. Indeed, if rejecting those beliefs is not irrational, it is important to forebear inculcating them. Of course, it would be wrong to insist that parents refrain from worship themselves, but they should not make a concerted attempt to initiate children into the doctrinal fold, and indeed into the practices which presuppose those doctrines (e.g. worship).

Some authors, such as Gareth Byrne, have wanted to advocate children's religious initiation within 'their own faith community'. Providing an aspirational description of denominational schools, he says: 'As well as learning about and from religion, these schools encourage their Christian young people to draw close to God in Jesus Christ' and acknowledges that 'other faith schools will form pupils of their religion within their faith tradition' (Byrne 2013, 213). He has in mind that children have a natural or default religion (namely, that of their parents or community), and that this is what it is right to initiate them into. But it follows from this that a mere accident of birth dictates how it is proper to influence someone, with respect to religion(s), even where the state of knowledge is universal. However, the idea that children ought to be opted into religious initiation by default because they have a religion in the sense of doctrinal commitments just by birth is to be resisted, even though it is to be admitted that they may well belong to some community or criss-crossing communities by birth. Clearly, children are not religious until you initiate them into religion, any more than they are mathematicians, carpenters or competitive swimmers until initiated into those practices. Nobody is of a religion, unless they accept at least its key doctrinal elements (or something close enough to them). Children do not, from birth, accept those doctrinal elements (they do not come innately packaged), and so are not of any religion. If children are only to be initiated into a faith which is already theirs, and yet do not have a faith (by virtue of lacking even the most basic belief), it follows that children ought not to be initiated into a faith.

Supposing that all religious instruction in schools were voluntary in the sense that any and all students could if they wish (and are aware that they could) decline to accept religious instruction at any time, and indeed, had to opt in to it in the first place, that would make it less morally objectionable it seems. However, even if less than literally captive, it still seems that initiating children into beliefs which it is not irrational to deny, especially ones so comprehensive in scope, is not a moral educational aim. Where religious education does not attempt religious initiation (but instead hopes to promote deep understanding through explanation, existential engagement and critical reflection), there seems to be scant reason why children should have scope to exempt themselves from religious education any more than they should have scope to be exempt from history, maths or science. Indeed, it seems that they ought initially to be opted in to such an education on the grounds of the momentousness of religious beliefs, their degree of rationality and the requirement of intervention to promote rational deliberation on their truth or falsity. It seems to betray insecurities about the ability of one's faith to survive a critical scrutiny, or investigation of alternatives to it insofar as parents do.

The primary focus of this enquiry has been whether, morally, children should be initiated into faith at all, and our finding has been that children shouldn't be, irrespective of whether it might be attempted in the context of the home or the school. It is debatable as to whether a school could be distinctively religious without attempting to initiate children (Hand 2012; Gardner 2014). To the extent that it could not, then, there shouldn't be any religiously distinctive schooling while the epistemic picture is such as it is. I have also argued that children shouldn't be dissuaded from religious belief tout court, even if they ought to be encouraged to assess religious propositions rationally, since it seems that it need not be irrational to deny atheism.

I have discussed how children ought to be influenced, with respect to religions. It is an interesting question as to whether there exist any non-religions which are apt for similar moral consideration in how children ought to be influenced with respect to them (similar because of their comprehensive formative role and epistemic credentials). If this were the case, it would seem that we would not be interested in religion *qua* religion, but in religion *qua* some other phenomenon (e.g. worldviews or comprehensive doctrines).[7] Concordantly, the scope of this book ought more properly to have been: children, comprehensive doctrines and the ethics of influence.

---

[7]   There is a strain of thought which claims that non-religious objects might be appropriate in Religious Education classes. The British Humanist Association, for instance, argues that humanism ought to be studied in RE, and for RE to have its name changed; I take it that this is essentially to push for a whole new subject (see Tillson 2011b).

References

Alexander, H.A. and Agbaria, A.K. (eds) (2012), *Commitment, Character, and Citizenship: Religious Education in Liberal Democracy*, London: Routledge.

Anderson, L.W. and Krathwohl, D.R. (eds) (2001), *A Taxonomy for Learning, Teaching, and Assessing: A Revision of Bloom's Taxonomy of Educational Objectives*, New York: Pearson and Allyn & Bacon.

Anselm, St (1903), *Proslogion* in *The Devotions of St. Anselm*, trans. Webb, C.C.J., https://en.wikisource.org/wiki/Proslogion (accessed 10 August 2018).

Aristotle, *Nicomachean Ethics*, trans. W.D. Ross, http://classics.mit.edu/Aristotle/n icomachaen.html (accessed 10 August 2018).

Austin, J.L. (1962), *How to Do Things with Words: The William James Lectures delivered at Harvard University in 1955*, J.O. Urmson and Marina Sbisà (eds), Oxford: Clarendon Press.

Beebee, H. (2004), 'Causing and Nothingness', in *Causation and Counterfactuals*, L.A. Paul, E.J. Hall and J. Collins (eds), Cambridge, MA: MIT Press.

Blackburn, S. (2012), 'Motivated Belief', in *What Do We Really Know? The Big Questions in Philosophy*, London: Quercus.

Blackmore, S. (1999), *The Meme Machine*, Oxford: Oxford University Press.

Bloom, B.S., Engelhart, M.D., Furst, E.J., Hill, W.H. and Krathwohl, D.R. (1956), *Taxonomy of Educational Objectives: The Classification of Educational Goals. Handbook I: Cognitive Domain*, New York: David McKay Company.

Bourget, D. and Chalmers, D.J. (2013), 'What Do Philosophers Believe?', *Philosophical Studies*, 170 (3): 1–36.

Bridges, D. (1979), *Education, Democracy, and Discussion*, Slough, UK: National Foundation for Educational Research.

Brighouse, H. and McAvoy, P. (2010), 'Do Children Have Any Rights?', in Richard Bailey (ed.), *The Philosophy of Education: An Introduction*, Continuum: London.

Brighouse, H. and Swift, A. (2009), 'Legitimate Parental Partiality', *Philosophy & Public Affairs*, 37 (1): 43–80.

Byrne, G. (2013), 'Encountering and Engaging with Religion and Belief: The Contemporary Contribution of Religious Education in Schools', in Gareth Byrne and Patricia Kieran (eds), *Toward Mutual Ground: Pluralism, Religious Education and Diversity in Irish Schools*, Dublin: Columba Press.

Byrne, P. (1988), 'Religion and the Religions', in Stewart Sutherland et al. (eds), *The World's Religions*, London: Routledge.

Byrne, P. (1989), *Natural Religion and the Nature of Religion: The Legacy of Deism*, London: Routledge.

Callan, E. (2009), 'Why Bring the Kids into This?', in Graham Haydon (ed.), *Faith in Education: A Tribute to Terence McLaughlin*, London: IoE Press.

Callan, E. (2014), 'Integration as Stealth Assimilation', in Judith Suissa, Carrie Winstanley and Roger Marples (eds), *Education and Philosophy: New Perspectives on the Work of John White*, London: Routledge.

Catechism of the Catholic Church, http://www.vatican.va/archive/ENG0015/_INDEX. HTM (accessed 10 August 2018).

Cialdini, R.B. (1993), *Influence: The Psychology of Persuasion*, New York: Morrow.

Clack, B. and Clack, B.R. (1998), *The Philosophy of Religion: A Critical Introduction*, Oxford: Polity Press.

Conklin, J. (2005), 'A Taxonomy for Learning, Teaching, and Assessing: A Revision of Bloom's Taxonomy of Educational Objectives', *Educational Horizons*, 83 (3): 154–9.

Cooling, T. (2012), 'Contestable Beliefs in Education: Fairness and/or Neutrality?', *Oxford Review of Education* 38 (5): 551–66.

Cooper, D.E. (2008), 'Teaching and Truthfulness', *Studies in Philosophy and Education*, 27 (2–3): 79–87.

Crane, T. (2012), 'Mindful', interview for *3: AM Magazine* by Richard Marshall, http://www.3ammagazine.com/3am/mindful/2/ (accessed 10 August 2018).

Dancy, J. (2012), 'Ethics without Principle', interviewed for *3: AM Magazine* by Richard Marshall, http://www.3am magazine.com/3am/ethics-without-principles/ (accessed 10 August 2018).

Davie, G. (1994), *Religion in Britain since 1945: Believing without Belonging*, Oxford: Blackwell.

Davison, S.A. (2012), *On the Intrinsic Value of Everything*, London: Continuum.

Dawkins, R. (1989), *The Selfish Gene*, 2nd edn, Oxford: Oxford University Press.

Dawkins, R. (2013), 'Q&A with Richard Dawkins: "I Guess I'm a Cultural Christian"', interviewed by Paul Bowers for *Charleston City Paper*, http://www.charlestoncity paper.com/charleston/qanda-with-richard-dawkins-i-guess-im-a-cultural-christian/ Content?oid=4581071 (accessed 10 August 2018).

Dennett, D.C. (1995), *Darwin's Dangerous Idea: Evolution and the Meanings of Life*, New York: Simon and Schuster.

Dennett, D.C. (2013), *Intuition Pumps and Other Tools for Thinking*, London: Penguin.

Department for Education (DfE) (1994), 'Religious Education and Collective Worship', 31 January 1/94, London.

Descartes, R. (1968), *Discourse on Method and the Meditations*, trans. with an introduction by F. Sutcliffe, Harmondsworth: Penguin.

Dubos, R. (1972), *A God Within: A Positive Philosophy for a More Complete Fulfillment of Human Potentials*, New York: Charles Scribner's Sons.

Eliot, T.S. (2000), 'Burnt Norton', from *The Four Quartets*, http://www.davidgorman.co m/4Quartets/1-norton.htm (accessed 10 August 2018).

Eshleman, A. (2008), *Reading in Philosophy of Religion: East Meets West*, Singapore: Blackwell.

Evans, D. (2003), *Emotion: A Very Short Introduction*, Oxford: Oxford University Press.

Finlay, S. and Schroeder, M. (Winter 2012 Edition), 'Reasons for Action: Internal vs. External', in Edward N. Zalta (ed.), *The Stanford Encyclopedia of Philosophy*, http://plato.stanford.edu/archives/win2012/entries/reasons-internal-external/ (accessed 10 August 2018).

Fitzgerald, T. (1996), 'Philosophy and Family Resemblances', *Religion* 26 (3): 215–36.

Flew, A. (1975), *Thinking about Thinking: Or, Do I Sincerely Want to be Right?*, London: Collins Fontana.

Fodor, J.A. (2001), 'Language, Thought and Compositionality', *Mind & Language*, 16 (1): 1–15.

Foss, S.K. and Griffin, C.L. (1995), 'Beyond Persuasion: A Proposal for an Invitational Rhetoric', *Communications Monographs*, 62 (1): 2–18.

Foucault, M. (1991), *Discipline and Punish: The Birth of the Prison*, London: Penguin.

Gardner, P. (2014), 'Hand's Academy Challenge: Some Starter Questions', *Journal of Philosophy of Education*, 48 (4): 637–45.

Giussani, L. (1997), *The Religious Sense*, John Zucchi (trans.), Montreal: McGill-Queen's University Press.

Green, J. (2012), *The Fault in Our Stars*, London: Penguin.

Gupta, A. (Spring 2014 Edition), 'Definitions', in Edward N. Zalta (ed.), *The Stanford Encyclopedia of Philosophy*, http://plato.stanford.edu/archives/spr2014/entries/definitions/ (accessed 10 August 2018).

Hacker, P.M.S. (2011), *Wittgenstein*, London: Hachette.

Hand, M. (2002), 'Religious Upbringing Reconsidered', *Journal of Philosophy of Education*, 36 (4): 545–57.

Hand, M. (2003), 'A Philosophical Objection to Faith Schools', *Theory and Research in Education* 1 (1): 89–99.

Hand, M. (2004), 'Religious Education', in John White (ed.), *Rethinking the School Curriculum: Values, Aims and Purpose*, London: Routledge Falmer.

Hand, M. (2006a), 'Against Autonomy as an Educational Aim', *Oxford Review of Education* 32 (4): 535–50.

Hand, M. (2006b), *Is Religious Education Possible?* London: Continuum.

Hand, M. (2007), 'Should We Teach Homosexuality as a Controversial Issue?', *Theory and Research in Education*, 5 (1): 69–86.

Hand, M. (2008), 'What Should We Teach as Controversial? A Defence of the Epistemic Criterion', *Educational Theory*, 58 (2): 213–28

Hand, M. (2009), 'On the Worthwhileness of Theoretical Activities', *Journal of Philosophy of Education*, 43(2).

Hand, M. (2010), 'What *Could* Go on the School Curriculum?', in Richard Bailey (ed.), *The Philosophy of Education: An Introduction*, London: Continuum.

Hand, M. (2011), 'Should We Promote Patriotism in Schools?', *Political Studies*, 59 (2): 328–47.

Hand, M. (2012), 'A New Dawn for Faith-Based Education? Opportunities for Religious Organisations in the UK's New School System', *Journal of Philosophy of Education*, 46 (4): 546–59.

Hand, M. (2013), 'Framing Classroom Discussion of Same-Sex Marriage', *Educational Theory*, 63 (5): 497–510.

Hansson, S.O. (Fall 2008 Edition), 'Science and Pseudo-Science', in Edward N. Zalta (ed.), *The Stanford Encyclopedia of Philosophy*, http://plato.stanford.edu/archives/fall2008/entries/pseudo-science/ (accessed 10 August 2018).

Hess, D.E. and McAvoy, P. (2014), *The Political Classroom: Evidence and Ethics in Democratic Education*, New York: Routledge.

Hession, A. (2015), *Catholic Primary Religious Education in a Pluralist Environment*, Dublin: Veritas.

Hobson, P. (1984), 'Some Reflections on Parents' Rights in the Upbringing of their Children', *Journal of Philosophy of Education*, 18 (1): 63–74.

Hofling, C.K. et al. (1966), 'An Experimental Study of Nurse-Physician Relationships', *Journal of Nervous and Mental Disease*, 143 (2): 171–80.

Irenaeus of Lyons (1885), *Against Heresies*, in Alexander Roberts, James Donaldson and A. Cleveland Coxe (eds), *Ante Nicene Fathers*, Vol. 1, Alexander Roberts and William Rambaut (trans.), Buffalo, NY: Christian Literature Publishing Co.

James, W. (2008), *The Varieties of Religious Experience: A Study in Human* Nature, Abingdon: Routledge.

Johnson, B. (2014), 'The Children Taught at Home about Murder and Bombings', in *The Telegraph*, http://www.telegraph.co.uk/news/politics/10671841/The-children-taught-at-home-about-murder-and bombings.html (accessed 10 August 2018).

Kant, I. (1933), *Critique of Pure Reason*, 2nd edn, N. Kemp-Smith (trans.), London: Macmillan.

Kant, I. (1996), *The Conflict of the Faculties* in *Religion and Rational Theology*, Allen W. Wood and George di Giovanni (eds and trans.), Cambridge: Cambridge University Press.

Kelman, H.C. (1958),'Compliance, Identification, and Internalization: Three Processes of Attitude Change', *The Journal of Conflict Resolution*, 2 (1): 51–60.

Kelman, H.C. (1998), 'The Place of Ethnic Identity in the Development of Personal Identity: A Challenge for the Jewish Family', in P.Y. Medding (ed.), *Coping with Life and Death: Jewish Families in the Twentieth Century*, *Studies in Contemporary Jewry: An Annual*, XIV, Oxford: Oxford University Press.

Kierkegaard, S. (1941), *Concluding Unscientific Postscript to Philosophical Fragments*, David F. Swenson and Walter Lowrie (trans.), Princeton, NJ: Princeton University Press.

Kleinig, J. (1983), *Paternalism*, Manchester: Manchester University Press.

Krathwohl, D.R. (2002), 'A Revision of Bloom's Taxonomy: An Overview', *Theory into Practice*, 41 (4): 212–18.

Krathwohl, D.R., Bloom, B.S. and Masia, B.B. (1964), *Taxonomy of Educational Objectives: The Classification of Educational Goals. Handbook II: Affective Domain*, New York: David McKay Company.

Latané, B. and Darley, J.M. (1968), 'Group Inhibition of Bystander Intervention in Emergencies', *Journal of Personality and Social Psychology*, 10 (3): 215–21.

Lewis, D. (1994), 'Reduction of Mind', In Samuel D. Guttenplan (ed.), *A Companion to the Philosophy of Mind*, Oxford: Blackwell.

Lewis, D. (2000), 'Causation as Influence', *Journal of Philosophy*, 97 (4): 182–97.

Lippitt, J. (2003), *Kierkegaard and Fear and Trembling*, London: Routledge.

Locke, J (1966), 'A Letter Concerning Toleration', in J.W. Gough (ed.), *The Second Treatise of Government and a Letter Concerning Toleration*, 3rd edn, Oxford: Blackwell.

Lowe, E.J. (2000), *An Introduction to the Philosophy of Mind*, Cambridge: Cambridge University Press.

Lowe, E.J. (2002), *A Survey of Metaphysics*, Oxford: Oxford University Press.

Lowe, E.J. (2008a), *Personal Agency: The Metaphysics of Mind and Action*, Oxford: Oxford University Press.

Lowe, E.J. (2008b), 'Essentialism, Metaphysical Realism, and the Errors of Conceptualism', *Philosophia Scientiæ*, 12 (1): 9–33.

Lowe, E.J. (2008c), 'How Are Identity Conditions Grounded?', in C. Kanzian (ed.), *Persistence*, Frankfurt: Ontos.

Mackenzie, J. (2004), 'Still Irrelevant to Us', *Journal of Philosophy of Education*, 38 (4): 639–48.

Mackie, J.L. (1982), *The Miracle of Theism: Arguments for and against the Existence of God*, Oxford: Oxford University Press.

Maier, J. (Fall 2011 Edition), 'Abilities', in Edward N. Zalta (ed.), *The Stanford Encyclopedia of Philosophy*, http://plato.stanford.edu/archives/fall2011/entries/abilities/ (accessed 10 August 2018).

Matthews, G.B. (2008), 'Getting beyond the Deficit Conception of Childhood: Thinking Philosophically with Children', in Michael Hand and Carrie Winstanley (eds), *Philosophy in Schools*, London: Continuum.

Matthews, G.B. (Spring 2014 Edition), 'The Philosophy of Childhood', in Edward N. Zalta (ed.), *The Stanford Encyclopedia of Philosophy*, http://plato.stanford.edu/archives/spr2014/entries/childhood/ (accessed 10 August 2018).

McDonald, W. (Fall 2012 Edition), 'Søren Kierkegaard', in Edward N. Zalta (ed.), *The Stanford Encyclopedia of Philosophy*, http://plato.stanford.edu/archives/fall2012/entries/kierkegaard/ (accessed 10 August 2018).

McDowell, J. (1983), 'Aesthetic Value, Objectivity, and the Fabric of the World', in Eva Schaper (ed.), *Pleasure, Preference and Value*, Cambridge: Cambridge University Press.

McKinney, S.J. (2011), 'Is Religious Education Possible? By Michael Hand', *Journal of Philosophy of Education*, 45 (1): 163–5.

McLaughlin, T.H. (1984), 'Parental Rights and the Religious Upbringing of Children', *Journal of Philosophy of Education*, 18 (1): 75–83.

Mill, J.S. (1906), *Utilitarianism*, Chicago, IL: University of Chicago Press.

Miller, A. (2013), '"Beyond Belief" Review of Brian Leiter Why Tolerate Religion? (Princeton University Press 2013)', *Morning Star*, 11 March, p. 11.

Millgram, E. (2008), 'D'où Venons-Vous, Que Sommes Nous, Où Allons-Nous?', in Daniel Callcut (ed.), *Reading B. Williams*, London: Routledge.

Monk, R. (1991), *Ludwig Wittgenstein: the Duty of Genius*, London: Vintage.

Mulligan, A. (2014), 'Constitutional Parenthood in the Age of Assisted Reproduction Technology', *Irish Jurist*, 51 (1): 90–122.

Nagel, T. (1979), 'Moral Luck', in *Mortal Questions*, New York: Cambridge University Press.

Nagel, T. (2001), *The Last Word*, Oxford: Oxford University Press.

Nagel, T. (2012), 'A Philosopher Defends Religion', in *The New York Review of Books*, http://www.nybooks.com/articles/archives/2012/sep/27/philosopher-defends-religio n/#fnr-2 (accessed 10 August 2018).

Nietzsche, F. (2009), *Beyond Good and Evil*, Helen Zimmern (trans.), http://www.gute nberg.org/files/4363/4363-h/4363-h.htm (last accessed 30 June 2015).

Nolan, D. (2005), *David Lewis*, Acumen: Chesham.

Nozick, R. (1971), *Anarchy, State, and Utopia*, Oxford: The Clarendon Press.

O'Hear, A. (1997), *Beyond Evolution: Human Nature and the Limits of Evolutionary Explanation*, Oxford: Oxford University Press.

O'Neill, O. (1988), 'Children's Rights and Children's Lives', *Ethics*, 98 (3): 445–63.

O'Neill, O. (2013), 'How to Trust Intelligently', http://blog.ted.com/how-to-trust-intelli gently/ (accessed 10 August 2018).

Papineau, D. (2013), 'There Are No Norms of Belief', in Timothy Chan (ed.), *The Aim of Belief*, Oxford: Oxford University Press.

Pascal, B. (1925), *Pensées*, in *Œuvres*, ed. L. Brunschvigg, Paris: Hachette.

Peters, R.S. (1966), *Ethics and Education*, London: Allen and Unwin.

Peters, R.S. (1973), 'The Justification of Education', in Richard Stanley Peters (ed.), *Education and the Education of Teachers*, London: Routledge & Kegan Paul.

Pinker, S. (2013), 'Science Is Not Your Enemy', *The New Republic*, http://www.newrepubl ic.com/article/114127/science-not-enemy-humanities (accessed 10 August 2018).

Plantinga, A. (1974), *The Nature of Necessity*, Oxford: Oxford University Press.

Plantinga, A. (1989), *God, Freedom, and Evil*, Grand Rapids, MI: Eerdmans.

Plantinga, A. (1991), 'Reason and Belief in God', in *Faith and Rationality*, 3rd edn, Paris: University of Notre Dame Press.

Plantinga, A. (1993), *Warrant and Proper Function*, Oxford: Oxford University Press.

Plantinga, A. (2000), *Warranted Christian Belief*, Oxford: Oxford University Press.

Plantinga, A. (Spring 2014 Edition), 'Religion and Science', in Edward N. Zalta (ed.), *The Stanford Encyclopedia of Philosophy*, http://plato.stanford.edu/archives/spr2014/ entries/religion-science/ (accessed 10 August 2018).

Plato, *Euthyphro*, Benjamin Jowett (trans.), http://classics.mit.edu/Plato/euthyfro.html (accessed 10 August 2018).

Plato, *The* Republic, Benjamin Jowett (trans.), http://classics.mit. edu/Plato/republic. html (accessed 10 August 2018).

Putnam, H. (1973), 'Meaning and Reference', *The Journal of Philosophy*, 70 (19): 699–711.

Ramsey, F.P. and Moore, G.E. (1927), 'Symposium: Facts and Propositions', *Proceedings of the Aristotelian Society*, 7 (1): 153–206.

Rawls, J. (1972), *A Theory of Justice*, Cambridge: Harvard University Press.

'Reasons My Son Is Crying', http://www.reasonsmysoniscrying.com/ (accessed 10 August 2018).

Rorty, R. (1991), *Objectivity, Relativism, and Truth: Philosophical Papers*, Vol. 1, Cambridge: Cambridge University Press.

Ryle, G. (2000), *The Concept of Mind*, London: Penguin Book.

Saler, B. (1993), *Conceptualizing Religion: Immanent Anthropologists, Transcendent Natives, and Unbounded Categories*, Leiden: E.J. Brill.

Saltman, B. (2006), 'The Temple of Reason: Sam Harris on How Religion Puts the World at Risk', *The Sun*, http://thesunmagazine.org/issues/369/the_temple_of_reason?page=1 (accessed 10 August 2018).

Sartre, J.P. (1973), *Existentialism and Humanism*, London: Methuen.

Sauvage, G. (1909), 'Fideism', in *The Catholic Encyclopedia*, http://www.newadvent.org/cathen/06068b.htm (accessed 10 August 2018).

Shields, C. (Spring 2014 Edition), 'Aristotle', in Edward N. Zalta (ed.), *The Stanford Encyclopedia of Philosophy*, http://plato.stanford.edu/archives/spr2014/entries/aristotle/ (accessed 10 August 2018).

Sibley, F. (2001), 'Aesthetic Concepts', in J. Benson, B. Redfern and J. Roxbee Cox (eds), *Approach to Aesthetics: Collected Papers on Philosophical Aesthetics*, Oxford: Oxford University Press.

Singer, P. (1972), 'Famine, Affluence, and Morality', *Philosophy & Public Affairs* 1 (1): 229–43.

Smart, N. (1973), *The Science of Religion and the Sociology of Knowledge*, Princeton: Princeton University Press.

Smeyers, P., Smith, R. and Standish, P. (2007), *The Therapy of Education*, Hampshire: Palgrave Macmillan.

Stanley, J. and Williamson, T. (2001), 'Knowing How', *The Journal of Philosophy* 98 (8): 411–44.

Strawson, G. (2012), 'We Live beyond Any Tale That We Happen to Enact', *The Harvard Review of Philosophy* 18 (1): 73–90.

Styron, W. (2010), *Sophie's Choice*, Open Road Media.

Swinburne, R. (1989), *The Coherence of Theism*, Oxford: Oxford University Press.

Swinburne, R. (2004), *The Existence of God*, Oxford: Oxford University Press.

Taliaferro, C. (Fall 2013 Edition), 'Philosophy of Religion', in Edward N. Zalta (ed.), *The Stanford Encyclopedia of Philosophy*, http://plato.stanford.edu/archives/fall2013/e ntries/philosophy-religion/ (accessed 10 August 2018).

Tertullian (1956), *De Carne Christi (Treatise on the Incarnation)*, Ernest Evans (ed. and trans.), London: S.P.C.K.

Thaler, R.H. and Sunstein, C.R. (2009), *Nudge*, Penguin Books: London.

Thiessen, E.J. (1993), *Teaching for Commitment: Liberal Education, Indoctrination, and Christian Nurture*, MQUP: McGill-Queen's Press.

Thiessen, E.J. (2011), *The Ethics of Evangelism: A Philosophical Defense of Proselytizing and Persuasion*, Milton Keynes: Paternoster.

Tillson, J. (2011a), 'Religious Education and the Floodgates of Impartiality', in Robert Kunzman (ed.), *Philosophy of Education Society Yearbook*, 118–23, Urbana, IL: Philosophy of Education Society.

Tillson, J. (2011b), 'In Favour of Ethics Education, against Religious Education', *Journal of Philosophy of Education*, 45 (4): 675–88.

Tillson, J. (2013), 'Elmer Thiessen and the Ethics of Evangelism'. *Journal of Education and Christian Belief*, 17 (2): 243–58.

Tillson, J. (2017), 'The Problem of Rational Moral Enlistment', *Theory and Research in Education*, 15 (2): 165–81.

Tillson, J. (2018), 'Is all Formative Influence Immoral?', *Ethics and Education*, 13 (2): 208–220.

Tillson, J. (forthcoming), 'Might Knowledge Be Insertable?', *Educational Theory*.

Tolkien, J.R.R. (2012), *The Fellowship of the Ring: Being the First Part of the Lord of the Rings*, New York: Houghton Mifflin Harcourt.

Tylor, E.B. (1871), *Primitive Culture: Researches into the Development of Mythology, Philosophy, Religion, Art, and Custom*, Vol. 1, London: John Murray.

Vryhof, S.C. (2012), 'Between Memory and Vision: Schools as Communities of Meaning', in Hanan A. Alexander and Ayman K. Agbaria (eds), *Commitment, Character, and Citizenship: Religious Education in Liberal Democracy*, London: Routledge.

Williams, B. (1981a), 'Persons, Character, and Morality', in *Moral Luck*, Cambridge: Cambridge University Press.

Williams, B. (1981b), 'Moral Luck', in *Moral Luck*, Cambridge: Cambridge University Press.

Williams, B. (1985), *Ethics and the Limits of Philosophy*, Abingdon: Fontana Press.

Williams, B. (1989), 'Internal Reasons and the Obscurity of Blame', *Logos* 10: 1–11.

Williams, B. (1993), *Morality*, Cambridge: Canto.

Williams, B. (2006a), 'Tertullian's Paradox', in A.W. Moore (ed.), *Philosophy as a Humanistic Discipline*, Princeton: Princeton University Press.

Williams, B. (2006b), 'The Human Prejudice', in A.W. Moore (ed.), *Philosophy as a Humanistic Discipline*, Princeton: Princeton University Press.

Williams, B. (2009), 'Plato: The Invention of Philosophy', in Myles Burnyeat (ed.), *The Sense of the Past: Essays in the History of Philosophy*, Princeton: Princeton University Press.

Williams, B. and Magee, B. (2001), 'The Spell of Linguistic Philosophy', in Bryan Magee, *Talking Philosophy: Dialogues with Fifteen Leading Philosophers*, Oxford: Oxford University Press.

Williams, K. (2014), 'Conscripts or Volunteers? The Status of Learners in Faith-Schools', in Marianna Papastephanou (ed.), *Philosophical Perspectives on Compulsory Education*, London: Springer.

Wilson, J. (2003), 'Can Sex Education be Practical?', *Sex Education: Sexuality, Society and Learning* 3 (1): 23–32.

Wilson, T.D. (2011), *Redirect: The Surprising New Science of Psychological Change*, London: Allen Lane.

Wise, K. (2001), 'Kurt P. Wise, Geology', in John Ashton (ed.), 'Six Days: Why 50 Scientists Choose to Believe in Creation', https://answersingenesis.org/answers/boo ks/in-six-days/kurt-p-wise-geology/ (accessed 10 August 2018).

Wittgenstein, L. (1969), *On Certainty*, G.E.M. Anscombe and G.H. von Wright (eds), Denis Paul and G.E.M. Anscombe (trans.), Oxford: Blackwell Publishing.

Wittgenstein, L. (1984), in G.H. von Wright and Heikki Nymam (eds), *Culture and Value*, Peter Winch (trans.), Oxford: Blackwell Publishing.

Wittgenstein, L. (2010a), *Philosophical Investigations*, Oxford: Blackwell.

Wittgenstein, L. (2010b), *Lectures and Conversations on Aesthetics, Psychology and Religious Belief*, Cyril Barret (ed.), Oxford: Blackwell Publishing.

1856 August 27, 'Kelvedon School', in *The Essex Standard, and General Advertiser for the Eastern Counties*, Colchester: England.

Wright, A. (2000), 'The Spiritual Education Project: Cultivating Spiritual and Religious Literacy through a Critical Pedagogy of Religious Education', in Michael Grimmitt (ed.), *Pedagogies of Religious Education*, Essex: McCrimmon.

Film and television

Blow (2001), Ted Demme (dir), New Line Cinema.

A Clockwork Orange (1971), Stanley Kubrick (dir), Warner Bros.

Goodfellas (1990), Martin Scorsese (dir), Warner Bros.

Interstellar (2014), Christopher Nolan (dir), Paramount Pictures.

The Last of the Mohicans (1992), Michael Mann (dir), Morgan Creek Productions.

Lord of the Rings: The Fellowship of the Ring (2001), Peter Jackson (dir), New Line Cinema.

There Will Be Blood (2007), Paul Thomas Anderson (dir), Paramount Pictures.

Titanic (1997), James Cameron (dir), Paramount Pictures and 20th Century Fox.

The Root of All Evil (2006), Russell Barnes (dir), Alan Clements.

Planet Earth (2006), Alastair Fothergill (producer), BBC Natural History Unit.

The World at War (1973–6), Jeremy Isaacs (creator), Thames Television.

Audio and visual

Blair, T. and Hitchens, C. (2012), 'Is Religion a Force for Good in the World?', https://www.youtube.com/watch?v=ZSJ5CrZ_3Pg (accessed 10 August 2018).

Broome, J. (2008), 'Rationality', http://podcasts.ox.ac.uk/john-broome-rationality (accessed 10 August 2018).

Craig, W.L. and Hitchens, C. (2014), 'Does God Exist? William Lane Craig vs. Christopher Hitchens – Full Debate', https://www.youtube.com/watch?v=0tYm41hb48o (accessed 10 August 2018).

Dennett, D.C. (2011), 'On What Should Replace Religion', https://www.youtube.com/watch?v=m5tGpMcFF7U&t=44s (accessed 10 August 2018).

Ladyman, J. (2014), 'Pseudoscience and Bullshit', https://www.youtube.com/watch?v=32ZaTKa2IRg (accessed 23 June 2015).

Minchin, T. (2009), 'If You Open Your Mind Too Much, Your Brain Will Fall Out (Take My Wife)', https://www.youtube.com/watch?v=PkLGMyYbz4I (accessed 10 August 2018).

Index